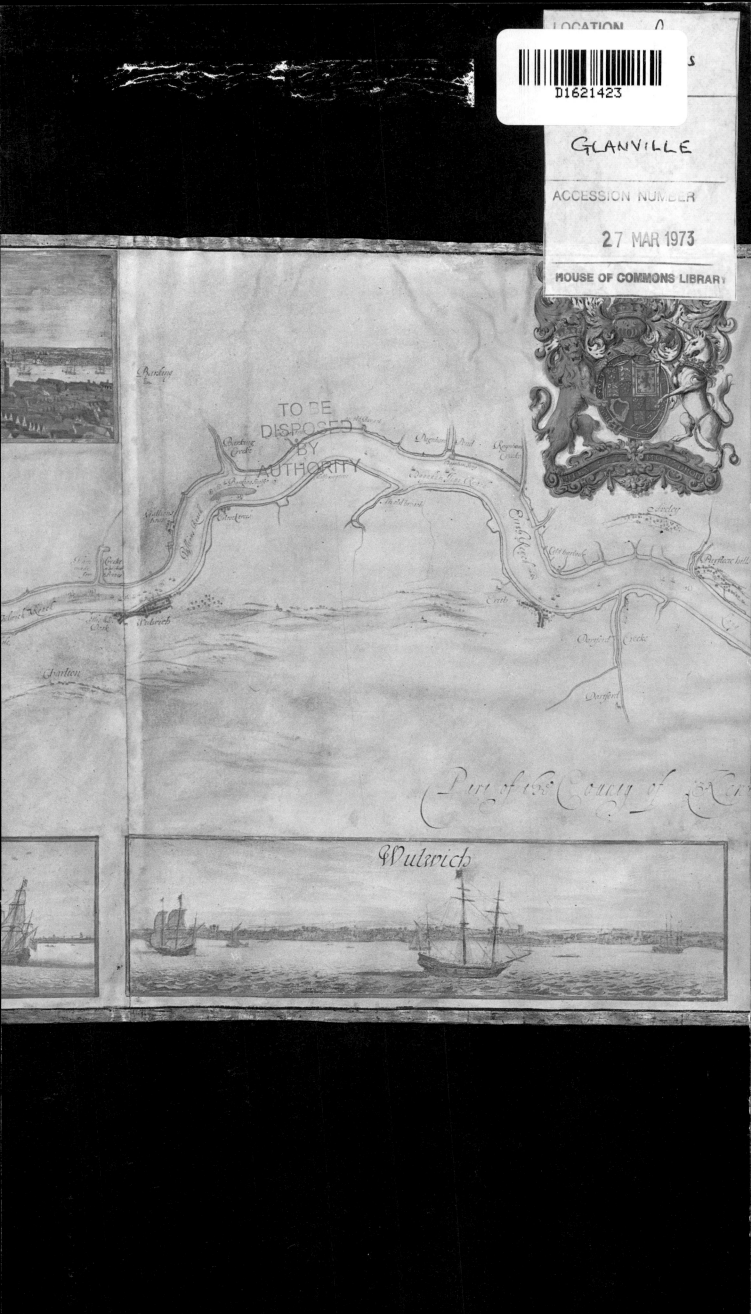

TO BE
DISPOSED
BY
AUTHORITY

Barking

Barking
Creeke

Dagenham Reach

Rainham
Creeke

Aveley

Purfleete hill

Erith

Dartford Creeke

Dartford

Charlton

Part of the County of Kent

Woolwich

Endpaper map: Chart of the Thames prepared for the Navy Office by Jonas Moore, 1662. The watercolour views of London and of the Thames-side towns with naval yards are attributed to Wenceslaus Hollar: see Chapter III for notes on the map of London.

Endpaper map: Chart of the Thames prepared for the Navy Office by Jonas Moore, 1662. The watercolour views of London and of the Thames-side towns with naval yards are attributed to Wenceslaus Hollar: see Chapter III for notes on the map of London.

LONDON IN MAPS

LONDON
IN MAPS

Philippa Glanville

*Maps . . . which doe allure the eies by pleasant portraiture, and
are the best directions in Geographicall Studies, especially when
the light of learning is adioined to the speechlesse delineations*

CAMDEN, *Britannia,* 1610

THE CONNOISSEUR
LONDON

First published 1972 by
The Connoisseur, Chestergate House,
Vauxhall Bridge Road, London SW1V 1HF

© *Philippa Glanville 1972*

Photography by Barnet Saidman, FRPS, FIBP
Edited by Elsie Cannon
Consultant Editor for Connoisseur Books David Coombs
Designed and produced by Derek Morrison

Filmset in 11/13 pt Garamond (Mono series 156) by
BAS Printers Limited, Wallop, Hampshire
Lithography and printing by
Grafische Industrie Haarlem B.V., Haarlem, The Netherlands
Printed on woodfree machine-coated Satijn Extra paper
made by Koninklijke Nederlandse Papierfabriek N.V.
Maastricht, The Netherlands
Bound in Buckram by Webb Son and Co. Ltd
London and Glamorgan

To G.H.G.

Contents

INTRODUCTION   *page* 9

Chapter I
London before the Map-maker   11

Chapter II
Early Plans and Surveys   17

Chapter III
The new London – post-Fire changes   25

Chapter IV
The Century of Squares   33

Chapter V
Metropolitan Improvements and the Transport Revolution   41

Chapter VI
The Twentieth Century   50

Chapter VII
Map-maker and Map Seller: the trade through four centuries   55

Techniques of Map Reproduction   61

The Surveyor's Task: *by D. J. Bryden, Curator of the*
Whipple Science Museum, Cambridge   63

BIBLIOGRAPHY   66

INDEX   69

MAPS: PLATES 1–69   72–211

  Medieval and Tudor London   72–81

  Stuart London   82–115

  London under the Hanoverians   116–171

  Victorian London   172–199

  Twentieth-century London   200–211

ACKNOWLEDGMENTS   212

List of Maps

PLATE 1 Section of an itinerary from London to Rome *page* 72

PLATE 2 Finsbury from a lost map of London 72

PLATE 3 *Londinum Feracissimi Angliae Regni Metropolis* 78

PLATE 4 Westminster in 1593 78

PLATE 5 Bird's eye view of London from the *Particular Description of England* 81

PLATE 6 An estate in Tothill Street, Westminster, surveyed for Christ's Hospital 82

PLATE 7 *The Cittie of London* 86

PLATE 8 Northwest of the city from the woodcut *Civitas Londinum* 86

PLATE 9 Northwest of the city from *London* 88

PLATE 10 Gray's Inn to the river from *West Central London* 90

PLATE 11 *A Map or Ground-plot of the Citty of London . . .* after the Fire of 1666 94

PLATE 12 Rebuilding Scheme 94

PLATE 13 The road from London to St. Albans from *Britannia . . . Principal Roads Thereof* 96

PLATE 14 Blackfriars from *A Large & Accurate Map of the City of London* 98

PLATE 15 London Bridge to the Royal Exchange from *A Large & Accurate Map of the City of London* 100

PLATE 16 Plan of tenements in Cheapside owned by Christ's Hospital 102

PLATE 17 East of London Bridge from *London etc. Actually Survey'd* 104

PLATE 18 The West End from *London etc. Actually Survey'd* 106

PLATE 19 Western section of the home counties from *A Map . . . Twenty Miles Round London* 108

PLATE 20 An estate off Bishopsgate Street, from the Survey taken for the Goldsmiths' Company 110

PLATE 21 Central London from the *Actuall Survey of London, Westminster and Southwark* 112

PLATE 22 *An Actual Survey of the Hamlet of Lime-House* 114

PLATE 23 *A New Plan of the City of London, Westminster & Southwark* 118

PLATE 24 *Farringdon Ward Without* 118

PLATE 25 Westminster from *A New and Exact Plan of the Cities of London and Westminster* 120

PLATE 26 North of Oxford Street from a *Plan of the Cities of London & Westminster* 122

PLATE 27 Park Lane from a *Plan of the Cities of London & Westminster etc.* 124

PLATE 28 Greenwich from *An Exact Survey of the City's of London, Westminster . . . and the Country near Ten Miles Round* 126

PLATE 29 *South London* 128

PLATE 30 Part of Hyde Park from a *Survey of Kensington and Hyde Park* 130

PLATE 31 East London from *A Topographical Map of the County of Middlesex* 130

PLATE 32 Holborn to Lambeth from *A New Plan of the City and Liberty of Westminster etc.* 134

PLATE 33 The defences of London during the Gordon Riots in 1780 138

PLATE 34 The country to the southwest of London from *The Country Twenty-Five Miles Round London* 138

PLATE 35 Southwark from the *Plan of the Cities of London and Westminster, the Borough of Southwark and Parts adjoining* 140

PLATE 36 Finsbury from the *Plan of the Cities of London, and Westminster, the Borough of Southwark and Parts adjoining* 142

PLATE 37   *Islington*   146

PLATE 38   East London from the manuscript drawings for the first Ordnance Survey of Essex   146

PLATE 39   Land use in the London region from the *Plan of the Cities of London and Westminster*   150

PLATE 40   The roads from London to Hendon and London to Finchley from the *Survey of the High Roads from London*   150

PLATE 41   The Isle of Dogs from *London and Westminster*   152

PLATE 42   Edgware Road to Chelsea from the *New Two-Sheet Plan of the Cities of London & Westminster*   154

PLATE 43   Regent's Park to Pimlico from the *New and Accurate Plan of London*   156

PLATE 44   Holborn and the Strand from the *Plan of the Cities of London and Westminster*   158

PLATE 45   Central Kensington from the *Plan of the Parish of St. Mary Kensington Reduced from Actual Survey*   160

PLATE 46   Northeast Surrey from the county map   162

PLATE 47   Westminster from the *Map of London from an Actual Survey*   166

PLATE 48   Marylebone from the *Topographical Survey of the Borough of St. Marylebone*   167

PLATE 49   Kentish Town and Regent's Park from the *New Plan of London and its Vicinity*   170

PLATE 50   Proposed changes on the Chelsea waterfront from the *First Report of the Commissioners for Improving the Metropolis*   172

PLATE 51   Central London from a *Balloon View of London as seen from Hampstead*   174

PLATE 52   Bloomsbury to Whitehall from *London*   176

PLATE 53   West London from *London and its environs*   178

PLATE 54   Railway Proposals and Miscellaneous Improvements from the *Library Map of London*   180

PLATE 55   St. John's Wood from Sheet XVI of the first edition 6 in. Ordnance Survey of London   182

PLATE 56   Sydenham from the *Library Map of London*   184

PLATE 57   Administrative Boundaries in East London from the *Administrative Map of London and the Suburbs*   186

PLATE 58   Routes in Central London from the *District Railway Map*   190

PLATE 59   Public Houses in Central London, from *The Modern Plague of London*   190

PLATE 60   Diphtheria cases in East London from *A Map of London Shewing the Several Sanitary Districts*   192

PLATE 61   *Proposed New Road from Charing Cross to the Mall*   194

PLATE 62   Old Westminster from the social survey map of London   196

PLATE 63   Canonbury from the social survey map of London   198

PLATE 64   Central London from the *Monumental Map of London (Industrial & Commercial)*   200

PLATE 65   Section from a *Map of a German night aeroplane raid 31 October 1917*   202

PLATE 66   Targets in East London from the *Stadtplan von London mit militärgeographischen Objekteintragungen*   204

PLATE 67   Post-war reconstruction in the City from *A Report on Improvements Prepared by the Town Planning Committee*   206

PLATE 68   Age/sex structure of the London boroughs from *The Atlas of London*   208

PLATE 69   Central London from the *Greater London* one-sheet map published by the Ordnance Survey   210

Introduction

My aim in writing this book has been to convey some of the enthusiasm I feel for an unjustly neglected subject – urban cartography. Although there is an extensive list of books on county maps and map-makers, virtually nothing of a general nature has been written on the maps of our capital city.

London has inevitably appealed to many writers and artists, and for the past four centuries topographers have been at work depicting its growth with pen and brush. Stow, Strype, Hollar, Scott – their names are familiar and their work is universally known. But maps, too, are pictures of a sort, capturing the state of the capital at one point in time. In the past their appeal has been restricted to a limited few, topographical specialists, but I hope to show in the following pages the wealth of fascinating detail they offer to anyone interested in London's past. For me the concentrated atmosphere of the London world of Pepys, of Hogarth, of Dickens, springs vividly to life when I see on a contemporary map the streets they knew and the coffee houses and taverns which were the background to their lives. Maps indeed are a vital clue in reconstructing the history of London: what better way to see at a glance its development from the compact medieval town to the vast sprawl of today?

As the capital of England and the setting of great national events, London naturally interested map-makers from the first, although the very earliest English town-plans, prepared for Henry VIII and showing strategic coastal towns and ports, slightly ante-date the first printed map of London. This was made in the mid-16th century, and demonstrates how small the walled 'square mile' of the city actually was, although its rôle in national history has been so great.

The first group of maps reproduced here shows a town already mature, but little larger than a market town, and more or less confined by its walls. The medieval commercial centre clustered above London Bridge had not yet spread along the Strand to absorb the separate city of Westminster – home of Parliament, of the law and of three royal palaces. Later maps chart that development through the following centuries as London grew, her spreading skirts taking in the surrounding villages to east, west and north, and southwards across the river. The Fire of 1666 gave fresh impetus both to the western expansion of London, as new houses sprang up in the fields of Soho, and to the demand for up-to-date and accurate maps of the capital; the magnificent surveys of London, Westminster and Southwark published by Ogilby and Morgan set a standard not to be surpassed before the late 18th century.

Town-planning in Georgian London fell to the great land-owners, the Bedfords, Grosvenors and Harleys, whose orderly squares and terraces dominated contemporary maps as they still dominate so much of central London. The violent arrival of the transport revolution in Victorian England provoked an even more dramatic change in the maps, as London sent feelers outwards to create new suburbs on the new omnibus and railway routes.

The 19th-century maps show a city struggling with a fresh difficulty – pressure from a nation drawn to the centre of the Empire: a metropolis of several millions demanded slum clearance, new roads and more rational administrative boundaries to deal with the accumulated problems of 1900 years – all of which required new and accurate maps to the standard of the Ordnance Survey. The pressure still continues; London is now too large and complex to be satisfactorily expressed in a single map, but specialized surveys cover every conceivable aspect of the capital above and below ground.

Certain problems of urban life continually recur; conflicts over water supply, communications, zoning, over-crowding, are characteristic of the urban situation. Maps of London epitomise these recurring themes, and the examples in this book have been chosen partly for the way in which they illustrate the social history of each period.

No-one can say the final word on London, but I have hoped at least to draw attention in this book to a useful and decorative yet often forgotten mirror of its past.

Throughout the book and in all my studies of London maps I have been heavily indebted to the invaluable catalogue of printed maps of London compiled by James Howgego and the late Ida Darlington. Uniquely placed as they were – the one Keeper of the important collection of London maps and prints in the Guildhall Library, the other until 1967 Head Archivist to the Greater London Council – they have created an essential source for all those interested in London maps.

I am particularly grateful for specific advice and information generously given by the following people: Arthur Corfe, British Museum Map Room; Brigadier G. Cox, Archivist at Claydon House, Buckinghamshire; Brian Curle, Kensington Reference Library; Miss Susan Hare, Librarian to the Goldsmiths' Company; Ralph Hyde, Guildhall Library Print Room; David Johnson, House of Lords Record Office; John Phillips, Greater London Council Map Room; and by the staff of the London Museum. I am also grateful to Miss Elsie Cannon, who thought of the topic initially and has encouraged me ever since. Finally, I must thank my husband, who has borne patiently with me during the writing of this book and still finds it interesting.

CHAPTER I

London before the Map-maker

We have, alas, no map of London in its first fifteen centuries. Either no-one felt one to be necessary, or it has not survived the chances of time and decay. Perhaps other sketches of the city, more elaborate and detailed versions of the little drawing by Matthew Paris (Pl. 1) were made, but apparently none exists today; this drawing is thus our only visual clue to the appearance of London before the end of the middle ages. Already the salient features of the capital – its encircling wall, the river and great churches – dominate the scene, but the sketch is not very informative; Matthew Paris did not feel it necessary to provide more geographical detail for his pilgrim-reader than a mileage-table of the distance to the next town.

However, as London has fortunately kept an astonishing degree of continuity, we can, in the absence of contemporary evidence, work back from the known to the unknown.

London's Natural Setting

Although the first settlers left us no account of how the site appeared to them, the combined evidence of geology and archaeology allows us to visualise it before the changes brought by man's occupation.

At first glance the site offered no invitation to found a city. A broad, and of course unbridged, river, with the sea-tide flowing in no further than the present London Bridge, formed both a boundary and an obstacle to the creation of a unified Britain. The Thames, where it flows through London, was in prehistoric times both shallower and several hundred feet wider than now; as South-East England gradually sinks, in a movement imperceptible except on a geological time-scale, so the fading of the last Ice Age has raised the level of the sea and propelled the tide further and further up the Thames, until today only the presence of a weir at Teddington prevents its further progress. The river has risen between 10 and 15 feet in relation to the land in the past 2000 years; mud flats excavated on Bankside, about 10 feet below London Bridge Station, were repeatedly flooded by the river in the Roman period, until by the end of the 4th century A.D. the silt deposited had built up the ground several feet above the then water level. For 1200 years the river crept up, until at the beginning of the Tudor period the area was again an inhospitable, waterlogged marsh. Since 1500 the Thames has risen another five or six feet, so that this part of London is once more at risk of flooding; at the spring high tides the water is inches above the roadway along Bankside, confined only by the river wall.

Now largely conquered by modern drainage and built over, in earlier centuries those low-lying alluvial marshes which flanked the Thames on either side in the London region defied development. In the 19th century the mean streets of Pimlico, built on the flood plain of the Thames within half a mile of the Houses of Parliament, were regularly flooded at high tide, and even today the repeated calls for a Thames barrage are a pointed reminder that many of London's inhabitants live at risk from the Thames. The marsh is not entirely inhospitable; this alluvial soil has been turned to good effect in East London's dock-filled loop of the Thames – now itself gradually to be reclaimed for housing. A glance at the modern map shows open spaces close to the centre of London along the river, at Fulham and Battersea, spaces which, unsuitable for building, have been used for parks, power stations and football grounds.

The marsh is pierced at intervals by low, gravel-capped plateaux, the Taplow terraces, which run particularly behind the north bank. To the south the marsh extends in a wider band, by the river, the gravel uplands being most clearly recognised in the great open spaces of Wimbledon Common and Richmond Park. The well-drained terraces close to the north bank were perhaps less heavily wooded than the surrounding clays, which must have presented an almost impossible obstacle to primitive settlement. Epping Forest is now the last surviving fragment of the ancient woods of the London region: as Defoe commented in his *Tour through England and Wales*: 'this forest of Epping has been a wild or forest ever since this island was, before the Romans landed in Britain'.

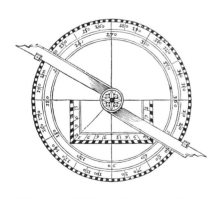

Diagram of 'Theodolitus' from *Pantometria* by L. Digges, 1571

The Thames – Celtic highway into Britain

The Celtic and Belgic settlers of Britain avoided the heavily wooded London area; the Thames to them was merely a boundary for quarrelling tribes and a means of access for traders from Europe; the true potential of the river-bank site was to be realised later by a centralised power coming from the open sea and needing to control the heart of Britain. Nothing that can be called a substantial early settlement has yet been discovered nearer to London than Heathrow. The 'Cæsar's Camp' of Wimbledon is also prehistoric – not Roman as the name suggests – but whether a homestead or simply a defensive site is not certain. Those Iron Age objects, metalwork and pottery, which have been found on the bed of the Thames are not in themselves strong evidence for settlement, only indications of the river's use as a highway.

The Roman settlement

But to the Romans invading in A.D. 43 the gravels of Middlesex did not appeal; their first essential was a defensible bridgehead on the Thames, the focus of routes through Southern Britain. The invading power had at all costs to protect its supply-and-command chain back to the heart of the Empire.

The first Roman town, described by Tacitus as a colony of Continental merchants, may have received a Celtic name, but it was an alien growth; as such it was burnt by Boudicca in the revolt only 17 years after the Romans arrived. A thick layer of destruction containing blackened pottery and household goods turns up under the archaeologist's trowel in the City and Southwark, indicating that even in the few years since their arrival the Romans had established a southern suburb across the river. The exact site of the bridge connecting the two has never been found, although it must have been at or near the then tidal limits of the Thames. All trace of it may have been destroyed in the many subsequent relayings of the bridge piles, but it is possible that the forthcoming redevelopment in Southwark may give a chance to plot the Roman roads leading to the bridge from Kent and Surrey, so pinpointing at least its southern end. We can be sure that it stood somewhere on the narrow gravel ridge on the Southwark bank, since the alluvial marsh does not provide an adequate footing; it ran north to the gravel plateau east of the Walbrook valley and St. Paul's, which still rises steeply from the riverside. The river Thames then lapped at the south side of Thames Street against a steep gravel bank, but reclamation through the centuries has pushed out the shore many feet into the river's width. (The process still continues; at Blackfriars 150 feet of foreshore is at present being converted to dry land for a developer, at great cost, but with the promise of great profit in over-crowded central London.)

Half a century or more after the invasion, an elaborate town-planning scheme was imposed on London – as yet an unwalled cluster of houses, shops and wharves concentrated in the eastern half of the city around Cornhill. There is no historical reference to this, and archaeology cannot provide a precise date, but sometime late in the 1st century or a little later, as part of this development, a forum and a magnificent basilica were built. The latter, by far the longest in Britain, lies partly under Leadenhall Market, and indicates London's contemporary standing among the Roman towns of the British province. It may already have achieved in effect the status of a provincial capital; although we lack a written account of Roman London, stamped tiles and bricks give evidence for three major administrative buildings in London. Made at a local brickworks, they are stamped P.PR.BR.LON. or variants of these letters, equivalent perhaps to our familiar MPBW for the Ministry of Public Building and Works. Authority there must have been to lay out the street grid, which sadly survives less clearly in London than in other Roman towns (for instance, Chester). The massive building discovered under Cannon Street Station on the river front is assumed from its size and magnificence to have been the Governor's palace or *praetorium* of the British province.

The 12-acre stone fort at Cripplegate in the north-west corner of the city contained a garrison of 1500–2000 men, too large for purely defensive purposes, but probably appropriate for the ceremonial of a provincial capital. Certainly the many town houses discovered in the city equipped with fine mosaic floors and elaborate bath-houses indicate a wealthy and sizeable community. Oddly, no sign of those other adjuncts to civilised living, an amphitheatre and theatre, has yet been discovered in London; perhaps as in later periods these places of entertainment stood in the south bank suburb. Probably the best-known of the Roman buildings of London is the Mithraeum, which stood on the east bank of the Walbrook, just behind Walbrook

Street running down to the river. This temple, the only building of Roman London whose plan is preserved above ground, has been partially raised from under Bucklersbury House where it was excavated, and reconstructed on a terrace in Queen Victoria Street, 60 yards away from and many feet above the original site.

Walls, Gates and Roads

The Roman town was not walled in stone before the end of the 2nd century or a few years later, but the defences then built were to determine the shape of London for over 1000 years. Medieval re-building of the wall has ensured that the line of Roman work survives, even if only in the lower courses, and it can be seen in several places round the city, notably in St. Alphage Church-yard, Noble Street and the Tower. Digging since the last war has added to the story, so now we know that the Romans built bastions only in the eastern sector of the wall, perhaps the direction from which they expected danger. There is no evidence that they felt it necessary to protect the river frontage, although it was from this vulnerable direction that London was repeatedly attacked later, in the Viking period.

Six of the gateways in the wall certainly have Roman origins; we are unfortunate in that none has survived re-building (although FitzStephen recorded several double gateways still standing in the 12th century). The superb road system which radiated from London for rapid marching to the rest of the province still to some extent determines the lines of the roads today; Ermine Street or the Kingsland Road still points straight into the eastern section of London as it has done for 2000 years. Within the city, however, the chaos into which London lapsed during the dark ages, and particularly its repeated destruction by fire in the 9th century, led to the disappearance of Roman street-lines under building rubble. The continuous build-up of the ground level due to man's dumping of rubbish within the walls has buried Roman layers as much as 20 feet down, so that the Roman street-lines lie under our feet. Still, there are considerable coincidences of direction which must indicate some degree of continuity of use, at least of the site of a road, if not of its actual surface. For example, a thickly metalled Roman street runs for at least 370 yards east to west, 300 yards north of and parallel to the river, largely under Lombard Street; Wood Street is on the line of the central roadway of the Cripplegate Fort, and Cheapside, Newgate Street and Cannon Street all overlie sections of Roman metalling. Edgware Road or Watling Street, although a Roman road, points towards the river-crossing at Westminster and makes no deviation towards London, bending sharply east at Marble Arch; it may follow an earlier trackway from Kent to the tribal capital at St. Albans.

The Saxon city

London's layout in the centuries up to the Norman Conquest and beyond is far less easy to reconstruct. Later intensive re-building has destroyed the Anglo-Saxon levels, so preventing rescue by the spade; the earlier Roman layers have been protected by later accumulations of soil and débris, but in central London it is rare to find undisturbed even late Roman, let alone medieval, sites. There are exceptions: isolated finds indicate that the earliest settlement by the Saxons was in the emptier western half of the city; perhaps the Walbrook or 'stream of strangers' represented to the Saxons a genuine boundary between their area and that still inhabited by the Romanised Britons in the crumbling ruins of London. Professor Grimes has found a dark age hut, a solitary reminder of the Saxon community within the walls. On the western side of the city, St. Bride's, Fleet Street, marks the beginnings of suburban development; the first Saxon church, whose walls stand to a height of 3 or 4 feet in the crypt, itself covers a Roman building. Further west again, London's other half, Westminster, traces its first beginnings as a community to the Anglo-Saxons. The re-building of the Treasury early in the 1960's produced an unexpected discovery behind Whitehall; a 9th-century timber hall was revealed which had once stood on an oak raft in marshy ground by Treasury Green, half a mile from the community 'aet Westminster' which was granted land by Offa. This watery, low-lying area, through which the two streams of the Tyburn ran, offered a small gravel plateau first occupied by an obscure monastery destroyed by the Danes; on this site Edward the Confessor's church was to be built, to form the nucleus of the later great abbey and royal palace.

For more substantial knowledge of London's plan during this pre-map period we are forced to turn to contemporary or later documents, to early church dedications and to clues from the site-continuity of certain buildings;

for instance, London was given a bishop by Augustine in 604. Perhaps a church existed already on the site of St. Paul's, although Bede gives an account of King Athelberht, acting as patron, having built a church; certainly in all the subsequent rebuildings of the magnificent cathedral the memory has persisted of that first little wooden structure. Several other churches preserve hints of their Saxon ancestry, perhaps in the form of stonework, which is least likely to be touched by remodelling of the body of the church, as at All Hallows, Barking, or in their dedications.

From all this we know that throughout the centuries of attack and destruction by successive invaders, first from Frisia, later from Scandinavia, London kept its identity and some form of community life. The wall was never destroyed and was repaired by Alfred; a bridge survived, either that built by the Romans or a later structure – although the former is more likely, since the unsettled times were not suited to such a major undertaking. London retained trading links with Europe, as the contents of pagan Saxon graves indicate, and by the Norman Conquest it was again the leading city of Britain, although probably there were fewer inhabitants within the walled 330 acres than 800 years before. Each of the twin hills of Ludgate and Cornhill, on either side of the Walbrook valley, had its market place, East and West Cheap, and its quay, Billingsgate and Queenhythe. Clear ground abounded within the walls; north-east of St. Paul's was the great meeting place for the folkmoot. When William I built his White Tower to dominate the City he did not need to clear away citizens' houses as he did at Lincoln.

London under the Normans

From the century after the Conquest our knowledge of London increases dramatically, as the city itself increased in wealth and in new buildings. Deeds and charters provide the minute evidence on which a plan of London, recreated from property boundaries, might eventually be based. Scholars have for many years been studying these medieval records, with fascinating results, though as yet no overall detailed plan of the city has been prepared.

We have, however, William FitzStephen's description of London, written in c. 1180 as introduction to a panegyric of that great Londoner Thomas Becket; this gives a vivid word picture of a populous city crowded with churches – almost 100 within the walls – drawing on the fertile cornfields of Middlesex for its markets, but with the bulk of its trade river-borne. The river highway carried not only bulky provisions and merchandise from Queenhythe (the oldest dock), Dowgate, Billingsgate and the mouth of the Fleet, but also passenger traffic to and from Westminster and the villages further upstream, which were more accessible by water than by foot along rutted country tracks as yet unmapped and still to be dignified by the name of road.

Charing Cross, so called from the cierring or turning in Akeman Street (the ancient road from the city to Bath and the west, which here bends north up Haymarket) was already a road junction when FitzStephen wrote; here the King's road from Westminster, now Whitehall, met the highway to Kensington and the west. An Eleanor cross was erected here by Edward I between 1291 and 1294 in memory of his dead wife's last resting place before her burial in Westminster Abbey. Within 70 years the hamlet had become Charing Cross. (The cross was pulled down in the Civil War, and the replica outside Charing Cross station is quite wrongly placed, as the original cross stood where Whitehall meets Trafalgar Square.)

London's riverside was dominated from east to west by three great structures, the looming mass of the Tower standing within its own moat, the Custom House and quaysides stacked with cranes, and, near the mouth of the Fleet river, Baynard's Castle, the royal tower whose site passed to the Black Friars in 1279, and which was rebuilt by Paul's Wharf (Pl. 15). When the friars bought the property they also obtained permission to pull down the Roman city wall in the south-west corner of London, to extend their precinct, so creating one of the largest estates within the city and changing its walled line for the last time. The wall as rebuilt by the citizens stood further to the west.

Great Medieval Houses

Blackfriars was only one of the sizeable precincts within the medieval city created by religious houses and noblemen, which swallowed up the available space in gardens and orchards and large churches and forced men to build houses outside the walls. In 1222 London formally extended its jurisdiction to the Bars, points on the main roads out of London which are still marked today – as at Temple Bar in the Strand and by Staple Inn in Holborn – by the City's winged dragon on a pedestal. These liberties mark the extent to which the city grew in the middle ages, although they did not confine it; Fleet Prison stood outside the wall, and already the Strand, although low-lying and badly drained, was lined on the south by the White Friars' church and cemetery and the Old and New Temples before Temple Bar was reached. Beyond this point to the west lay Middlesex and the Liberty of the Savoy, flanked by the London houses of the bishops of Llandaff and Carlisle. (Traces still exist of these distinguished owners in the street names of this area, although all the estates had changed hands several times before the 17th century – apart from the Savoy, continuously part of the Duchy of Lancaster since the 13th century.) (Pl. 4)

Episcopal and private inns lie under Charing Cross station, and the Hospital of St. Mary Rouncevall under Northumberland Avenue. In spite of the narrow river frontage and the flat, marshy ground, this area along the bank exerted a tremendous pull in the middle ages, because it was so near to Westminster and the palace. In 1240 the Archbishop of York bought the stretch between the present Westminster Tube Station and Scotland Yard as an official London residence; incidentally, some of this estate, extracted by Henry VIII from Wolsey and so now part of the concentration of administrative buildings which replaced the royal palace of Whitehall, is soon to be excavated, one of the few sites on the north bank ever likely to be available for detailed investigation.

At the far end of King Street or Whitehall lay the royal palace of Westminster, the place where Parliament met, interlocked building by building with the precinct of the abbey and dominated by its church. Even their different functions, administrative and religious, were confused, from lack of space to expand on the cramped site; the Chapter House of the Abbey remained the meeting place of the House of Commons until the death of Henry VIII. Very little survives of the medieval palace, apart from the magnificence of Westminster Hall and a moated three-storey tower, the Jewel Tower, in the western corner of the old royal garden – the palace was largely destroyed by fire in 1512, and Henry did not choose to re-build.

Behind the palace and abbey of Westminster on its gravel island stretched empty flats to the riverside hamlets of Chelsea and Fulham. The Domesday references to the lands of the Bishop of London at Fulham underline the treelessness of that marshy area; he owned no pannage for swine there, but had enough for a herd of 1000 in woodlands near Finchley.

Facing Westminster across the river stood (and still stands) London's greatest ecclesiastical palace, the London home of the Archbishop of Canterbury, Lambeth. This 13th-century palace did not become the focus of a village before the 16th century, but stood isolated on the south bank, cut off by marshes from its hinterland of Surrey. (Pl. 3)

This brief description of London's earlier growth has inevitably taken greater account of institutional buildings than of the houses of the ordinary Londoner; after all, the perpetual corporations maintained their estates intact through many generations and so substantially influenced the course of London's layout. Private individuals were less influential; families rose and fell in two or three generations, and no large private enclaves were created and preserved in the city comparable to those of the religious houses. Certain wealthy merchants did build great houses, but a part of one only survives, and that not on its original site – Crosby Hall, now part of an international hostel in Chelsea, was once the hall of the great town house built by Sir John Crosby in 1468 adjacent to the churchyard gate of St. Helen's, Bishopgate.

The Tudor Discovery of England

So much for our picture of early London, pieced together with help from archaeology, from scattered and often obscure documentary references and a few surviving structures. Indeed, this relative blank is true of almost all England before the 16th century; scholars, with a few exceptions such as Matthew Paris, were uninterested in topography, and maps did not exist.

Two notable exceptions were the 15th-century topographers, John Rous and William of Worcester. In the 1470's when the latter was writing about a journey from Norwich to St. Michael's Mount, he gave distances between towns, the course of rivers and a detailed description of Bristol from which has been reconstructed a plan of the medieval town. His methods were not scientific (he used his own pace as a measure of distance), but his intentions were original and his achievement unique in its time.

Some half a century after William of Worcester came the traveller John Leland, determined to bring English topography 'oute of deadely darknes to lyvely lighte'. He planned his itineraries with an eventual map of the country in mind, and proposed to have engraved for Henry VIII 'this your world and impery of England so set forth in a quadrate table of silver'. Unfortunately Leland went mad and left his notes incomplete, but his is the first scientific detached account of England as he found it, relatively uncluttered by legends of Brutus and Lud.

In Queen Elizabeth's England, a host of antiquaries and topographers were at work, and specialist fields had begun to emerge. Although John Norden combined both the preparation of maps and the gathering of information for his *Speculum*, his contemporary William Camden relied on professional cartographers to produce maps for the *Britannia*. English mapmaking was by then fully launched.

London itself shared in all this new topographical enthusiasm, and from the end of the 15th century our knowledge increases dramatically. A flood of information about the city is available, some methodically gathered, as in John Stow's *Survey*, some impressionistic but none the less intriguing, such as the reports of the Venetian ambassadors, and it is supplemented for the first time by maps and map-views. The self-conscious spirit of curiosity characteristic of the Renaissance Englishman is reflected in his new interest in his surroundings.

The earliest printed view of London.
Woodcut by W. de Worde,
Westminster, 1497

CHAPTER II

Early Plans and Surveys

The English impetus to map cities was at first the fruit of antiquarian enthusiasm, and the results to a modern eye are less informative than decorative; contemporary taste preferred a perspective or bird's-eye view, not a measured ground plan, at least until the very end of Elizabeth's reign. The herald and topographer William Smith drew 'plats' or profiles of English cities in this style; his London is a city crammed with spires and great palaces, dominated by St. Paul's and the Tower, none of which would have stood out so impressively in a true map. Although he had lived for several years in Nuremberg and evidently acquired there considerable knowledge of the German conventions of true map-making, he preferred the more picturesque form of map-view. (Pl. 5).

The compromise achieved by most map-makers until at least the end of the 17th century was to draw the roads, river and outline of property or parish in flat plan, but to give a three-dimensional view of buildings so as to emphasise their full splendour. The art of map-making 'consisteth rather in describing the quality and figure, than in the bignesse and quantitie of anything', Cuningham commented in his *Cosmographical Glasse* of 1559.

This preference for the picturesque extended to the filling of the open spaces which skirted London, not only with such necessary cartographic information as a scale and a compass rose, but also with figures of humans and animals. On Braun and Hogenberg's well-known map of Tudor London, a true plan, but with the addition of buildings in elevation, the cartographer has lovingly delineated laundresses in Moorfields and deer grazing in the royal parks, and has also shown the bull- and bear-baiting rings of Bankside so totally out of scale that Maid Lane runs quite hopelessly out of line and disappears behind the Londoners in the foreground, instead of meeting Deadman's Place as it should. (Pl. 3)

In 16th-century England the science of map-making was new; the instruments and techniques for accurate surveying barely existed and their use was misunderstood. Fitzherbert's handbook of advice to the surveyor, published first in 1523, describes in elaborate detail how the traditional written survey of an estate should be prepared, but ignores the potential value of a drawn plan. Such medieval plans as we have seem to be mere memory-joggers, rough sketches to supplement the full and detailed written account or to illustrate the details in a lawsuit. In this class is the early 15th-century sketch plan of Chertsey Abbey in the Public Record Office, or the well-known diagram of the Charterhouse water supply. They are not the result of a measured survey on the ground, but merely a visual reminder or note for office use; this type of sketch barely merits the title of map, but the detail given is often fascinating and too obscure to have been recorded on larger and more formal maps. A crude sketch plan of Southwark of *c.* 1542, also in the Public Record Office and unfortunately too faint for reproduction, marks and names the famous taverns and noble houses of the riverside suburb, names which are familiar to us from Elizabethan plays, yet whose sites would but for this plan not be ascertainable.

The Surveyor Comes into his own

Economic pressures increasingly encouraged the improving land-owner to set out in plan form the exact boundaries and acreages of his estate. In London this process was given impetus by the high price of land within the city, resulting from the pressure of a population rising more rapidly than ever before. The subdivision of great city houses into tenements became commonplace; the aftermath of the Reformation threw onto the land market vast walled precincts which were rapidly split up, to the confusion of traditional boundaries. In this situation the professional surveyor found work, establishing the exact bounds and extent of properties previously never planned, whose new owners were not content to use merely the traditional written record.

The earliest examples in London of the new scientific approach to property surveying are a series of late 15th-century house plans from south of the river, part of the Bridge House estates; a century later surveyors were at

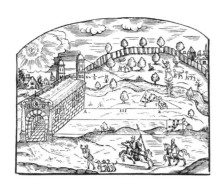

Surveyors at work from *Pantometria*
by L. Digges, 1571

work all over London for the Crown, the City and the great land-owning institutions, laying the foundations of a great series of property surveys, still largely unexploited, but potentially of enormous value to the London topographer. The conventions of these manuscript surveys are strange at first sight to the modern eye, since the draughtsman combined his ground plan with sketches of house-fronts, perhaps as a quick reminder as to the exact location and identity of each property. (Pl. 6)

The precise purpose for which any given survey was drawn up is not always apparent, and so it is not possible to say exactly what the draughtsman might have omitted as irrelevant; in many of them, however, the incidental matter is of great interest. A delightful example is the small watercolour 'plat' of Cheapside dated 1585 by Ralph Treswell – an artist from a notable family of contemporary London surveyors; in plotting and measuring the line of pipes to the Cheapside conduit (as preparation perhaps for relaying or repairs to it as a result of Barnard Randolph's donation of £900 two years earlier), he has depicted in large and loving detail a group of the wooden water 'cans' or barrels customarily left standing at the conduit by the street water-sellers. They do not detract from the accuracy of his plan, however, and he has provided the necessary additional matter of a compass rose and a scale of feet. A series of plans revealing a much greater section of London, but with a similar combination of naïvety and accuracy, were prepared by an anonymous surveyor for St. Bartholomew's Hospital in about 1617; they cover not only the Hospital precincts, but also its house property beyond the walls, identifying other owners and including such details as the bowling alley under London Wall at the north end of Chick Lane. Another such plan, prepared by Aaron Rathborne in 1618 to show disputed roads in Southwark, is of considerable incidental interest, as it settles the vexed question as to whether the Globe Theatre stood north or south of Maiden Lane.

These plans prepared for lawyers' and land-owners' purposes survive in relatively large numbers, in many cases still in the hands of the institution, hospital or inn of court for which they were originally made; unfortunately, due to the chances of heredity, families are less likely than perpetual corporations to preserve intact plans from early periods. Examined side by side and reduced to a common scale, such plans, if available, could form the basis of a street-by-street, even house-by-house, study of the oldest parts of London.

The first printed Maps

No manuscript plan, however, shows more than a part of London; to see the city's past at a glance one must turn, as did the Tudors, to the maps and panoramas which were being published from the mid-16th century onwards.

Printing presupposes a popular demand, but in England a market for maps had been slow to grow. The earliest European printed map was engraved on copper in Italy about 1473; not until a century later, in 1572, did an Englishman engrave and publish a map. A few maps had already been published in London, crude woodcuts like the map of England sold by Bagford to Pepys for 5 shillings; dated 'between 1520 and 1530', it was 'Printed from a wooden cut by Winkin de Woorde wch is an extraordinary Rarity, and was so contrived as to be folded up in an Almanack'. A rarity indeed, and one which sadly Pepys has not preserved for us. Better known, and sometimes called the original of the 'Agas' map, is the 'Carde of London' entered at Stationers' Hall in 1562–3. This was one in a list of popular prints, mainly portraits of royalty and saints, entered by Giles Godhed or Godet, indicating perhaps an awakening interest in maps as ornament. As no contemporary English pictures show us maps used as wall decoration, we cannot argue with certainty that they were so used before the 17th century, but the court taste for topographical pictures, indicated by Henry VIII's ownership of a painted 'plat' of London, may have stimulated the production of cheaper versions for those unable to afford the services of a Wyngaerde or some other contemporary topographical artist.

In 1572 came the first English map made by engraving, that technique which is so much more appropriate than woodcut for the precise detail required in a town map. It was published by Humphrey Cole, protégé of Matthew Parker, that Archbishop of Canterbury who had surrounded himself with continental topographical artists and engravers. Some seven maps of London appeared between 1550 and 1600, four published abroad, and all but one most probably engraved by foreigners. All but two of the surviving printed maps were prepared for cosmographies or similar accounts of the world and its cities, a tribute to contemporary curiosity about England in Europe, but all are derived from a common original now lost, and not surveyed afresh for each publication, so that the different maps give no fresh information; they show in fact a city already vanishing.

Certainly the best-known of these early maps of London is that engraved on copper and published in Germany in 1572 by Braun and Hogenberg in volume one of their atlas *Civitates Orbis Terrarum*. From internal evidence it is clear that the map shows London in the 1550's; for example, the spire of St. Paul's appears, a famous landmark which was struck by lightning in 1561 and never replaced; the map was not brought up-to-date in later editions or when republished by François de Belle Forest and Sebastian Munster in 1575 and 1598, and only one modification was ever made to the original plate: the Royal Exchange, London's great pride, was opened by the Queen in 1571, and since this important addition could not be ignored, a neat insertion was made, visible on plate 3. Many copies of this map were printed; as late as 1660 Janssen of Amsterdam published it in a collection of maps of European cities.

The German publishers of the *Civitates*, who rarely had a town re-surveyed if they could obtain and copy an existing map, had used as their basis an earlier and much larger copper-engraved map, adding to it details of interest to their German public, such as the figures in the foreground, typical Londoners in the costume of the mid-16th century, and a cartouche with an account of the Hanse in London.

Lost Tudor Treasure

No copy of this large map of London now exists, but fortunately it seems to have been drawn and engraved by a master-cartographer, and even in the greatly reduced plate of Braun and Hogenberg's map its quality can be gauged. By chance, two worn-out copper plates, of the 20 from which it was printed, have survived intact because the warm tone of copper was popular with certain contemporary Flemish artists; the reverse of each copper plate has been used as the base for an oil painting, one of the Tower of Babel by Martin von Valkenburgh, the other a Madonna and Child by an unknown artist. Presumably, unless the map was engraved abroad, these old copper plates were exported from London to Flanders and bought by the artists for the sake of their metal.

The two surviving copper plates cover the centre of the city, from Bow Church to Spitalfields, and the countryside outside the city wall to the north, where now office blocks loom; there the engraver has depicted groups of Londoners at work and play in Finsbury Fields – laundresses, milkmaids and youths at archery practice. (Pl. 2) The large scale of three chains to the inch (comparable with the Ordnance Survey 25-inch to the mile sheets) allows the three-dimensional drawings of houses and churches to supplement without swamping the purely cartographic detail as to street direction and width, and the combination enables one to walk around Tudor London in the mind's eye and to recognise familiar narrow streets and angles and intersections hardly changed in four centuries. The city wall, ditch and posterns are clearly marked (with traitors' limbs displayed on Moorgate), as is the line of spacious suburban houses and gardens outside Bishopsgate, in dramatic contrast with the cramped roofs within the wall. Although the wall has gone – demolished as an inconvenience during the 18th century – its name persists, albeit applied now to a five-lane highway on a new alignment. On the copper plate summer houses and tenter grounds line the west side of Bishopsgate Street where today Liverpool Street Station stands. Other streets visible on the map today still obstinately follow their own crooked lines, reminding us that once these rural lanes had to curve round the walled precincts of Austin Friars and St. Bartholomew's Hospital.

Thanks to John Stow's loving and elaborate description of London in his *Survey*, both as he knew it and as it had been in former times, we are able to identify very many of the houses in the map and give at least an approximate date as to when the unknown map-maker was at work surveying and sketching London. For example, the cross in St. Botolph's churchyard, removed as part of the Protestant reaction in 1559, is clearly marked. The cartographer knew London's streets, although he mis-spelt some familiar names, such as St. Miguelis and St. Taphins for St. Michael Bassishaw and St. Alphage; these misunderstandings may indicate that he was an Italian. The extraordinary dearth of native topographical artists in Tudor England has encouraged the attribution of this map to Anthony van den Wyngaerde, who in the reign of Philip and Mary drew the magnificent panorama of London now in the Ashmolean Museum. He was later to prepare topographical drawings of cities in all Philip's domains, and perhaps London was to be the first of the series, but the political reversals on Mary's death put paid to Philip's hopes of England. Apart from the coincidence of date, there is no evidence to link Wyngaerde with the copper-plate map; his style is that of the topographical artist, not of the cartographer. It is still possible that another plate giving more information – even the name of the cartographer – might emerge from some private collection.

Although presumably many copies of this great map were printed, since the plates are buckled and so worn that it is now impossible to take an impression from them, none survives today. The loss is irreparable; even in so small an area the map-maker has demonstrated not only his detailed knowledge of London topography, but also his graphic skill. Its quality must have been apparent at the time; apart from the smaller derivations published abroad by Braun and Hogenberg and others, a woodcut version (known as the *Civitas Londinum* map from its 17th-century title, and mistakenly attributed by George Vertue to Ralph Agas the Elizabethan map-maker) was published in at least two editions, the second in the reign of James I. (Pl. 8)

Three copies of the Jacobean edition survive, one in the Pepys Library, Magdalene College, Cambridge, thanks to Pepys's assiduous collecting of Londoniana, one in the Public Record Office and one at the Guildhall. Though of comparable size with the estimated dimensions of the copper-engraved map, the woodcut is not an identical copy of it: the spire of St. Paul's is missing and the Royal Exchange has been inserted, two London landmarks of such importance that no map-cutter working in London could ignore them. However, although the map was brought up-to-date by the insertion of a block containing James's coat of arms, the royal barge on the river still flaunts the Tudor flag untouched, and the woodcut map shows London largely unchanged since 1553–9 when Agas was only a boy.

Vertue's re-engraving of the woodcut in 1738 is perhaps better known than its Tudor progenitor; under the title of *Civitas Londinum Circiter Ano Dni MDLX* or *London about the year 1560*, his engraving was reproduced by several London publishers in the 18th and 19th centuries. Initially, Vertue used as his original a large map belonging to Sir Hans Sloane, which may have been a copy of the copper-engraved map; unfortunately he later altered his plates to agree with the woodcut, itself a derivation from the earlier map. It is tantalising to think that had Vertue not changed his mind, he might have preserved for us a version of the complete copper-plate map. His mid-18th century engraving has itself had a numerous progeny, each cruder than the last, but far better-known that their carefully drawn Tudor ancestor.

Books of Maps – Country and Town

During the reign of Elizabeth I contemporary interest in geography and history stimulated a burst of enthusiasm for county maps and histories. Saxton's atlas of 1579, the best-known and finest of the series, was the first of a line of printed county maps, some published as separate sheets, but most collected into book form. The map-makers provided what their customers wanted: decorative hand-coloured maps, lacking roads and mileage scales, but marking clearly the noble seats, parks and market towns. In the absence of any more accurate maps, these were seized on and bought not only by collectors like Dr. John Dee, but also for professional purposes; Burleigh's proof set of Saxton's counties bears annotations in his own hand as to the homes of the justices of the peace in each shire, and Saxton himself had been sponsored in his work of mapping England from 'Towre Castle, highe place or hill' by Thomas Seckford, Surveyor of the Court of Wards, a man with a professional interest in the plotting of England's great estates.

The famous English county historian William Camden in his *Britannia* discoursed brilliantly on the antiquities of the English counties, but in Latin; more popular in both size and approach was the projected *Speculum Britanniae* of John Norden, in which each county was to be the subject of a separate study, illustrated by a map. The only county published was Middlesex, due to Norden's inability to attract adequate patronage. English patrons were slow to appreciate the practical value of town plans; Norden in vain urged Lord Treasurer Burleigh to patronise the mapping of England, 'the most principall townes Cyties and Castles within every shire should be briefly & expertly plotted in their estate and forme as at this day they are.' Fortunately Norden surveyed for the book (a neat pocket- or saddlebag-sized volume published in 1593) maps of London and Westminster that were outstanding for the time in their accuracy and detail. 'The more things (as I take it) are observed, the more like is the discription to the thing discribed'; a sound principle for a map-maker and one to which Norden adhered. Since the crowded detail of Westminster and the Court was too great for his small scale, he used a key of numbered and lettered references, the first English map-maker to do so; he was also the first and almost the only one to find a neat if unorthodox solution to the perennial problem for London map-makers of how to represent both cities, London and Westminster, on one small sheet of a map without compressing or distorting the awkward bend in the river between the Strand and Whitehall. He simply published a separate map of each. (Pl. 4)

The convenience of Norden's London map was obviously appreciated; it was re-issued separately in 1623, entitled 'A guide for cuntreymen by the helpe of wich plot they shall be able to know how farr it is to any street. As also to go unto the same, without forder troble.' Two of the smaller 17th-century maps were similarly re-issued later with the visitor in mind, those originally published by Dankerts in 1633 and by Porter in 1655; presumably the ignorant countryman would eagerly snap up this modern aid, unaware that the map he bought might be up to half a century old and out-of-date.

Several other schemes for publishing collections of town maps as well as county maps were in the air late in the reign of Elizabeth; Speed is well-known for the town plans published in his *Theatrum Orbis Terrarum*, but he used the work of earlier map-makers, notably Norden, and did not initiate any new survey of London. A slightly earlier but abortive attempt to assemble maps and profiles of British cities into an atlas which would have pre-dated Speed's has recently been recognised; Jodocus Hondius, early in the reign of James I, engraved several town profiles which had been originally drawn by the herald William Smith. Smith's manuscript volume of notes on and maps of English towns, now in the British Museum, was prepared about 1588; several of the town plans are in his own hand and betray considerable knowledge of cartographic techniques common in Germany but only gradually becoming familiar in England, such as the grid for map references and the table of symbols, the result perhaps of his decade's residence in Nuremberg. London is represented not by a true map, but by a profile or bird's-eye view on three leaves, which emphasises the splendid buildings along the river front. (Pl. 5)

Had William Smith succeeded in publishing the volume his would have been the earliest atlas of English town plans; William Harrison, in his famous *Description of England* prefixed to Holinshed's *Chronicles*, refers hopefully to 'Mr. Seckford's' scheme for publishing town plans, but presumably, unlike the county maps, this failed to come off.

The Map-maker's Problems

This lack of printed town plans, at a time when county and maritime maps were popular, is explained partly perhaps by lack of demand, but more probably by the sheer inability to make them. Until the middle of the century the English surveyor was unlikely to have any more sophisticated measuring device than a line coated in wax. Even Saxton probably used nothing more elaborate than a plane table on which he sketched the countryside around him, as he saw it from some high place; just before Saxton began his survey, Leonard Digges' *Pantometria* was published, the first English handbook on surveying to describe the use of the circumferentor, under the name of 'theodolite', an instrument vital for the survey of large areas; but its use was slow to spread, in the preparation of printed maps at least.

The criticisms offered to map-makers may be gauged from Norden's revealing defence of his techniques in the *Preparative*, a prospectus for his proposed *Speculum Britanniae* published in 1596; he gives a vivid picture of the weaknesses of English mapping techniques at that time. One major problem was the lack of a standardised mile; 'the ordinary miles of England (especially such as are remote any way 30 miles from London) contain neere $1\frac{1}{2}$ miles of the greatest account'. He therefore defended his omission of a mile scale on the grounds that 'the true content of an English mile is not anywhere extant . . . but received by tradition', an inadequate authority for a mathematical man. None of the London maps before the Fire provides more than a scale of paces or a scale of feet, both copied from bad or poorly-equipped surveyor's usage.

'Some errors of necessitie will be committed, especially by reason of hills, dales, woods and other impediments which intercept the view from station to station;' in mapping London this surveying problem noted by Norden was aggravated by the impossibility of obtaining a clear view from any vantage point into all the cramped and narrow streets and alleys of the city. The surveyor's rod alone was not enough, and the picturesque profile inaccurate; while each generation appreciated the need for an exact survey and criticised the efforts of its predecessors, none before the Fire succeeded in improving on them.

In any case, whether the map-maker could produce a true plan or not, the public wanted something more attractive and more expressive of their pride in London; Fitzherbert had summed it up and rejected the true cartographic method earlier in the century: 'if the citie of London sholde be surveyed, the surveyor may not stande at Hygate, not at Shotershylle, nor yet at the Blackheth, nor suche other places, & overlooke the citie on every syde. For if he do, he shall not see the goodly stretes, the fayre buyldings nor the great substance of rychesse conteyned in them!'

Ralph Agas implicitly criticised the ever-popular romanticised profile when he stressed the need for a map with practical uses; he saw no point in 'setting out a Citie Borough and Towne, except you so lay out the streets, waies and allies as may serve a just measure for paving thereof, distance between place and place and such other thinges of use'. Agas never achieved his projected map of London, so we do not know whether it would have conformed to his principles, and London continued to lack such a map.

Another man who planned to survey and publish a map of London on up-to-date scientific principles but whose work, if completed, has not survived, was the experienced land steward Aaron Rathborne, who published a handbook on the use of mathematical instruments in surveying which went into many editions. He first mentioned his proposed large-scale copper-engraved map of the cities of London and Westminster in 1617: 'there hath never been made or taken any true or perfect description, but false & mean drafts cut in wood' – perhaps a side-swipe at the *Civitas Londinum* woodcut.

Even the most scientifically-minded surveyors continued to combine in their professional work the elements of a true survey or flat plan and the bird's-eye house-elevations delightful to the modern eye, and this dual convention survived on both printed and manuscript maps until the end of the 17th century and beyond. Hayward's plan of the Tower of 1597, which has been preserved in an early 18th-century manuscript copy, outlines exactly and accurately the ground plan of the individual buildings, but adds their elevations. The numerous surveys of property in and around London prepared by the Treswell family between 1585 and 1617 all share common technical features, and also indicate the widening range of employers requiring professional surveys of their valuable London properties – the Crown, Dulwich College, the Clothworkers' Company, Christ's Hospital, the Duke of Northumberland. John Gosling's post-Restoration plan of land in Nevill's Alley behind Fetter Lane belonging to Sir Nicholas Bacon continued the tradition, and may represent the work of a surveyor by then old-fashioned and out of touch with contemporary practice. He uses the combination of elevation and plan, gives a scale of feet and a compass rose, and calculates the area in perches and square feet 'being cast up together'.

The first 60 years of the 17th century saw a decline in the quality of London maps; only seven were published, and two at least of those were re-issues of Tudor maps, Norden's and the *Civitas Londinum* woodcut. 'The Scales but Small, Expect not truth in all': this apologetic qualification from a map of 1685 might well describe the Stuart group. No new surveys were made in the period and the quality of engraving was with one exception abysmal, after the clarity and beauty of the copperplate and Braun and Hogenberg's

Scalebar from a Dutch map of London, c. 1685

map. Map-makers aimed at and achieved only an approximation to London in map form; the results were on the whole cruder and less detailed than their predecessors achieved and certainly not necessarily more accurate, despite the grandiose claims of the publisher. Indeed, the more ambitious the title, the less useful the map: Richard Newcourt's, an eight-sheet map published by William Faithorne in 1658 to a scale of about 14 inches to the mile (the largest, apart from the woodcut map, before the Fire), claimed to be 'Composed by a Scale and Ichnographically described', but failed to differentiate any individually recognisable houses, which the engraver of Braun and Hogenberg had succeeded in doing on a far smaller scale. Westminster Abbey is a mere block half an inch long on Newcourt's map; on the German map, though minute, Henry VII's chapel is clearly distinguished. (Pls. 9, 3)

Although Newcourt's map does illustrate the extent of building to the north-west, showing houses along ' Howlburne' linking the village of St. Giles in the Fields with the city and developments into the fields around Westminster – areas often excluded from maps before the 18th century – his 'Exact Delineation' of the city is derived from earlier maps and virtually useless to the student of London topography. Another, Dankert's map of London apparently published about 1633, stops short at Fleet Street, ignoring Westminster as a separate community, but in effect cutting away an integral part of London, if not of the City. (Pl. 7) Porter's *Newest and Exactest Map* of 1655 is unusual in extending out to the east, to show houses lining the river bend to Rotherhithe and the limekiln at Limehouse, but his map, like Newcourt's, merely renders those houses as crude blocks resembling a child's building toy, with no pretensions to accuracy.

Lack of artistry in the delineation of building may have been caused by the feeling that printed maps, particularly pocket-sized ones, were ephemeral and not worthy of great skill. The relatively small numbers existing and the repeated re-issues of maps imply that they had a short life and were easily replaced; possibly some finer examples have not survived at all. Hollar's map-view of the West Central area of London, of which a unique impression is in the British Museum, supports this belief. (Pl. 10) It was presumably intended to form part of a larger map-view, whose loss we can only regret, since this section towers head and shoulders above all other maps of the period in accuracy, detail and vitality, as might be expected of Hollar. In the convention of the time he has drawn not a ground plan of this fashionable quarter, but a view as if from a helicopter hovering somewhere over the Thames, although he allows himself to see more of the streets to the north than would ever be physically possible. In Holborn a solitary carter whips up his lumbering team, a reminder of the heavy traffic clogging that important east-to-west route before the New Road from Marylebone was built a century later. Coaches stand 'at the Meypoole' in the Strand; the west end had filled up rapidly with new houses, despite repeated building restrictions, even before the Piazza in Covent Garden was laid out on the old convent orchard. Each narrow house had its own long garden behind, indicating the high value attached to land on the street front in a developing suburb, where however the back gardens still merged into fields. Little hint here of the gradual infilling and downgrading of this area to take place over the next two centuries: Hollar has brought into focus the old adage of one law for the rich and another for the poor. The rich bought pardons for evading the building restrictions, and so could move into spacious new-built houses to the west of the city; the poor, forced to build on old foundations, were confined to the old walled area.

What do these survivals from the first century of London's mapping tell us about the changing city? The earliest are, paradoxically, the most informative; from maps alone we know more about the London of Mary Tudor than that of Charles I, although the written record is far fuller for the later period. In Braun and Hogenberg's map we see a town still in the late 1550's recovering from the aftermath of the Reformation; the great walled precincts of dissolved religious houses were being broken up into industrial buildings, storehouses and tenements for the city's teeming population. Blackfriars, the vast 13th-century Dominican Priory below Ludgate, traditionally the home of printers (where the Times office now stands in Printing House Yard), still preserved its integrity unbroken by any intersecting street or alley. The Charterhouse and St. Bartholomew's Hospital – the latter refounded as a hospital by the Mayor in 1552 – flanked Smithfield; even today Goswell Street and St. John's Street curve round these two estates, preserving the line of a vanished boundary wall, originally built over green fields.

In Westminster, during the 30 years since Henry VIII seized York House from Wolsey for a palace, his Whitehall had doubled in size, spreading to St. James's Park and along the river bank to Scotland Yard. Between King Street, the modern Whitehall and St. James's Park lay the tennis courts, bowling alley and cockpit of Henry's palace; towards Charing Cross (where now the Horse Guards parade) was the tilt yard, that vital adjunct to Tudor royal pageantry. Along the river bank jetties stretched into the Thames, called 'bridges' and 'stairs', where wherries moored to land their passengers. On Braun and Hogenberg's map the royal barge is being towed laboriously upstream by a boatload of oarsmen, perhaps from a day's hunting in the park at Greenwich. Westminster stands on an island encircled by two branches of the Tyburn; one flowing invisibly into the Thames somewhere under Palace Yard, the other emerging behind the Abbey on Millbank, carrying away refuse from the Queen's slaughter house and powering the mill which has given its name to the spot. (Pls. 3, 4)

To interpret the Tudor maps we need a guide; we are fortunate that at the time John Stow, that indefatigable lover of London, was walking the city and recording the disappearance of the medieval town as he saw it happen. He refers constantly to the effects on the topography of the city of a rapidly increasing population, confined within the walls, and to gardens built over and houses 'lately new built with a number of small tenements letten out to strangers and other mean people', a criticism in which he is borne out by ward assessments of the time. The intermingled and subdivided properties within the walls show clearly on contemporary manuscript surveys.

The population was growing by immigration both from the countryside and from abroad, and as it grew those who could afford it left their small town houses and built anew in the spreading skirts of London to east and north, but particularly to the west, towards the Court. Stow saw the process as one not of growth but of destruction; London's fields were disappearing under houses – a familiar complaint even today. He referred wistfully to the loss of country pleasures possible only in a town whose walls met the open fields and flowing streams of Middlesex. 'On May Day in the morning every man would walk into the sweet meadows and green woods, but now the countryside is much pestered with building and with enclosures so that by the closing in the common grounds, our archers for want of room to shoot abroad, creep into bowling alleys and ordinary dicing houses nearer home'. Moorfields, where the Tudor archers and gunners are seen practising on the copper-plate map, had been enclosed and laid out as gardens by 1605. (Pl. 3)

The maps tend to give an impression of London as a peaceful, static place, the river the main scene of activity; but this is misleading. The streets were crowded, noisy with squeaking wheels and dogged with through traffic forced to cross the river by London Bridge; the nearest alternative bridge lay far upstream at Kingston. The streets were further narrowed by encroaching buildings, as Stow bitterly commented, 'Cars, drays, carts & coaches, more than hath been accustomed the streets and lanes being straitened, must needs be dangerous, as daily experience proveth'. The picture is of a city bursting at the seams.

Attempts to build a second bridge were made during Elizabeth's reign but were foiled, perhaps by those same vociferous and muscular watermen who successfully resisted the building of a bridge at Westminster until 1736. It is hard to see where a bridge could have stood, unless at Lambeth (an important ferry point), since the Strand bank of the Thames was entirely enclosed in noblemen's gardens. Today only a few names remain to remind us that this was the Court suburb, equivalent to St. James's in the 18th century. Arundel House, Somerset House, York House, all have gone; of the last palace, a Stuart watergate, the work of Nicholas Stone, still stands in the Embankment Gardens at the foot of Villiers Street, a landlocked reminder that once the river lapped over the site of Charing Cross Underground Station. Northumberland House, the latest of these mansions to survive, did not disappear until 1874, with the building of Northumberland Avenue in response to the demand for better traffic facilities.

Today governments can remove some streets from the map and alter the lines of others in a wholesale manner impossible in other centuries; the old street-lines have been preserved for us only because before the days of the motorcar the City had not the power to make sweeping changes, however much planners such as Wren urged them. The result is that even modern maps show a city preserving in its streets and alleys the lines of country lanes winding to villages that are now mere postal districts in London.

Scalebar from the map of London by
R. Newcourt, 1658

CHAPTER III

The new London – post-Fire changes

Restoration England saw a dramatic surge of interest in map-making, reflecting perhaps Charles II's own liking for collecting maps. For the first time a close-knit circle of individuals existed, all Englishmen, and many of them associated with the Royal Society, who combined both the necessary knowledge of contemporary scientific advances and the curiosity about their surroundings to produce plans and surveys of the capital, and from whose enthusiasm sprang a wealth of maps which enable us to recreate a dynamic period in London's past.

The Thames mapped

The earliest map of Charles II's London to be considered here is more strictly a chart, the manuscript survey on whose preparation for the Navy Office Pepys was engaged in July and August 1662; it showed 'the river Thames from Westminster to the sea with the falls of the Rivers into it, the several creekes soundings and Depths therof and Docks made for the use of his Maties Navy'. Given his declared purpose, it is no surprise to see that the draughtsman has displayed little interest in details of the rural landscape beyond the river bank; roads taper off into blank areas of parchment, and the thriving villages of Kent and Essex – apart from those riverside communities such as Erith and Deptford with naval connections – might not exist. London, however, the cartographer could not or would not ignore. Although the plan of the capital is presumably not original, but based on some other man's work, as yet unidentified, London is depicted entirely as it stood in 1662, with all the latest buildings and streets, so that this map is a valuable if fortuitous checkpoint in a decade of rapid changes, not merely in the heart but also on the fringes of London. (See endpapers)

At Greenwich the new Charles II building, forerunner of Wren's later hospital, rises on the site of the ruinous Tudor palace. In Southwark, ribbons of houses are spreading out along the marsh lanes in defiance of the Tudor and Jacobean building restrictions resignedly renewed by Charles II on his accession. Lincoln's Inn Fields, originally laid out as a park 40 years before and still surrounded by open land in Hollar's West Central view of the 1650's, are on this plan flanked by houses on two sides, while further north in Bloomsbury stands Southampton Buildings, a little-studied speculation started by Thomas Wriothesley, 4th Earl of Southampton, in 1661, which converted fields and rough houses 'ruinous and decayed and very dangerous in cases of fire', typical shanty-town dwellings on the outskirts of the city, into a formal square of elegant houses, with the addition of markets and subsidiary streets, and so for the first time providing not merely town houses for the wealthy, as in St. James's Square, but a complete community. To the south-west London fades away beyond 'Foxhall' and 'Tutile Fields', Westminster.

This map is the only one accurately to record the position of one of the Civil War forts that encircled the city; the earthworks of this fort were incorporated into the gardens of Southampton House. George Vertue's later engraving of the lines of the City's fortifications has little basis in fact; the forts were razed within a year of their construction in 1647 and have left only vague reminders of their existence, as in Mount Street, so-called from Oliver's Mount Fields.

The Thames chart hung for many years in the Office of Works, which suggests that it was an official copy, 'finely set out and hung up'; if so, perhaps the watercolour views of London and of naval depots along the Thames ornamenting the map (which may or may not be by Wenceslaus Hollar), were added as a flourish of that decoration characteristic of 17th-century maps, which were rarely sold without a panorama of London or views of individual buildings.

Planning and Re-planning

The rapid growth of London as a place of resort under the later Stuarts would no doubt have stimulated a demand for maps even without the dramatic impulse given by the Great Fire; Hollar at least, as Pepys knew, was engaged on 'a great map of the City, which he was upon before the City was burned, like Gombouts of Paris, which I am glad of', but John Evelyn was not alone in regretting the lack of a completed accurate map on which to base his proposals for re-building London. 'An exact plot . . . ought in the first place to be taken by some able Artist, and in that accurately to be described all the declivities, eminences, watercourses, etc., of the whole Area. The Gent. who performed that of Tangier [i.e., Jonas Moore, for whom the chart of the Thames referred to above was prepared] . . . might I suppose be a very fitting person for that employment'. Evelyn is here requiring on his map elements that were not supplied for some two centuries, until the Ordnance Survey Skeleton Plans of 1848–51, which were the first to express in print at least the uneven contours of the city. He also required 'some more particular ichnographical plan of the whole city *membratim*, as it were, with the principal streets', on which he and other planners might plot their piazzas, churches and quays. Apart from embodying his ideas for the re-building in the pamphlet *London Reviv'd*, quoted above, Evelyn also sketched them out and presented the re-building scheme and plan to the king on 13th September, only days after the Fire; Charles was 'extremely pleased with what I had so early thought on'. Evelyn was not alone in this attempt to persuade Charles to recreate London along new lines. His and Wren's idealistic schemes for the re-built city incorporated many desirable ideas, such as drastic street-widening, although neither advocated the removal of the medieval wall and gates, and levelling-off of such notoriously steep approaches to the city as Ludgate Hill, which was not fully conquered until the building of Holborn Viaduct in 1869.

'Everybody brings in his idea'; Wren's and Evelyn's plans, both familiar in the form of 18th-century engravings prepared by Vertue for the Society of Antiquaries, are only two of many proposals for rebuilding. Another planner, little known but of comparable interest, was Richard Newcourt, a Somerset man who is associated with an earlier map of London, that published by Faithorne in 1658. His manuscript volume of proposals, with three sketch plans, is in the Guildhall Library. He has been described by the late Professor Reddaway as the only one among the planners to have 'imagination, education and an understanding of the needs of the ordinary man'; he saw the desperate need for more space in London, which had within its walls 'a multitude of bye-lanes, rooks and alleys, huddled up one on the neck of another so that some houses scarce ever saw the sun and the inhabitants lived comfortless and unwholesome,' a description which Dickens might have echoed. The cost of his proposals, which included moving the wall outwards and laying out the enlarged area in rectangular blocks, each with its central market-place, church and square, ruled them out as practical propositions until the massive public improvements and private building schemes of the 19th century created a comparable system of squares as a desirable town landscape. (Pl. 12)

Newcourt's plan, prepared in remote Somerset, apparently received no official recognition in London; others, like Evelyn, were more fortunate. Robert Hooke, the energetic curator of experiments to the Royal Society, was appointed City Surveyor in 1666 to help with the re-building, as a result of his having exhibited his proposals to the Royal Society. His 'exquisite model and draft for re-building' was apparently circulating in London immediately after the Fire, since it appears in at least two of the many prints and views of *Verbrandt London* published in Holland by the exulting Dutch, with whom the English were then at war.

Emergency Survey   These idealistic proposals for wholesale re-planning all had their merits, but none was realistic or even feasible in the City of the time. Every day that the markets remained empty and the shops and warehouses closed, the City lost money. It had to attract back its inhabitants as fast as possible, to arrest the drift to the fashionable west end which the Fire's devastation had only accentuated. The wealth of London, its citizens, was 'running out at its gates' while it remained in ruins. The first need was for an overall survey of the burnt area, in anticipation of disputes between returning householders over property boundaries obscured by rubble. The City and the king both provided surveyors, the former six men to plot individual house sites, the latter Hollar and Sandford to make a street survey. Charles took particular interest in street-widening and the removal of markets from such vital thoroughfares as Newgate Street and Cheapside into more appropriate sites elsewhere, and he was presented with the City's draft proposals in February 1667, plotted probably on that lost six-sheet map of London of which Hollar engraved a one-sheet version, to be published by John Leake later in the same year. (Compare Pl. 11)

The team working in the burnt area included not only humble men, trained as carpenters and bricklayers, like Edward Jarman and Peter Mills, sworn surveyors to the City, but also eminent scientists and mathematicians from the Royal Society, Jonas Moore and Robert Hooke. The knowledge of London gained by these men perhaps encouraged them to publish maps based on their work; several feature as publishers of maps in the decade or so after the Fire, and others, such as Hooke and William Leybourne, are closely associated with that celebrated name in later 17th-century map-publishing, John Ogilby. The manuscript volumes in which fair copies of the site plans were entered are preserved in the Guildhall, a minute house-by-house record of London property-ownership and a mine of fascinating information on the great city estates in the hands of such diverse institutions as St. Paul's School, Pembroke College, Cambridge and the Goldsmiths' Company. They also disclose details of the boundary adjustments made necessary by street-widening so that, for instance, the site of the church of St. Michael le Querne disappeared into Blow Bladder Street.

The Map-maker's Opportunity

The destruction of map-stocks in the Fire was a concealed blessing, since it discouraged printers from merely re-issuing London maps taken from out-dated plates, as was their custom; some of Speed's county maps, for example, originally drawn by Norden before the death of Elizabeth I, were still being issued nearly two centuries later. Compared with the relatively stagnant market of the first half of the 17th century, the post-Fire years saw a great increase in published maps based on new surveys, together with such in-novations as road-books. Technical improvements, such as the virtually universal adoption of Gunter's chain for surveying, were fruitfully coupled with the concentrated practical experience gained in the re-building of London, in which so many of the map-makers were concerned, to produce a generation of map-makers whose work was to stand alone until the 19th century. William Leybourne, one of the six commissioners for the re-building survey, acknowledged his debt to the Fire and profited by it, in his treatise for the surveyor, published in 1667, which was 'intended for persons concerned in the letting, buying and selling and building of or upon ground then in the Ruins of the City'.

Little is known in detail of the day-to-day process of surveying for town maps, which was presumably regarded as a workman's skill very little different in essence and in method from that used for estate surveying. There are some occasional glimpses of the surveyor at work; thus, brief references in their accounts to a survey of manors in the estate of the Dean and Chapter of Canterbury at Walworth and Vauxhall, carried out by Thomas Hill in 1681 give payments 'for Carrying ye Chain at fauxhall'; this survey, of which a facsimile was published by the London Topographical Society in 1932, retains the traditional picturesque details of houses sketched in perspective, but when Miss Darlington compared it with other later maps of the same area, notably the Ordnance Survey, she found an astonishing degree of accuracy. 'Considering Hill's lack of modern instruments, his careful delineation of the property of the Dean and Chapter is remarkable'.

Property surveys of this type are an invaluable source of information on the outskirts of London; as houses spread over the fields, new developments were often excluded from printed maps of the capital, whose publishers were reluctant to extend their borders or to cut new plates, so that these manu-script surveys may give, incidentally to their main purpose, a picture of new streets half a century or more before they appeared in any printed map. The process of development itself spurred land-owners on to create accurate and up-to-date surveys of their property, which was potentially far more valuable laid out in streets than left in fields. It is no coincidence that in the expansive post-Fire building period, the Goldsmiths', together with other land-owning city companies, ordered a survey of their urban and semi-urban properties. (Pls. 16, 20)

John Ogilby's Map

The Fire, 'however disastrous it might be to the then inhabitants, had prov'd infinitely beneficial to their Posterity'; in no field is this benefit more visible than in that of London maps. No doubt the piecemeal house-by-house survey produced by the City was the stimulus for the outstanding map of London by John Ogilby, published posthumously in 1676. Certainly in making the map Ogilby was closely associated with three of the Fire surveyors, Robert Hooke, Richard Shortgrave and William Leybourne, although their contribution was not acknowledged by Ogilby and it is impossible to say how closely he based his map on the official surveys for which they had been responsible. The greater proportion of the map's area (which, at about 52 inches to the mile, is on a scale far larger than any other printed map, apart from the Ordnance Survey Skeleton Plan of the mid-19th century) would in any case not have been covered by the post-Fire surveyors, who confined their official attention to the burnt area. (Pls. 14, 15)

Ogilby's map is a true plan, in that he resisted the temptation to raise buildings in elevation, so departing from contemporary practice, although his partner William Morgan was to revert to the older and more picturesque style a few years later, in his map of London, Westminster and Southwark. An invaluable record of the city's medieval past, the names and lines of the smallest and most obscure streets and alleys are indicated on the map as they were before the inexorable redrawing of the last three centuries, but the map also lays out for us the post-Fire innovations of the City's planners. The sites of 35 forgotten churches not rebuilt after the Fire, whose parishes were to melt away, absorbed into larger units, are here laid out; the widened streets, such as Gracechurch Street, strike into the heart of the city from the country and from the river.

The new Thames Quay intended to emulate the splendid waterfronts of Genoa and Holland, replacing the smelly, muddy foreshore recorded in Hollar's drawings, was never to be fully cleared, since the focus of river-borne traffic was already shifting downstream below the bridge, but Ogilby's map records the partial clearance achieved by 1676. A further impulse had transformed the Fleet river, before 1666 a ditch 'very stinking & noisome', into a fine canal lined with broad quays reminiscent of those in Holland, to form a haven for the lighters seen moored in Ogilby's map. But this potential amenity soon suffered from the City's limited authority; above Holborn Bridge 'Turnmill Brook' became the responsibility of the Middlesex justices, who were not over-fastidious in dredging the river and keeping it free of débris. The consequent silting-up drove industrial traffic away, and the building of new Thames bridges sealed the dominance of road over river. In 1733 the Stocks Market was opened between Fleet Bridge and Holborn Bridge, bridging over the canal, and 30 years later the lower reach was to be covered in, finally converting the Fleet to an underground sewer.

Only one edition of Ogilby's great map was ever published; less decorative than many of its contemporaries and inconveniently large to be framed and hung, perhaps it did not enjoy a ready sale except among those with a professional interest in the city. Robert Hooke, who had recommended the scale ultimately used and who had designed the layout on 20 sheets, no doubt drew the attention of his fellow members of the Royal Society, who would appreciate its pretentions to accuracy, and Ogilby himself offered to present the original manuscript to the City 'so that London may be an example for the rest of the cities'. Whatever the contemporary demand for the map, few copies have survived to the present.

The only criticism that can be levelled at Ogilby's map is that it omits much of Stuart London. His claim that the map showed 'The Liberties of London at 100 Foot in an Inch' was justified, but it stopped short to the west at Somerset House, so excluding the surrounding communities such as Westminster and St. Martin's in the Fields, not to speak of the borough of Southwark, which were in effect if not administratively integral to the capital.

William Morgan and Expanding London

This omission was being made good even before Ogilby's map went on sale late in 1676; his partner William Morgan (who incidentally was his wife's grandson) had, during the previous few years, organised a survey of Westminster by Gregory King, son of a Lichfield surveyor, and others. Apart from the names of those engaged in it we know little of the progress of this survey. Although the bulk may have been completed before Ogilby's death, the map *London, Westminster and Southwark Accurately Surveyed*, published by William Morgan early in 1682, shows streets not named until 1681, such as Essex Street and Glasshouse Street, indicating that revision continued to the last possible moment; Morgan was in this as in other respects notably more conscientious than many map publishers before and since. (Pls. 17, 18) Although on a smaller scale than Ogilby's, the map gives in its 16 sheets an even more valuable picture of the capital just at a point of change, but it is less well-known than it deserves to be, both for its quality and its interest.

This may be because, like so many of the large maps designed to be made up and displayed as a picture, the sheets have decayed as they hung, or eventually disappeared under whitewash. One of the few surviving copies, purchased by the London Museum some years ago, had long been stored in a loft with other engravings and apparently never exhibited as a whole, since the individual sheets remain untrimmed and so retain the key numbers provided by the printer as a guide to the frame-maker in assembling the map.

In one of his many advertisements in the *London Gazette*, Morgan claimed to have 'garnished H M Palaces etc' with his map, and the royal patent of February 1682 quoted King Charles' recommendation of the map to the Universities, to 'sett up in their Respective Halls or other Publique Roomes', a recommendation which if followed should have resulted in many more copies of the map surviving, as a copy of Morden and Lea's later edition has, in the Stone Gallery of the Vyne in Hampshire, where it hangs varnished, as 'a usefull Ornament' to the large room. Sadly, there is no indication that any copies of the first edition, at least, still exist, apart from those few in public institutional libraries, although the greater number of later editions surviving must indicate a considerable contemporary demand. The plates remained in use, with slight alterations, for at least 40 years after Morgan's original publication date.

London was growing in area faster than ever before, spreading to absorb outlying hamlets as formal squares moved out over the intervening countryside. The boundaries of Morgan's map illustrate his awareness of London's satellite villages – now become mere localities in the sprawl of Greater London; an extension into the northern border shows Myddleton's New River Head at Islington, and the parish of St. Leonard, Shoreditch, while to the east Stepney 'alias Stebenheath' church marks the heart of a new point of growth. Contemporaries regarded this process with horror; Fletcher of Saltoun's comment in 1703 is characteristic and may stand for a common attitude: 'this vast city is like the head of a ricketty child which. . . . becomes so overcharged that frenzy and death unavoidably result'.

Problems of Growth

The pressure put on London's resources by the rapid rise in population took some unexpected forms; a proclamation of 1671 pinpointed one, that of the need for an adequate water supply. References to conduit fields and to streams are dotted on the maps all round the fringes of London, especially in the vicinity of 'Windmill Fields and So-hoe'. The proclamation criticised the increase in building in that area, with special emphasis on the threat to the royal water supply from builders damaging, blocking or fouling the conduits running through the fields to Whitehall 'whereof some decay is already perceived by his Majesties Sergeant-Plummer'. (Compare Pls. 21, 23)

Water supply was a perennial problem, and the activities of the water companies a source of constant complaint; an early 18th-century bill for the repair of roads in Westminster was opposed since 'as the Publick Companies for raising the Thames water were perpetually laying down their Pipes or amending them such a Bill would prove to little or no purpose'.

London's greatest weakness, which was not to be overcome until the 19th century, was that through this period of rapid uncontrolled expansion the administration of the fringes of the capital was divided among a score of authorities, vestries and commissions; Westminster and the City in the centre maintained their jealously guarded separatism intact and distinct from the county authorities of Surrey, Middlesex, Essex and Kent. The extension of

Scalebar from the map of London and Westminster by W. Morgan, 1682

Westminster in 1604 to include the manors of Ebury, Neyte and Hyde, to its limit near the Albert Hall, was fully justified a century later when this overall control made easier the task of estate development and provision of roads, water and drainage in this area, but the concept of an overriding authority was glimpsed only by a few theorists such as William Petty. He anticipated the need for wholesale planning and recommended the extension of London's administrative boundary to include not only Westminster but also 'so much of the built ground in Middlesex and Surrey whose houses are contiguous huts, or within call of those aforementioned', but even he did not foresee the total disappearance of Middlesex which was to take place three centuries later.

Meanwhile the problems created by the swelling and shifting population were resolved piecemeal. In 1668 Charles II granted a new burial ground, where the National Portrait Gallery now stands, to St. Martin's in the Fields, since this medieval country parish now served a substantial suburban community; 20 years later the church of St. James was consecrated for the use of those living in the new streets built by Frith, Barbon and Bond both north and south of Piccadilly. The pace of change was rapid; in 1683 William Earl of Craven gave three acres in the fields on the western edge of London 'for the entertainment of people that shall have the plague'. By 1733 the site of his Pesthouse, to the east of Carnaby Street, was covered in houses, and the charity moved to Paddington, though it was to be ousted again, by elegant terraces, in 1815. On its site now stands Craven Hill Gardens.

Maps by their nature are static; they merely freeze the story at one point in time. But by comparing maps made at sufficient intervals and with some claim to accuracy, a vivid picture emerges of London as a living organism, stretching out tentacles over the fields, the existence of a new centre of population belatedly acknowledged by the opening of a church or chapel of ease. Thus the sites of the 12 churches consecrated as a result of Queen Anne's Act of 1711 mark the growing areas – Greenwich, Limehouse, Bloomsbury, Westminster, Southwark, Hanover Square. The Strand, which gave St. Mary's Church a most unusual site in the middle of a busy thoroughfare, was no new community, but the subdivision of the site of Arundel House into streets by Nicholas Barbon, 'inventor of this new method of building by casting ground into streets and small houses, and to augment their number with as little front as possible' created here a population density astonishing to contemporaries.

The piecemeal growth of the west end in a half-century or more after the Restoration is easily recognised on the modern map, where the streets of Soho still wriggle confusingly across the page, recalling ancient boundaries between estates which were developed at diverse times and by different landlords, in striking contrast to the regular street-grid of those areas controlled by one landowner, such as the Grosvenor family in Belgravia. (Pls. 18, 47)

Pocket Maps for Visitors

Increasingly the map publishers recognised and responded to the demands of a new market. As London grew, so also the flow of visitors increased, and the visitor was exceptionally well provided for; the many small 18th-century folding maps, each sold in a pocket-sized slipcase, were often attractively hand-coloured and showed at least the most significant of the recent buildings, although the passion to be up-to-date in the street-plan might lead to the inclusion of streets which were never actually built.

From 1720 at least, few of these single-sheet maps lacked a list of watermen's and later hackney coach fares, Georgian equivalent of the official tariff carried in taxis, a useful guide for the unwary and gullible visitor. The watermen were a notoriously vigorous lobby; they had effectively blocked Elizabethan and Stuart attempts to build a badly needed second bridge over the Thames, until the passing of the Westminster Bridge Act in 1736, and even then fought a strong rearguard action, with propaganda about the evil effects which the bridge would bring, culminating in 'the Danger and Delay, which it will create to the conveyance of Goods and Passengers, more especially in and about the New Bridge', surely a misunderstanding of its intended function, of speeding traffic and improving communications between Parliament, the Court and southern England. The bridge was to appear on London maps almost immediately, although the foundation stone was not laid until 1738–9 and it was not to be opened to the public for 14 years; it was added to copies of Jefferys' maps from 1736, and appeared on almost all maps published from 1739, whatever their other omissions. (Pl. 25)

The new demand for maps came not only from tourists but also from gentlemen who required them either for their ornamental value or for reference. For the former market, maps were published with engraved views of buildings, panoramas of London from the river, or portraits of the reigning sovereign, either on separate sheets or decoratively filling empty spaces on the map, all features of Morgan's map and of others later in the century, but perhaps a speciality of the Dutch map-sellers who dominated the late Stuart market; those of de Ram, Moll and Homann are typical.

New Kinds of Map

Historians of London, or those with even a mild interest in its past, had a wide choice of maps in the early 18th century. Hatton's *New View of London*, for example, a popular guide-book published first in 1708, contained two maps, one of London at the time, the other, on a comparable scale, of Tudor London, based on Braun and Hogenberg's elegant map-view of 1572. The author unwisely 'Advises comparison', an exercise in which the older map is without doubt the winner. In a century and a half cartography appears to have made no progress; on Chiswell's map, which Hatton used for contemporary London, fewer place names are given than on the Tudor map, and the engraving is so crude that Lambeth Palace is unrecognisable, a child's building block. Hatton was perhaps aiming at the cheaper end of the market. A version of a Tudor map pasted in Strype's magnificent illustrated two-volume edition of Stow's *Survey of London* (first published in 1720) provides a similar contrast between maps of contemporary and Tudor London, but the map he reproduces of 18th-century London is of a far higher standard than Hatton's (although very little larger in scale) and far more informative. A further 18th-century map of Tudor London *About the Year 1560*, is based on the woodcut map attributed to Ralph Agas; this map, engraved by George Vertue and published for the Antiquaries in 1738, produced a flood of imitations, few of which were as clear as the earlier version. In 1741 the enterprising Millward brought historical demography a shade closer when he published a map of Georgian London on which 'The line mark't thus. . ., encompasses ye City of London as it was in Q. Elizabeth's Reign by which the vast increase in ye Buildings since that time may be nearly estimated'. (See Pls. 24, 25, for Strype's map)

An earlier innovation on the map market, and one which achieved lasting popularity very rapidly, was due to John Ogilby's initiative. A man of great and varied abilities, he had travelled abroad and was perhaps familiar with the printed road-books which had been used in France for a century or more. No English equivalent existed before 1675, the nearest parallel being Norden's triangular mileage tables which were published with lists of routes in *The Intended Guyde for English Travailers* in 1625. Ogilby pioneered a series of pictorial road maps, in strips radiating from London along the main post roads of the country, marking off not only the miles, but relevant features along the route – hills, bridges, crossroads, gentlemen's residences – with comments of historical and topographical interest. Their value for London lies not in their depiction of the built-up area, which is merely schematic and on too small a scale to be useful, but rather in the outskirts of

Travellers using a road map: from the title page of *Britannia* by J. Ogilby, 1676

the city, where individual houses are named and identified and the positions of milestones recorded. The road-book principle, once established, was to be extremely persistent; even today the AA produces route-maps on the same lines, differing only in detail from those given in Ogilby's *Britannia*. (Pls. 13, 40)

A further speciality was originated by Ogilby and Morgan at this period and widely imitated later, notably by Benjamin Cole in the mid-18th century; they volunteered to provide 'at Reasonable Rates the Draft of any Ward, Parish Liberty or Particular Estate', lifted presumably from the plates of their maps of London and Westminster. No such sheets from their maps are known, but Richard Blome engraved several ward maps for Strype, before his death in 1705, which bear a strong resemblance in size and style to sections of Morgan's map. (Pl. 24) The numerous descriptions of London published in the 18th century all include ward maps, most, like Benjamin Cole's, lifted from other men's work; Morgan, Ogilby and Rocque, as the only men to publish large-scale maps, were obviously vulnerable to copyists, given the feeble operation of the copyright laws introduced in 1734.

After this quarter-century of invention and enterprise, the first part of the 18th century saw little improvement in the quality of London maps. A few new features were introduced, maps became cheaper and more were printed, but they were not noticeably more accurate. Indeed in many cases the maps are markedly inferior to those published in the flush of Restoration London's scientific awakening. (Pl. 25) The duty on all imported maps imposed in 1712 reduced the Dutch and French share of the market, which at the turn of the century had been substantial and had perhaps provided useful competition. The greater number published is evident in the wealth of maps of this period in the national collections, but their contribution to our knowledge of London's topography is small, and some are positively misleading. Repeated editions of certain maps only preserved inaccuracies fossilised on the out-of-date plates, whose borders alone were occasionally recut to incorporate recent building on the fringes of London – in for example, Islington and Westminster.

CHAPTER IV

The Century of Squares

'A somewhat colourless and uneventful period in which landmarks are few, . . . marked by a certain degree of competence rather than by brilliance of conception or beauty of craftmanship' – so Thomas Chubb dismissed the map-maker's art in the 18th century. His comment on British cartography in general holds good for London maps in particular, with Rocque's and Horwood's maps as notable exceptions.

Town maps were no longer rich in pictorial effects, but had not achieved a compensating accuracy; hardly surprisingly perhaps, since most were produced as a sideline by print-sellers. The Bowles family, Overton and Sayer, names familiar to the student of Georgian prints, published many maps of London, but mostly as single sheets, and derived from older and larger originals. (Pls. 32, 33) Given this lack of specialisation, it is perhaps too much to expect fresh surveys. Henry Overton's map of the country 30 miles round London, first published in 1720, was re-issued 74 years later from the old plates – then in the possession of Laurie and Whittle – completely unaltered, except in the imprint.

Unjustified Claims Contemporaries were well aware of these weaknesses; each map title emphasises in defiant capital letters and heavy print its unique claim to accuracy and exactness, to be taken 'from the latest survey, with all the additions to the present year'. In many cases the 'latest survey' referred to is that of Morgan in 1682, though it is rarely acknowledged; even in 1735, 50 years after the first edition of William Morgan's map, Thomas Jefferys published a reduced version of it entitled 'A New & Exact Plan . . . Laid down in such a manner, that any place may readily be found . . . the like not Extant'. Attempts were occasionally made to add to the maps when important changes had taken place since the plates were originally cut; however, fortunately for the map-makers who wished to avoid the expense and inconvenience of a fresh survey and recut plates, the greatest alterations to London's plan occurred on the outskirts, where formerly blank areas of the map and its borders could be filled with new streets – in, for example, Islington and Mayfair. This could give rise to strange apparitions on the maps; several of the streets north of Cavendish Square, for example, were being built in the 1720's, at the time when Lea and Glynne were re-issuing Morden and Lea's map of 1700. Whether proposals for the layout of these streets were circulating in London is not certain, but the publishers, determined to show recent improvements where potential customers might live, gave their own version of the street plan. This was copied by Overton in his *Pocket Plan*, which went through at least three editions before 1741, and again by Foster. Not until 1756, when Foster published a revised map showing the streets correctly replaced by the 'Marylebone Basin', were they removed from the plates – having never in fact been built as shown on those maps.

George Foster was remarkable, even given the low standards of his fellow map sellers, for publishing maps with many omissions and inaccuracies; he failed to be consistent in what he showed even on two maps published within a few years of one another. His maps of 1738 and 1739 were both republished several times, by his widow Elizabeth among others; each leapfrogs over the other in the dates of issue, but neither is ever wholly up-to-date, nor agrees entirely with the other: for example, the 1752 edition ignores the approach roads to Westminster Bridge, completed in 1750, yet that of four years later marks them in, while Blackfriars Bridge appears on one in 1760, as 'The intended new Bridge', but not on the other until 1768.

In 1780 Richard Gough, himself a notable collector of fine maps, including many of London, which are now in the Bodleian Library, wrote disparagingly of his contemporaries' work; 'Notwithstanding the assertions of Bowen Kitchin and other modern map-makers, that their maps are formed from actual new surveys, there is scarce a single one which does not abound with faults'. There was no real justification for this lack of originality; encouragement, both scientific and financial, existed for the map-maker prepared to undertake the risk and effort of an original survey. The Society of Arts attempted to stimulate cartography by offering a series of prizes between 1759 and 1801 for county maps on the one-inch scale based on original surveys; London maps were of course ineligible, but although several notable map publishers such as Jefferys, Cary and the Greenwood brothers were to win the coveted prize for their efforts, the vast improvement in the surveying and engraving of county maps was slow to influence those of the capital. From 1791 the Ordnance Survey was to have a greater though still indirect effect by providing for the first time a national series of triangulation tables, to which lip service at least was paid by map-makers after 1800.

The 18th-Century Giants

In the mass of small-scale and derivative maps published in the 18th century, two names as already mentioned stand out, those of John Rocque and Richard Horwood: the latter was to be responsible for one work only, the massive survey of London undertaken in the last two decades of the century and dedicated to the Phoenix Fire Office. The other man, a Huguenot émigré surveyor, was to publish a range of maps of enormous interest not only for central London, but for its environs also. His great mid-century map of the country 10 miles round the capital, from Chislehurst to Woodford, from Molesey to Harrow-on-the-Hill, is deservedly well-known.

The idea was not new; the earliest printed map to show London in the centre of its surrounding countryside was issued in the reign of Charles II, that fruitful period for London cartography, by Ogilby and Morgan, to be rapidly followed by Robert Morden and Philip Lea. But none of their single-sheet maps showed much improvement on Saxton's county maps of a century earlier; roads alone were added. (Pl. 21)

Rocque's map, on 16 sheets, shows in fascinating and elaborate detail the villages of Middlesex and Surrey, straggling along country lanes which are now major routes. His background as a '*dessinateur de jardins*' and as a surveyor of such estates as Wanstead, Wrest Park and Hampton Court, perhaps inclined him, more than other cartographers, to take an interest in land utilisation and to record in the map the existence of heath, ploughland, orchards and pasture by means of differentiated stippling, a feature new to England but familiar to continental surveyors. The vertical shading of hills was not entirely unknown, but his extensive and effective use of it no doubt popularised this technique for expressing contours. (Pl. 28)

The appeal of the map was considerable; from the *Proposals* inviting subscriptions which were published in 1741, five years before the map itself appeared, it is clear that Rocque was aware of the interest in large-scale maps, an interest which had been unsatisfied since Morgan's venture of 60 years before: 'Such a Map will be of great use to all Directors of Insurance Offices, and Commissioners of Turnpikes, to all Church-Wardens and Overseers, to all Persons who have occasion to travel round this Metropolis for business, health or pleasure; and lastly to curious persons at home and abroad'. The radius chosen was particularly appropriate in that the villages and hamlets inside it all lay within a comfortable daily ride of London, and some at least were becoming rural retreats for the wealthy. The owners of villas in fashionable Twickenham or Richmond, like 'Mr. Pope's Gardens' and Marble Hill,

Surveyors at work: from the map of Middlesex by J. Rocque, 1757

could admire on the map the elegant layout of their estates, some of which Rocque had no doubt surveyed as part of his professional duties before he turned to map-making.

By 1769 at least eight editions of the map had been published, the later ones by Rocque's widow Mary, the map being brought up-to-date in respect of various new routes, including the important Marylebone by-pass road (now the Pentonville, Marylebone and Euston Roads) and Blackfriars Bridge, with its connecting network of roads in St. George's Fields. The details of the map make it an absorbing and rewarding study, in part for the unexpectedly rural names appearing in familiar suburbs: for instance, in Blackheath Park, the present railway station stands near a hollow known to Rocque's fellow-Londoners as Dowagers Bottom. By the barn at Highbury is a moated site, presumably a medieval farmstead, whose traditional name is still known to us, as Jack Straw's Castle. On Kensington Gore the very mile-stones are drawn in, recording the distance from Hyde Park Corner; one at least, or its replacement, still stands set in the wall of the Royal Geographical Society, slightly to the west of the Albert Hall; another, half a mile further on, has given its name to a hotel on the roadside. At Shepherd's Bush and on Kennington Common, the gallows tree marks the approach to London.

A striking feature of the map is the great number of watercourses, much too small to be called rivers, which wind across the flatlands of Middlesex and Surrey and eventually drain into the Thames. Between Bow Church and the 'Decenters Chapel', Stratford, the road crossed five bridges over branches of the river Lea. The palace of Fulham, in a notoriously marshy area, still retained its water-filled moat, and a whole section of Lewisham is named simply 'the Watersplash', an indication of the hazards facing the traveller before the days of Macadam, once he left the paved streets of Westminster and the City.

Maps of the Home Counties

Perhaps Rocque recognised an unsatisfied demand for maps on a large scale of the area around London; he was to publish a couple more, one of Middlesex in 1754 and one of Surrey in 1757, and his friend and colleague André was to publish a superb map of Essex on 26 sheets in 1777, all of which are significant and useful for the study of London's environs. The Middlesex map is relatively little-known; as the first to show parish boundaries it is a valuable reminder of the vast parishes served by one church alone, with perhaps a chapel of ease, before the parochial subdivisions made in response to the 19th-century population explosion. (Pl. 31) The rector of St. Mary Abbot's had sole responsibility for all within his parish, which stretched from Kensal Green in the north to the river bank at Chelsea; St. Pancras, an ancient church which had already by this date been outgrown and rebuilt, served all the land from Tottenham Court Road to Highgate, an area which was no longer even at that date merely open fields.

Returns from the parish of St. Pancras were excluded from the weekly bills of mortality in London published by the parish clerks, and these by now no longer reflected accurately the true size of London. Rocque indicated on the easternmost of the 4 sheets which make up his Middlesex map the parishes within the area of the Bills of Mortality, 'which is bounded by a Strong dotted line with this Mark annex'd' i.e. appropriately, a pair of crossed bones. There were then 108 parishes in the city, 28 'Without the Liberty of the City' and 10 in Southwark; the same area, excluding the city, now contains nearly a couple of hundred.

Bound with the London Museum's copy of the map, as a key sheet, is the reduced one-sheet map of the county published 'by J. Rocque in the Strand, price 2s. 6d.' in 1757. On this the roads, streams and built-up area are attractively coloured, while to the north the rococo title cartouche is flanked by engravings of a surveyor with a 'perambulator' and a cherub taking his bearings with a theodolite.

More pertinent for those interested in central London, which inevitably is much reduced on county surveys, is the map on 24 sheets published in 1746, for which Rocque is best known. (Pls. 26, 27) From 1737 he was employed as surveyor on the map by John Pine, the map's engraver, and its publisher John Tinney. In its early stages the projected 'grand design of an ichnographical survey, or map of London and all the suburbs' had interested George Vertue, whose name is associated with so many of the important earlier maps, but William Oldys, after a meeting with Vertue in 1738, noted in his diary that 'Mr. Rocque and he are not yet come to an agreement': apparently they never did so.

This map attracted 400 subscriptions, at two guineas apiece, and presumably considerable shop sales, since it went into at least three editions. Possibly a fourth was planned, to include changes in the face of London to about 1770, but proof copies only are known of this edition. As a result of its success, various reduced versions were published, notably the one-sheet issue of 1749, the two comparing London with other European capitals in 1754 and 1761, and the 8-sheet map published in 1755, which acknowledged its debt to the earlier larger map, but claimed that it was 'improved by the Addition of all the new Roads made on account of Westminster Bridge, and all the new Buildings and Alterations made since'.

The scale of Rocque's London map, at 26 inches to the mile, allowed the delineation 'not only of an exact description of all the squares, streets, courts and alleys in their true proportions, but likewise of the ground plots of the several churches etc.'. To enable the fine detail of the map to be easily referred to, a grid of squares with numbered and lettered references was laid across it, and a 'contracted sketch' or key map provided, in itself a far finer engraving than the crude maps the Bowles family were content to reproduce.

In area the map stretched 'From beyond Marylebone turnpike, by Tottenham Court . . . to near Bow' and from Chelsea College (or Hospital) to the naval victualling yards at Deptford, six miles west to east and three north to south. It thus not only included the built-up area but extended beyond it, and unlike many of the smaller contemporary maps, most of which ended at Westminster in the west, it showed London's satellite villages. These were soon to be invaded by terraces, and the surroundings of London are dotted with those necessary companions to the building trade, gravel pits north of Marble Arch, lime-kilns in Limehouse, brick-kilns (one on the site of Grosvenor Crescent), and timber-yards, which line both banks of the Thames, especially in Westminster and Lambeth. These, and waterworks, mark the favoured areas of new building – Chelsea, Marylebone, and just north of Oxford Street, where Merchants Waterworks is prominently marked on the triangular site still defined by Upper Rathbone Place and Newman Street, west of Charlotte Street. The waterworks had already disappeared under houses when Horwood's map was published half a century later.

Rocque's own religious convictions, which had presumably driven his family to move to England in the 1730's, perhaps made him particularly conscious of the diversity of belief possible in London. In his list of abbreviations he provides letters for five varieties of nonconformist meeting house, apart from the many German, Dutch and French churches which also sprinkle the face of the map, and the Anabaptist meeting house in Winchester Street, near Bethlem Hospital. These were not all the religious variations available in London in the second half of the century. Entries for 1777 in the diary of John Allen, a Quaker brewer living in Wapping, refer to five Quaker meeting houses within easy walking distance of his home. This diary incidentally illustrated how small the built-up area of London still was: one afternoon Allen and his aunt, whom he collected from her home in Lambeth, walked together to the Quaker meeting in Hammersmith 'through the Park and Kensington Gardens', a pleasant semi-rural journey of at least seven miles.

Character of Urban Life
The restrictions on free movement in and around London were considerable at this date; on each of the main roads turnpikes blocked the traveller's progress. Rocque's map shows them half a century before the turnpike system reached its fullest extent, but already the man travelling from Westminster to Knightsbridge or Chelsea, from the City to Islington, or even from Lambeth to Camberwell, had to pass a gate and pay toll. All these gates and various others Rocque records, together with a reminder of the considerable inconvenience caused by the lack of an adequately wide and clear road from east to west, by-passing both the formal squares of the west end and the bottle neck of St. Giles and Broad Street, before the Marylebone Road was opened in 1756–7. This linked Paddington and Islington, and crossed the northern routes from Edgware and Highgate.

Holborn, on the old east-west road, was notoriously congested; Strype in 1755 described it as 'a place pestered with coaches which are a trouble to its inhabitants', and Rocque marks not only a watchhouse but also a block of houses, Middle Row, half-filling the roadway by Staple Inn. However, traffic was also impeded by the herds of country-bred stock brought down Gray's Inn Lane and Tottenham Court Road along Holborn to Smithfield Market, where Rocque has drawn a mass of sheep-pens. Great and Little

Title from the map of London and Westminster by R. Horwood, 1792

Turnstiles took their names from gates erected by the inhabitants of Lincoln's Inn Fields, determined to prevent cattle from straying into their pleasant and exclusive residential quarter. Another major interruption to free movement, London's wall, had finally gone by the time Rocque's map was published, although it was still marked on Thomas Jefferys' map a decade earlier, but the bars at the city limits noted by Rocque were still closed each night. The city ditch had disappeared 80 years before, victim of the relentless pressure on potential building land; already in 1681 Burton had commented that it was 'curiously arched over with brick and dothe nowhere appear'.

Rocque created a magnificent source for London social history, a vivid picture of the capital some two centuries ago. What his survey failed to achieve was absolute mathematical accuracy, despite his claim that 'The method followed . . . has been by ascertaining the position and bearings of the Churches and other remarkable buildings by trigonometrical and other observations. . . , by taking the Angles at the Corners of Streets Etc. with proper instruments and measuring the distances by the chain. . .' In its advertisements the smaller map he published in 1755 was highly recommended by the then President and Secretary of the Royal Society for the thoroughness of Rocque's and Pine's surveying methods: 'They have had the proportional Distances of a great many Points in different very distant Parts of the Town computed trigonometrically to which computations they have strictly confined their map', but when compared with Horwood's venture of 40 years later, which made no much extravagant claims, and with the town plans of the Ordnance Survey, few of the streets agree precisely in their alignment.

Accuracy at Last

Richard Horwood's map was the next milestone in London cartography. By 1792, when the first sheet appeared, London had become the cartographic centre of the world; English atlases, charts and maps were second to none. Nine years before, as prelude to the setting up of the Ordnance Survey of all England, General Roy had measured a base line and a series of triangulations 'for my own amusement' across the fields between Marylebone and St. Pancras. The sappers were beginning the massive process of national survey which still continues today, although London was not to receive their attention for a further half-century.

Horwood, unlike some other contemporary map-makers, did not make use of the Survey's triangulation in the London area, but the accuracy of his map, when compared with the later O.S. town map, establishes that he must have used similar methods. For the first time a town map showed not only every house site, but also the house numbers (required by Parliament from 1762). Perhaps he provided this new feature in response to the special need of the Phoenix Assurance Office, to whom the map is dedicated, to know exactly where its clients lived, for the better stationing of its reservoirs and fire-engines. (Pls. 35, 36)

The publication of the map took eight years, between 1792 and 1799, as sheets were issued singly when the survey and engraving of each was complete. For the first time the skeleton of modern London can be picked out on the map. The characteristic monotony of so many streets 'lined with common London houses, like so many boxes in a row' is glaringly obvious with the formal layout of Camden Town, Somers Town, the Bedford and Foundling Hospital estates in Bloomsbury, all developments of the previous decade or so, forming a solid block between the picturesque confusion of London's ancient centre and the open land of Middlesex. London was spreading and continually swallowing up its countryside. Like many former rural pleasure gardens, Marylebone Tea Gardens had been closed down in 1778, and now the houses of Beaumont and Devonshire Streets ran over the site. In South London the demand for houses in Camberwell had already forced the enlargement of St. Giles' Church in 1786 and – a true sign of a prosperous and respectable community – the first Act for paving and lighting the parish had been passed 10 years before.

In belated recognition of these new suburbs outside the London district's postal limits, the postal services were revised in 1794; in place of the original 13, 91 carriers were engaged to take letters to and from the out-parishes where over half London's population lived. Horwood does not indicate the limits of this inner postal delivery service, but many maps carried a broad red circle 'Shewing the limits of the Two-Penny Post Delivery'. Cary's *New Pocket Plan* of 1790 had included also 'the situation of the Receiving Houses, of the

General and Penny Post Offices'. The inner area was not extended to 12 miles round London until 1833, so that St. Pancras, Hackney and Brompton, for instance, remained until then country districts, excluded from the magic circle within which there were six deliveries a day. (Pl. 49)

The Thames – a Working River

The significance of the Thames as a highway was soon to reach its peak, before the railways arrived to compete for heavy transport; along its banks were moored hundreds of barges carrying stone and timber to the riverside builders' yards. A cluster of quays between the Horseferry and Parliament Stairs, Westminster, named for their various commodities – stone, brick, dung, coal and timber – reflect the range of materials required in one fast-growing area of London.

To the east of London the dock explosion was about to start, to relieve intolerable congestion at the Legal Quays. In 1794 it was estimated that over 400 Newcastle colliers, each making nine trips a year, had to push their way upriver to their wharves past the great East and West Indiamen moored in midstream. London needed docks; various schemes were in the air in the 1790's: one to straighten the river between Wapping and Woolwich and use the three resulting 'dead' bends as docks, another, proposed by the inhabitants of Southwark, to excavate a dock system on the south bank, between Limehouse Reach and the Pool, with a canal to Bankside as a by-pass avoiding the busiest stretch of the river. Neither of these schemes came about, although a comparable north bank by-pass running in the opposite direction was provided by the Regent's Canal, with its easterly outlet at Limehouse; the dock companies found the alluvial soil of the Isle of Dogs and Wapping Marsh easily excavated, and within a few years had created a massive ever-expanding dock system which only today is losing its function and gradually reverting to dry land.

The docks, as a major London achievement, were perforce added by the map sellers to their existing maps, either by including an inset at a smaller scale, as Bowles and Carver did on the 1805 edition of their *Two-Sheet Plan*, or by engraving and printing an extension sheet and sticking this to their existing maps, as Wallis and Cary did. The second edition of Horwood's map, published in 1807 by William Faden, who had acquired the plates, was similarly 'augmented with eight new copper plates extending the plan eastward to the river Lea'. Map-makers were forced to invent some element to fill the blank blue spaces of the docks, which lay bare in stark contrast to the busyness of the built-up area; Fairburn drew in a fleet of merchantmen on his plan of the docks in 1801 with the explanation 'This Dock of 30 Acres for Unloading Inwards capable of containing between two and three Hundred Sail of West Indiamen'. (Compare Pl. 41)

Development of Land Use Symbols

The use of semi-pictorial and other symbols to indicate the function of an area, such as ships and barges on the Thames, trees in parks and windmills on hills, was not new to London maps. Symbols distinguishing between villages, castles and market towns, comparable with those now standard in O.S. maps, had first been used by John Norden in 1593 on his map of Middlesex in the 'firste part' of the *Speculum Britanniae*. The range expanded only gradually, but when Rocque published his map of 10 miles round London in 1746 he used as many as 10 different land use characters, and even within the immediate environs of London, Horwood found it useful to distinguish between pasture, ploughland and marsh. The man who developed the most elaborate system to express land usage in the London region was Thomas Milne, described by George Adams, with whom he collaborated on a handbook of surveying techniques in 1791, as 'one of the most able and expert surveyors of the present day'.

In 1800 Milne published a fascinating land use map in six sheets, covering 240 square miles of the London region. (Pl. 39) His experience had been both as a surveyor and as a publisher of maps with William Faden, with whom he collaborated on maps of Hampshire and Norfolk in the 1790's; the former experience taught him the styles of lettering and colouring traditional to estate surveys, which he used both on his London map and on a manuscript plan of Walworth, now in the British Museum, carried out in 1794. The latter introduced him to the methods of the Ordnance Survey, for whom in their early years Faden was official publisher. This association gave him access to the triangulations radiating from General Roy's five-mile base-line on Hounslow Heath, carried out in 1788 specifically for 'the Improvement of the Plan of London and its Environs'. The links between commercial map publishers and military surveyors were particularly close in the early years of the Survey, before the Board of Ordnance took over the engraving and printing of its maps, and the shapes of Milne's fields in Middlesex and Essex bear too close a resemblance to those of the first O.S. sheets for the similarity to be merely due to chance. His triangulation and theirs must have been identical.

Milne's map reveals the substantial areas of inner London still given to farming, but farming closely geared to the London market – dairy farms, market gardens and orchards. His zone of market gardens, from Teddington to Chelsea, along the fertile soils of the flood plain, and manured with London's refuse, carried upstream from the laystalls of the east end, had traditionally supplied London with fruit and vegetables in season since the 17th century. Half his map is taken up with meadow and pasture; in this 'green and open tract, which gives a pleasing rural character to the immediate vicinity of the town' noted by the Rev. Henry Hunter in 1811, were the hayfields which fed the thousands of horses stabled in London's mews. In Battersea the ancient common field was still divided into strips, although these and the watercress beds were to disappear within 30 years.

Maps in Quantity

Milne's map represents a new departure in the mapping of London. From then to the present day, the range and quality of maps is sufficient to satisfy almost every need. The crude maps, fit only for tourists, that were characteristic of the preceding century, continued to be printed in ever-increasing numbers, but their standards gradually improved in the face of competition. In many cases the old plates were re-issued until they wore out, with only minimal alterations; Cary's *New Plan of London and its Vicinity*, first published in 1790, was still on sale in 1836. The Marylebone Road was still 'the New Road', although it had by then been open 80 years, and the map excluded from its scope Chelsea, St. John's Wood, developed between 1794 and 1830, and Brompton, but as a concession to modernity the line of the London to Greenwich railway was marked. It was, however, not provided with a terminal point or station at either end. (Pl. 49)

Other publishers similarly ignored the current facts about London. Cruchley was so determined to justify the claim of his *New Plan of London in Miniature* '. . . Showing the New Improvements . . . together with the projected improvements at Charing Cross and others not yet completed', published in 1830, that he recorded a scheme for the layout of Trafalgar Square which replaced Nelson's Column by a building labelled the Royal Academy, flanked by statues of George III and IV. At that time, admittedly, the Academy was planning its move from Somerset House. In 1837 it took over the eastern wing of the newly-built National Gallery. (Compare Pl. 47)

Even the most reputable publishers were guilty of re-issuing from outdated plates, to avoid the expense of a fresh survey; James Wyld, who had acquired the plates of Faden's map *The Country 25 Miles Round London*, re-issued it in 1838, blissfully ignoring the changes which had taken place in London's environs since the first edition of 1788. (Pl. 34)

In contrast to these derivative products were the fine large-scale maps, still conveniently folded for the pocket, but far larger and more accurate, produced by map-makers like Andrew Bryant, and Christopher and John Greenwood, by similar methods and almost to the Ordnance Survey standard. (Pls. 46, 47) Christopher Greenwood summed up his intention in preparing his county maps as being 'to delineate with consistency, that portion of (the Earth) we have been designed by Providence to inhabit', in contrast with the shortcomings of the past: 'A century ago surveys of counties were made by measuring (I daresay laboriously enough) different districts and laying them together, regardless of their true scientific bearings'. Greenwood's London map, published in 1827 after a series of successful county maps, was the finest and most beautifully engraved of all his work, but there were by then other publishers, such as the George Frederick Cruchley already mentioned, to divide the London market with him, and Greenwood was not to survive long. The later editions of his map were published by E. Ruff, who acquired the plates when Greenwood's Regent Street business collapsed in about 1835.

Growth of the Parish Map

Side by side with these large-scale town maps, a new type was emerging, stimulated perhaps by the tithe award maps of the early 19th century. These showed in considerable detail a particular locality, which was neither a town nor a single estate, but a parish, and satisfied a similar local market to that reached by the topographical and historical studies of particular parishes

published by Georgian antiquarians, whose subscription lists reflect their
local appeal. Often dedicated to the local landowner, like the map of Islington published in 1822 which was dedicated to the Marquis of Northampton,
they gave' information of parochial interest such as the parish boundaries,
field acreages and names of landowners. (Compare Baker's map, Pl. 37) Starling's Kensington map, also of 1822, marks the common sewer. (Pl. 45) These
maps were often produced by a local surveyor, with the co-operation of the
vestry; the vestry clerk himself, A. J. Roberts, in 1853, published a map of
Hammersmith as a guide to the tithe apportionment, which incidentally gives a
detailed picture of this area of London just before it lost its rural character.
The Marylebone map of 1834 not only marked the new parishes of that area,
but also illustrated, as a convenient sheet-filler, plans of the new churches
provided for its growing population. (Pl. 48)

CHAPTER V

Metropolitan Improvements and the Transport Revolution

Greenwood's fine map encapsules London in 1827 after a quarter-century of extensive change: street improvements, five new bridges, canals and the docks had all made their impact on the urban landscape. The following 25 years were to be a period of even more radical disruption, and the tempo established was to increase in pace until the end of the century, and the emergence of a metropolis relatively familiar to the modern eye. (Compare Pls. 47, 53)

The concept of a metropolitan area gradually emerged in this period, in response to the overwhelming necessity for an overall authority to deal with the urgent problems of public health, communications and security presented by the London region, which covered almost 100 square miles and contained nearly 2 million people at the beginning of Victoria's reign. Administration was split among a multitude of authorities, vestries, special commissions and private enterprise: the division of responsibility for the road system may serve as an example. Seventy-eight parish vestries in the environs of London, that is outside the city and liberties, had powers to maintain local roads; besides this, the Surrey, Kent and Middlesex justices of the peace maintained the ancient highways, while private boards of trustees controlled and charged for the use of turnpiked roads.

Coinciding with the slow general acceptance of a new administration for the London area, and perhaps helping to force it more rapidly into existence, came a revolution in public transport, with first the introduction of river steamers and horse-drawn omnibuses in the late 1820's, and a decade later the arrival of the railway, innovations of tremendous significance for the linking of London's isolated surroundings.

Pressures on and around the old city

Contemporaries recognised the importance of these developments and saw the beginning of a new age; in 1839 the metropolitan reformist William Bardwell commented in his *Westminster Improvements*: 'observe how (London) is throwing out her miles of houses and streets . . . and how the monster steam is chained to the car of science, which brings up whole hecatombs of oxen, entire flocks of sheep and the vegetable products of a hundred acres, for this vast multitude'. The greatest growth in population in the 30 years before 1861 was in the districts within three miles of the city and Westminster, accessible by omnibus and private carriage – Kensington, Chelsea, Paddington, Camberwell. Within this ring, areas once neglected by the developing builder because of their physical disadvantages became sites for new estates. Problems of drainage, water supply and access roads were overcome in the interests of profitability.

Westminster at first glance offered wide opportunities to developers. Behind St. James's Park, market gardens covered the open ground down to Chelsea and to the Grosvenor estates in Belgravia. (Pls. 42, 43) The area was still administered by the Elizabethan Court of Burgesses, a system which had worked with reasonable efficiency but could not be expected to adapt itself to the demands of the 19th century, particularly since they took the form of pressure for expenditure on Thames embankments and co-operative drainage schemes quite beyond the capacities of any single parish.

Low-lying, marshy and liable to flood at high tide, the country from Tothill Street to Chelsea was only built on under relentless pressure from London's expanding population. To make firm foundations for the new penitentiary built on Millbank in 1809 on the site of Belgrave House, the ground level had to be raised seven feet. Palmer's Village, a hamlet once standing near Victoria Station, lay a foot, and Tothill Street three inches below the 1832 high-water mark. Not only was there permanent risk of flooding, but since the ancient drainage sewers were inadequate, the recently-introduced private cesspits frequently overflowed into the street; in these conditions, the danger of epidemics, particularly the new menace of cholera, was tremendous.

Reforms were considered, although at the time they could not, for lack of both the necessary money and powers, have been carried through. George

IV, for example, had proposed razing the poor cottage district between St. James's Park, Vauxhall Bridge Road and the Thames and laying it out in a grid of spacious streets, but nothing was achieved, although this would have been a monument almost as impressive as the street and park named for him which Nash had created during the Regency. Others made similar, if less drastic, proposals. Sydney Smirke, writing in 1834, made several suggestions for the improvement of Westminster which anticipate later reforms, such as widening Whitehall by removing the island of houses between Parliament Street and King Street. Another idea of his, welcomed by members of Parliament in view of the poor drainage and consequent characteristic aroma of Westminster, was to shift the Houses of Parliament to Green Park.

Pressure to improve conditions in Westminster only really became effective after the accession of Victoria in 1837 – 'We have now a valuable life inhabiting Buckingham Palace'. Close by, in Belgravia, many other influential and wealthy people were now occupying Cubitt's newly built stucco palaces and added their strength to the pressure for reform. New instruments were needed to control a new situation.

Conditions elsewhere in London were little better; the slums of Agar Town and Somers Town, flanking the Euston Road, also lacked sewers and piped water. In central London the 1851 census revealed that the narrow streets and old houses of Soho held the highest population density of the metropolitan area – 327 per acre; only half the houses had drainage, and amenities were to decline further after the cholera outbreak of 1854, when those who could afford to took their prosperity elsewhere. One more statistic may be quoted, from the *First Report of the Metropolitan Sanitary Commission*, one of the statutory bodies set up to combat these intolerable conditions – in Lambeth average life-expectancy was only 24 years, whereas for the more fortunate inhabitants of Camberwell, traditionally although not necessarily a healthy district, it was 11 years more.

Beginnings of Metropolitan Government

Of the *ad hoc* bodies created to solve the problem of London's ever-growing skirts, the Metropolitan Police was the first, in 1829. It took over responsibility for public order in the most densely-populated region of England, which had contained, in 1801, over a tenth of the national population. Threats to the individual from highwaymen and thieves had been met in part from the middle of the previous century by the Bow Street horse-patrols and the runners, but the patrols worked only the main highways; districts between still fell to the parish beadles or constables, notoriously inadequate, and often physically incapable of carrying out their duties.

The police area defined in 1829 stretched well beyond London's immediate limits, to Acton, Bow, Greenwich and Streatham; 10 years later, perhaps in reaction to the impact of the railway on London's environs, it was extended to include all parishes within 15 miles of Charing Cross. The City was excluded; it set up and still retains its own police force, of 1,005 men. Perhaps the new police authority was not considered of interest to contemporary map-purchasers. It appears on only one map, Robert Dawson's *Metropolitan Boroughs Map* published in the year of the great Reform Bill. One modern map of London, in the *Handy Reference Atlas* published by Bartholomew's in many editions since its first appearance in 1907, carries the police area marked in red.

After preliminary skirmishes by social reformers such as Bardwell and Chadwick in the 1830's and '40's, and the setting-up of several commissions on metropolitan improvements, the desperate need for an authority with at least some overall powers was partially resolved by the creation of the Metropolitan Board of Works in 1854. It was ultimately to be responsible for much of London as we know it, drastically redrawing the face of the capital, with such schemes as the slicing of Victoria Street through the tangle of Westminster, and of Charing Cross Road and Shaftesbury Avenue through Soho and St. Giles. Communications in London were vastly improved – not before time – by the Board's freeing of all the Thames bridges from toll, building the Blackwall Tunnel and creating the Victoria, Albert and Chelsea Embankments, replacing the muddy foreshore by wide routes into the heart of London.

All this was not achieved without disruption of the original population. The embankments opened up central London without, on the whole, destroying homes or displacing people, since they were built into the river, but new roads driven through densely-populated central London inevitably increased overcrowding in adjacent slums. The creation of New Oxford

Paper slip case for the map of London and Westminster by C. Smith, 1816

Street in 1847 was estimated to have displaced 5,000 from the Rookeries of St. Giles – a mere handful compared with the major removals of the ensuing 30 years.

The Suburb is Born

Not only roadworks, but also and increasingly railway companies were responsible for 'shovelling out the poor', to gain ground cheaply both for lines and for termini. The earliest railway into north London, the London and Birmingham company line to Euston, came through open fields to within two miles of Westminster, but the development of those fields, called Fig's Mead, was already planned by the managers of the Bedford estates, whose steward commented shrewdly in 1834, 'the Railroad will be a more serious affair than contemplated'. By that year only two lines had been authorised, the Euston one and the London to Greenwich, but a flood of applications was to follow in the next half-century. Dyos has estimated that 69 schemes were put into effect between 1853 and 1901, affecting the homes of at least 76,000 people in London, most of whom received neither compensation nor alternative accommodation, since the vast majority lived in rented tenements.

The building of Broad Street Station in 1865 displaced 2000 people, and in preparation for the Fleet Valley railway 1000 houses, home to an estimated 12,000 people, were destroyed at the same date. Forty years later, the Great Central Railway Company shifted nearly 2000 Londoners from their houses, acquired to build Marylebone Station; they crowded into nearby Lisson Grove, whose decline into a slum was thereby hastened, since the company failed to provide alternative accommodation immediately, as it was their statutory duty to do since 1889.

Railways appealed primarily to those who could afford to move to the outskirts of London. The poor could not take advantage of rapid travel by rail to the new areas, 'suburb clinging to suburb, like onions 50 on a rope', despite the introduction of workmen's trains on many lines from 1861. As Charles Pearson, solicitor to the City of London, commented in evidence to the Commission on Metropolitan Termini in 1846, 'A poor man is chained to the spot. He has not leisure to walk, and he has not money to ride to a distance from his work'.

For thousands of the poor, their daily work was still within the city and so their homes were necessarily in 'the ill-ventilated culs de sac and dens of wretchedness in the vicinity of Shoe Lane and Saffron Hill', whose proposed replacement by the railway was welcomed in *The Times* in March 1861.

Apart from the destruction and involuntary movement of population the railways caused in the City, Southwark and Westminster, they were to have a dramatic effect on the communities around London.

The Impact of the Railways

The railway from London to Greenwich, the first true suburban line, appeared immediately on London maps, in the year of its ceremonial opening, 1836. The prospectus prepared by the company seized on what remains the most important element in suburban traffic, the saving of travelling time; it claimed that businessmen using the railway could save themselves up to eight hours' travelling a week and 'time constitutes wealth'. They did not mention the time taken to cross the river on foot; no south London terminus was built on the north bank until the 1860's, when for the first time the railways were able to bring their city and west end passenger to more convenient dropping points – Pimlico, or Victoria, in 1860, Charing Cross in 1864 and Cannon Street in 1866. (Pls. 53, 54)

The traffic pattern set on the Greenwich line, of frequent local trains at quarter-hour intervals, was to be popular for the future on all suburban services; railway policy was to play an important part in forming the characters of the new suburbs. In the 1850's, in contrast to the later working men's trains of north and east London lines, free passes and reduced season tickets were offered to first-class passengers to encourage them to use the railway and move to such desirable and rising residential towns as Harrow, Kingston and Watford, while the first late-night theatre train for the south-east region left Waterloo in 1849.

The Hammersmith to Farringdon Metropolitan line gave a good service to prosperous commuters from 1861, but provided no cheap trains for working men, so keeping that area relatively empty of extensive terrace housing until early in the 20th century, whereas the Great Eastern had, by 1881, through its policy of providing cheap trains early in the morning and of building many local stations – 68 within 12 miles of St. Paul's – stimulated the building of acres of small terraced houses in Edmonton and Tottenham, so creating the architectural and social character peculiar to those districts.

By contrast, in Wimbledon, seven miles from Waterloo as Edmonton was seven miles from Liverpool Street, lower middle-class and working-class housing was much less in evidence than the substantial semi-detached and detached villas characteristic of that prosperous suburb, whose occupiers could afford the higher rate per mile prevailing on southern London lines. Occasionally company enthusiasm for a new line outran public interest; the station at Penge West opened in 1839 prematurely and closed again the same year for lack of passengers. In 1863 it re-opened permanently – the commuter belt had moved out to it.

The population of London was not only shifting to new centres, it was also growing by immigration from the rest of the country and abroad throughout the 19th century, but especially in the latter half. The demands for maps increased proportionately, and quite new types appeared in response to this new situation.

The railway map of London today changes very little; the few additions there are, such as the Victoria line, are easily added to existing maps, particularly as the overall planning possible for a unified London Transport makes duplication of existing lines and stations unnecessary, but this was not so in the 19th century. At the height of the expansion of railway companies the firm of Edward Stanford at Charing Cross virtually monopolised one profitable section of the map business, by publishing annually large-scale maps showing both proposals for new lines and those sanctioned by Parliament in the previous session. (Pl. 54) These form a fascinating and informative series, giving a developing record of the network spreading over the capital, with the proviso that by no means all lines sanctioned were necessarily built; many have, of course, since disappeared in subsequent rationalisation of urban railway services. The *District Railway Map* of which a section is illustrated on Pl. 58 was from the 1870's published annually, showing on a single folded sheet the stations opened to date and the omnibus services connecting them.

Stanford's maps marked not only the railway proposals but also improvements to the road system under consideration by the Board of Works; the 1862 edition marks Cromwell Road as being then under construction. The increasing tempo of the Board of Works programme involved continual revision of London street maps, and no doubt Stanford's, from an authoritative publisher, were involuntarily useful to other map publishers in recording lines of new streets.

A new trend –
Travel for Pleasure

The railway and omnibus network created in the 19th century not only enabled Londoners to live further from their place of work in pleasant residential districts, but also encouraged them to travel for pleasure, a tendency further increased by the combination of a shorter working week and greater economic prosperity in the last 20 years of the century. Large retail shops such as William Whiteley's, 'the Universal Provider', in Bayswater, and Barkers in Kensington High Street, founded in 1870, attracted customers from outlying areas, who used off-peak capacity in trains and 'buses. The District Railway operated a parcels delivery service from 1892 until the First World War, primarily for the benefit of shoppers.

Excursion maps appeared, to satisfy a new market. Mogg's map of 1845 and John Bett's of 1847 may be cited as examples of typical early excursion maps, claiming to be such in their titles, and marking distances between rural towns and places of interest in Essex, Surrey and Middlesex accessible by rail. Of these, the ultimate descendants are the *Fourth* or *Popular Edition* of the Ordnance Survey maps, first published in 1919 in their familiar red covers, and the Ordnance Survey *Tourist Map of Greater London* which first appeared in 1921; they mark antiquities, transport services and other subjects of interest for the traveller in the London region. Weekend excursions soon caught the Londoner's fancy, and trains and 'buses ran special services to favoured spots. One of the earliest was the horsebus service which during the week ran between Kilburn and London Bridge; on Sundays it provided a special 6d. ride to the Welsh Harp, at Hendon.

Later in the century, in response to that new invention, the bicycle, maps appeared in print specifically for cyclists; Philips' *Cyclist's Map* of 1885 was 'Compiled specially to exhibit all the principal Gentlemen's Seats, Antiquities, and objects of interest to the Tourist', including cycle repair shops and dangerous hills in the environs of London.

So significant and fast-growing was travel for pleasure that the Brighton Railway Board was the most importunate lobbyist in the successful campaign to have the Crystal Palace re-erected at Sydenham in 1854, where it was served by two stations and attracted vast crowds (although decreasingly so after the turn of the century). (Pl. 56)

For visitors to central London the firm of Mogg published maps which folded into covers, containing lists of omnibus timetables, which together constituted a useful guide 'For Viewing London in eight days'. The 'bus routes were also marked on the map, as on most other pocket maps published with the tourist in mind from the mid-nineteenth century.

The Great Exhibition was only the first of a series of international and national exhibitions, held first on the South Kensington site, and then from 1886 at Earls Court, both substantially benefitting the District Railway, which served them. The main railway lines provided a relatively cheap and rapid journey from the provinces, encouraging the idea of travel amongst people who had formerly limited themselves to trips to the nearest market town. Cheap tickets further stimulated the flow of visitors to London – a five-shilling excursion return from Leeds was on sale for visitors to the Great Exhibition – and Euston Station handled 750,000 passengers in the months when the Exhibition was open. To judge from the enormous number and variety of map-titles published, and from the numbers surviving, most of these new Victorian visitors to London must have bought maps, particularly in the year of the Exhibition, when an exceptionally large number came onto the market. (Pl. 51)

By no means all the maps published were absolutely accurate or up-to-date, but they conveyed an increasingly large body of information, cramming in symbols to indicate anything from Board Schools to Police Courts, which might conceivably be of use to the public. Bacon's *New Map* of 1890, at four inches to the mile, used 14 different symbols, but since the map is printed entirely in black and white, it is virtually impossible to distinguish any individual item of interest without using a magnifying glass.

The Modern Specialised Map

To overcome this problem of super-abundance of information, more and more maps were published which conveyed specific limited information on a formalised skeleton street plan. The firm of C. Smith published in 1870 an illustrated *Map of London*, a single sheet of bright orange, on which only the major streets appeared, marked clearly by white lines, the railway lines in red, and assorted public buildings, ranging from Cannon Street Station to the Agricultural Hall in Islington, in full perspective. Its value to the user was presumably that any of the major buildings illustrated would be immediately recognisable in the flesh.

The *District Railway Map* used a similar formula, emphasising in crude, bold colours, the underground and other railways lines; the modern 'bus map produced by London Transport is a refinement of this type.

The innumerable commissions for the improvement of London which published reports during the 19th century created a completely new category of work for urban surveyors. The earliest project of the century, the making of a dock system for London, involved the preparation and publication of alternative plans and surveys to illustrate the eight schemes under consideration. From then on the pace of publication of these plans, usually reproduced by lithography, increased rapidly, particularly after the setting-up of the Metropolitan Commission for Sewers in 1847, and the Board of Works, eight years later.

A detail from one of these surveys is reproduced, a proposal for the new embankment at Chelsea published in 1844, nearly 30 years before the scheme was finally carried out by the Board of Works; it is characteristic of its class, with its soft colour, its appearance of scientific accuracy and its complete exclusion of irrelevant detail. (Pl. 50)

These published reports often contain valuable incidental information, in the form of subsidiary plans giving relevant historical background, and can be of unexpected value to the present-day London historian; for instance, the *Report for Improving the Metropolis* and 'providing increased facilities of communication within the same' from which the Chelsea bank survey comes, contains a fascinating plan of bankside encroachments into the river in central London since the 17th century.

Each planning proposal required the preparation of fresh surveys, at least until the middle of the century; then in 1848 the Board of Ordnance turned its attention to London, initially for the benefit of the Sewer Commissioners, who needed to know precisely where to place their magnificent and vital underground system. This request was very much resented by the civil surveyors of the time, but the need for an overall and accurate survey was undeniable. As Henry Austin, consulting engineer commented, supporting the Ordnance Survey's case, 'This . . . does not now exist in any shape'. The Royal Engineers, under Captain Yolland, completed their survey in just over a year, and the results, the first large-scale, contoured and entirely accurate map of central London, from Tottenham to Tooting, Barking to Hanwell, was published between 1848 and 1851.

The Ordnance Survey had not mapped London as such in its first half-century of work, although by 1820 its maps of the adjoining counties into which London spread included the environs and much of the built-up area. (Pl. 38) The scale of the early printed Ordnance Survey county maps, one inch to the mile, was quite inadequate for giving a true picture of an urban area; until the policy of making town surveys on a special scale emerged much later in the century Londoners were better served by the large-scale maps published by Greenwood, Cruchley and, later, Stanford during the 19th century.

Several contemporary publishers claimed to have copied the Ordnance methods, or used their triangulations, in preparing maps of London. Davies's map, published in 1843, had been 'drawn and engraved from authentic documents and personal observation' and Archer's of 1840 claimed in its title to be taken 'from Actual Survey, the Trigonometrical Points being accurately laid down from Gov^t. Documents', but this is improbable unless they were relying on the figures printed by Mudge and Dalby 40 years before, since Ordnance policy no longer allowed publication of their triangulations. However, there is no doubt that the standard of the Survey's published maps influenced contemporary commercial publishers, both in the use of symbols and in the quality of lithography. The improvement in the quality of printing was already apparent in county maps early in the century, but the custom of re-using worn plates (resulting in blurred, heavily inked lines) was only slowly abandoned by the publishers of London maps. Cary criticised in 1819 'The unnecessary degree of blackness which prevails in our best maps, confounds the objects and makes it extremely difficult to read the names or distinguish the features'. This problem was to be resolved by the middle of the century with the increasing use of lithography for map-reproduction, a method rapidly adopted by the Board of Ordnance and also used almost universally for the plans published in official reports. (Pl. 55)

The proposals for improvements to London, and those schemes finally accepted, were embedded in formidably fat volumes of official prose, inaccessible to the general public. Map publishers were quick to appreciate the potential market for up-to-date information on changes in the face of London; each of the administrative alterations of the century produced its crop of simplified maps. The earliest appeared in response to the great Reform Act of 1832, which created four new parliamentary boroughs, Finsbury, Lambeth, St. Marylebone and Islington; within the year Robert Dawson published a map of the new boroughs.

Not all publishers were so quick to grasp the reality of an emerging metropolis. In 1847 Hugh Hughes still entitled his map *A New Map of London, Westminster, Southwark and their Suburbs*, a clumsy circumlocution abandoned by more efficient publishers, such as Cruchley, in favour of the shorter and more explicit 'London' much earlier in the century. It is clear that official opinion was slower still to acknowledge that a whole new area could be called London; neither the Commission for Sewers nor the Board of Works used the word, preferring to call themselves 'Metropolitan' and it was first used officially in the title of the London County Council, in 1888.

Administrative Authorities Mapped

The firm of Edward Stanford, established at Charing Cross in 1852, secured a virtual monopoly in maps showing the boundaries of the several administrative districts which complicated London's government until the 20th-century rationalisation of local functions. A section is reproduced from a sheet showing the Metropolitan Board of Works area. (Pl. 57) This was one in a series of six maps of London published by Stanford in 1884, each showing the boundary of a different administrative body; they range from the Poor Law Commissioners to the Gas and Water Companies, with virtually no common boundary lines among them. This complicated system of local government was only partially resolved when the L.C.C. was created and took over some of these confused statutory functions.

Other administrative maps published by Stanford included one showing the ecclesiastical divisions of London on which, for no immediately obvious reason, nurses' residences are marked, and another of the Board and Voluntary schools in the London area. By the end of the century Stanford's dominated the market in large-scale maps of London of all types. Edward Stanford had quickly grasped the value of the Ordnance Survey sheets prepared for the Commission for Sewers and published at mid-century; he produced a map in 1862 on the 12-inch scale, closely based on their work, advertising it as 'the most perfect map of London that has ever been issued'. It is a clear and informative map, characteristic of the series of fine large-scale maps to be published by Stanford's during the following hundred years. (Pls. 54, 56, 57)

Edward Weller, a Fellow of the Royal Geographical Society, about whose professional antecedents very little is known, also published a large-scale map of London in 1862, for the *Weekly Despatch Atlas*. It would stand comparison with any Ordnance town map of the period and shows even more detail than Stanford's, concentrating particularly on details of industrial activity and local authority buildings such as parish schools and workhouses, useful to the local historian. (Pl. 52)

Mapping the People

A new type of map emerged during Queen Victoria's reign, the specialised survey of sociological and medical statistics. Among the earliest were those prepared by John Snow, and published in 1855, relating deaths in the cholera outbreaks of 1849, 1853 and 1854 to London's water supply. His pioneer application of cartography to the study of disease demonstrated the hitherto unproven relationship between polluted water and infection, and in particular the responsibility of the Southwark and Vauxhall waterworks for the high incidence of cholera in the lowlying areas which the company served. A few years later the Metropolitan Board of Health started publishing annual surveys showing the distribution of outbreaks of the more common epidemic diseases, information basic to any effective improvement of public health. (Pl. 60)

Little further development took place in the use of sociological maps by Victorian town-planners – the science was still in its infancy. Before Charles Booth's *Life and Labour of the People of London* appeared, between 1889 and 1907, the only published map showing statistics on urban conditions was a plan of Dublin accompanying the *Report of the Commissioners* for the Irish Census of 1841, which differentiated between types of accommodation, population densities, literacy and animals owned. Booth's revolutionary study of the people of London, their homes, incomes, religion, education and work, had dealt at first only with the East End, 'the focus of the problem of poverty in the midst of wealth', but he extended his field in the 1890's to cover all London. His private venture received very little official encouragement, although he was to exhibit at the Paris Exhibition of 1902 his vast poverty map, prepared to show the economic status of every private dwelling in London (two sections of which are reproduced in Pls. 62 and 63; compare also Pl. 59)

Booth's work was, however, an indication for the future; although the modern sociological maps of London are less accessible and perhaps consequently less familiar than some other forms of map, they, together with the planning schemes ultimately derived from them, are the characteristic map of the present century. (Pls. 67, 68)

The new 'Central London'

In 1827 Greenwood had portrayed a city still clinging to the Thames, no part of the built-up area more than a mile or two from the river, which was both highway, main sewer and an obstacle to north-south traffic. Seventy years later, when Edward Stanford published a revised edition of his pocket-map of central London, on a scale of four inches to the mile, the picture had altered radically. No longer was the Thames a barrier. Seven railway bridges crossed it between Putney and the Tower, all the foot and carriage bridges were free of toll, and new wide roads bisected London in all directions.

In 1896 Stanford's central London stretched from East Sheen to Willesden, Peckham Rye to Hackney. Seven years before, the London County Council had come into existence, the first comprehensive administration for the metropolitan area (although the City still remained aloof); by 1892 the county included not only the whole of Middlesex, but also those communities over the borders of Surrey and Kent which existed primarily as branches of the metropolitan tree.

Within the area of the map, which does not cover the entire county of London, still lived the majority of London's population, a little less than 6 million people. Redistribution and thinning-out of the overcrowded central districts had extended the lines of new streets in all directions. Only to the west appears open land, partly in the 'mud and water' districts of Fulham, Sands End and between Vauxhall Bridge Road and Hurlingham, and partly north of the Uxbridge Road, on the flat land dominated by Wormwood Scrubs, still at that date worked in two farms, Wormholt Farm and Old Oak Farm, although brickworks appear ominously close, to the west of Wood Lane, under the present B.B.C. complex.

Elsewhere the map is entirely covered with streets in regular terraces, criss-crossed with railway lines and interspersed with numerous gas and waterworks. The substantial reservoir and pump of the Southwark and Vauxhall Waterworks are particularly prominent, on the present site of the Battersea Power Station. On the north bank, running from Chelsea Bridge almost to Victoria Station, lay the Grosvenor Canal, a feeder to the Chelsea Waterworks which became redundant in 1852, when Parliament, in an attempt to improve the quality of London's water supply, forbade the creation of reservoirs taking Thames water from below Teddington. Part of the basin was used for the early railway lines into Victoria, and the remainder has now been covered in, substantially by the air terminal complex in Buckingham Palace Road, apart from a vestigial dock still visible on the present-day map.

The old Millbank penitentiary has disappeared; within its octagonal wall Stanford sketched a gasworks, three streets and the 'Nat. Gallery of British Art'. The present complex of streets and L.C.C. housing blocks around the Tate Gallery, from Regency Street to the river, had not yet been created to fill the space left by the departed prison.

The road pattern in central London looks familiar in the first glance at Stanford's map, but several important arteries are still missing. No direct route existed yet to the west along Cromwell Road. It was still blocked by the maze of railway lines at Earl's Court, whose station had been built on the site of a farm 40 years before. The road connecting Holborn and the Strand, whose necessity had been recognised as early as 1834 by the Commission on Metropolitan Improvements, was still not built, although as Kingsway it was to be opened within a decade. (For the 19th-century street plan, see Pl. 44)

In 1878, while the new Law Courts were being built, Temple Bar, the ancient bottleneck in Fleet Street which Wren had re-built in 1677, had been removed to Theobalds Park, where it still stands, and a few years earlier Northumberland House, the Percy family's Jacobean palace at Charing Cross, had been demolished to make ground for Northumberland Street, the connecting link between the new embankment and the roads meeting at Trafalgar Square.

To the north, the private gates which had preserved the character of the Bedford estate in Bloomsbury had finally been removed after a bitter parliamentary battle in 1893. Until then, the journey for rail passengers leaving London via Euston had been perforce circuitous. The direct route up Gower Street was closed to hackney carriages and omnibuses by a gate outside University College. Precincts are once again in fashion, and the 1943 County of London Plan threatened to recreate the Bloomsbury enclave, for the benefit of the University, by blocking 15 streets in this area and building underpasses for through traffic, to meet under Bedford Square. The plan remained a dream, but in other sections of London, such as Pimlico, traffic has at least been cut to the minimum by the device of creating a complex maze of one-way streets to baffle the motorist hoping for a short-cut. In such ways the planners attempt to preserve a little of the special character of particular districts.

At the close of the 19th century the railway dominated the map of London far more than today, partly from the close duplication of lines and stations by rival companies before their unification in 1933, and partly from the slowness with which central London lines disappeared entirely underground. The first true 'tube' or subterranean electric railway had been opened in 1890 between King William Street in the City and Stockwell. This pioneer was slow to attract passengers, but it was a herald of the future underground network. Within the decade the Central London Line or Twopenny Tube (so-called from its fixed rate), was opened, and carried 14 million passengers between Shepherd's Bush and the Bank in its first six months of operation – a staggering total, even when set alongside the 70 million travellers on the

Tradecard of T. Starling, map
engraver, 1818

Victoria Line in its first year's work, and an indication of the growing commuter district of Notting Hill and Shepherd's Bush. In 1905 there were seven stations within a quarter-mile of one another at Shepherd's Bush, rival lines competing for business in this fast-growing area.

The Inner Circle linked, by a circuitous route, the main London termini, but within this line rail transport was virtually non-existent. Attempts were made to extend services, notably by the City and West End Company in 1897, to obtain permission for a line from Hammersmith to Cannon Street via Kensington, the Albert Hall, Trafalgar Square and the Strand, but the District Line was already planning to run an extended line a little to the south into the City and beyond, so that this potentially useful line was quashed.

Within central London, despite the movement to the outskirts, large communities still lived either 'above the shop' or close to their daily work. Stanford marks no fewer than four Board Schools and three others, presumably private establishments, in the streets between St. Martin's Lane and Lincoln's Inn Fields, while six hospitals were founded to serve this area between 1851 and 1874. Four still remain, although the largest, Charing Cross, is in the process of moving all but its casualty department to a new site on Fulham Palace Road, in recognition of a continuing residential population shift which has accelerated since Victoria's day.

Outside the old heart of London, in Paddington, Kensington, Hampstead and to the east, the new communities have set their mark on the map, not only in their street-patterns, which vary from the large detached villas of the Ladbroke estate to the terraces of Dalston and Haggerston, but also in the churches, burial-grounds and power stations which their existence demanded.

There had been a burst of ecclesiastical building early in the century – 33 churches were opened between 1818 and 1832 to serve old parishes swollen beyond the capacity of the original church. Some, as in Marylebone, replaced chapels of ease, but are now redundant, as the process of decentralisation has continued in the present century. Lambeth parish gained four new churches, in Norwood, Kennington and Brixton, and now has more still. In the 1840's a further impulse gave 10 new churches to Bethnal Green. Meanwhile, the need for cemeteries to replace the ludicrously overcrowded central London graveyards was recognised as an important element in the public health programme. The vast acres of Brompton, Kensal Green and Highgate cemeteries were all laid out in the 1830's, with Brookwood, reached by special funeral trains from Waterloo, a High Victorian addition. (Pl. 53)

By the end of the 19th century contemporary maps of London have become brisk and informative, lacking in the idiosyncrasies which are characteristic of those published before the middle of the century. Relatively up-to-date, clearly printed and matter-of-fact, they are tools, not collectors' fodder. They are, however, almost more absorbing than earlier historic maps in the picture they give of a Victorian London which in this present century has already largely disappeared, wiped out by re-building and massive road-schemes, but which we feel we almost remember, the nostalgic background for so many of the Victorian writers. Mr. Pooter's London has gone, as surely as that of David Copperfield.

CHAPTER VI

The Twentieth Century

The first 70 years of the present century have brought more radical and more continuous change to the face of London than any preceding era. In central London the devastation of the Second World War only accelerated a process of renewal which had already been recognised as imperative in the 1930's. The residential population of the inner boroughs has been dropping since 1901, but the workers and visitors flowing daily into London's heart have increased disproportionately, making demands on road and rail services which have still not been met in full.

In greater London sprawling new communities have sprung up, some by planners' policy, such as the L.C.C.'s Becontree estate which increased Dagenham's population from 9000 to 89,000 between 1921 and 1931, and others created by Londoners in flight to semi-detached havens in almost rural surroundings – for example, at Edgware, where the Underground advertisements of the 1920's urged suburbanites to 'convert pleasant, undulating fields into happy homes'.

Piecemeal Re-building

In this dual process of urban renewal and growth deliberate official policy has played an increasing, if not always effective part. A series of development schemes have been prepared for the capital before and since the war, each attempting to solve London's problems but none coming to full effect, from lack of money or from political turns-about or a combination of both. (Pl. 67) The result has been not the wholesale change achieved in 19th-century Paris by Haussmann, for example, but haphazard and piecemeal alterations, the rise of one inner suburb as the prosperous middle-class move back into central London, and the blight of another under the long-anticipated threat of the motorway box. The present controversy over Covent Garden typifies the problem; while it is presumably no longer necessary to have the country's largest fruit and vegetable market in central London, the lack of a generally acceptable alternative use for this historic area, and the conflict of interests involved, commercial, preservationist and administrative, has led to several years of delay and discussion. Meanwhile the pleasantly run-down streets of Seven Dials are a quiet backwater, in contrast to Holborn and the Strand.

It has been estimated that four-fifths of all the buildings standing in the City and immediately adjacent districts in 1855 had been re-built by 1905, and a fifth replaced again by 1939, partly as advertisement and for reasons of prestige, and partly in the interests of more concentrated use of expensive and valuable ground-space. The 1920's and '30's were the most active decades – the reconstructed Regent Street, the Port of London Authority building, Bush House, the massive blocks of flats along the Edgware Road and most of the great department stores of Oxford Street and Kensington High Street arose then, in a flush of commercial self-confidence and cheap labour.

The L.C.C. was to play a major part in the reshaping of London, both in building and in massive street improvements. The earliest were also the most dramatic, before the wholesale replanning characteristic of the post-war years. The road linking the Mall with Trafalgar Square gave a traffic outlet to the west of London, popular with taxi-drivers and others wanting to by-pass Piccadilly and still not entirely saturated, even in the rush-hour. (Pl. 61) The other scheme, opened in 1906, was the long-awaited link between Holborn and the Strand named Kingsway, with the splendid crescent of Aldwych creating an architectural sweep comparable with Regent Street in the eyes of its Edwardian builders. Clare Market and the courts off Drury Lane were swept away in the process, 'to open and improve one of the most insanitary and decaying quarters of London'. The subway provided for trams as part of the scheme was soon opened to all traffic, in recognition of demands from the privately-owned car and the motor taxi, a frequent sight on London's streets after its introduction in 1905.

*Goodbye to the
Older London*

By the outbreak of the First World War the L.C.C., together with the City authorities, were to be responsible for the final destruction of the picturesque if squalid London evoked by Dickens. The grim walls of Newgate Prison were demolished in 1902 to give ground for the Old Bailey. In the same year the Bluecoat School, Christ's Hospital, moved from Newgate Street to Horsham, almost the last of the great schools to abandon the city and follow the population shift to the open country. St. Paul's had moved from the Cathedral Yard to Hammersmith in 1884. Five years after Christ's Hospital's move the Underground broke a tunnel through to Golders Green and Highgate – the northern heights ceased to control London's suburban development in that direction and, sign of the times, Hampstead Garden Suburb opened the same year. By 1914 the built-up area around London lay within a circle 18 miles across, from Edmonton to Croydon, Ealing to Woolwich, bursting the bounds of the county of London.

Before the L.C.C. itself disappeared in 1965, it had gone some way towards destroying the individual identities of the many pre-existing communities it had absorbed. Each village had had its own street names, some springing from ancient field and farm names, some from traditional usage – King Street, High Street, Church Street, West End. Inevitably this duplication created difficulties for the Post Office and for strangers to the district, so that the L.C.C. and its predecessor the Board of Works assiduously renamed streets. In 1935 the 4000 duplicates remaining, together with names offensive to the prudish as too redolent of a rural past, were replaced or adapted, so that many historic and evocative titles have disappeared. Burying Ground Passage, off Paddington Street in Marylebone, has become the innocuous and meaningless Ashland Place (although this might possibly conceal a reference to cremation). Twenty-two High Streets, from Lewisham to Kensington, were renamed by 1927, and 10 Grove Places, from Lambeth to Bethnal Green. In west London, Starch Green Road – a memory of the days when Starch Green, Acton, was London's laundry, 'soapsud island' – has become Becklow Road, Hammersmith.

A similar process of simplification took place in the City. Bishopsgate Street Within and Without were two ancient short streets, the point where they met being the site of Bishopsgate and the city wall. In 1911 they were amalgamated under the single name of Bishopsgate. Aldgate Avenue has swallowed up Bull Inn Yard, Old Cottages, and Zarah Buildings.

Plans and Counter-plans

In the 1930's the L.C.C. acquired far-reaching new authority, vital in its struggle to control the unwieldy monster London had become. The Town and Country Planning Act of 1932, which gave the L.C.C. power to zone new housing estates and industries, was only one in a series of L.C.C.-sponsored measures giving new planning powers to County Hall, such as the London Squares Preservation Act of 1931, which reduced property-owners' powers arbitrarily to destroy those necessary ventilators. Two years later came the first comprehensive town plan for London, in spite of enormous opposition from the member-boroughs whose autonomy was affected, the first in a series which culminated in the Greater London Development Plan recently (1969) published by the G.L.C.

Controls were badly needed; over 12,000 building applications poured into County Hall annually before the war, and the L.C.C. itself built nearly 100,000 homes between the wars, half of them on land outside the County of London. Although the population grew only by about 17 per cent. in this period, the inexorable expansion of the built-up area continued well beyond the administrative boundary.

The need to control London's sprawling outskirts, which threatened gradually to swallow south-east England, had been foreseen as early as 1845, the year of the General Enclosure Act, when the threat of creeping urbanisation was, not for the first time, recognised officially. By a special provision inserted into the Act, enclosures in the London region were to be under a particular restraint, and reports were required if commons within 15 miles of London were threatened. This had little effect; what the building contractors could not buy, the railway companies would. Wandsworth Common was bisected and virtually destroyed by a railway cutting within 20 years, and by the 1930's land outside the county had to be bought for the allotment-holders of Middlesex.

The Green Belt proposals of 1935 came only just in time to halt London's expansion. Two years before, the London Transport Passenger Board had been set up to co-ordinate 'bus and train services in an area covering almost 2000 square miles. Now this vast region is itself rapidly becoming saturated with people; within 40 miles of Charing Cross lives a quarter of Britain's population.

The interaction of new transport facilities and new estates is clear in the pattern of urbanisation in Middlesex and Surrey. Ealing, relatively close to central London, was slow to attract Londoners until the tube line was opened from Shepherd's Bush in 1920. The intermediate stations at North and West Acton were not opened for a further three years, since until then their communities were too small to justify even a halt. Several of the stations on this line still have a misleadingly rural air about them. In 1920 the *Railway Magazine* had commented on 'the relatively sparsely populated Park Royal and Greenford Districts', which as yet did not merit a through service to central London. The Central London Line beyond to Ruislip was not opened until 1949, although its need had been recognised before the war, and in the same year came its eastward extension to Epping and Ongar.

The demands of the Motorcar

Already in the 1920's the motorcar was devouring space in London; the North and South Circular Roads and Western Avenue were the forerunners of a whole new road system which threatens to destroy ancient communities still embedded in the heart of London, bisected, as Chiswick has been, to leave a fringe of quiet culs de sac along the river-bank whose inhabitants are isolated by the continuous traffic lines of the M4 from their village beyond the road.

In 1934 traffic lights, one-way streets and roundabouts were introduced, to help in controlling the motorcar, but its dominance continues. Roads now occupy over 20 square miles of the county of London, not to speak of the land given over to car parks. Some road-schemes have, fortunately for the preservationist, failed. The underpass in Cheapside, proposed as part of the post-war reconstruction of the city to relieve the notoriously congested Bank junction, was temporarily shelved in 1947 for lack of funds, since the City had many other more pressing reconstruction problems. (Pl. 67) The so-called Northern Boundary Route from Gray's Inn Road to Liverpool Street Station, a new east-west road badly needed to relieve Holborn, which was to fly over Smithfield Market on a double-deck, has also disappeared without trace. (For roads in central London, see Pl. 69)

Other less drastic street improvements of the past decade or so have helped the cars move around central London, to some extent at least; cars now shoot through the underpasses at Blackfriars, Hyde Park Corner and on the Euston Road, only to be halted by old and persistent bottlenecks at the Bank and Knightsbridge. London Bridge is being replaced by a dual carriageway, but the other 19th-century bridges of London, such as that at Putney, or the suspension bridge of which Hammersmith was so proud on its opening in 1827, still remain, picturesque and at certain times of day totally blocked with stationary traffic.

L.C.C. into G.L.C.

Repeatedly London's problems have been too great and too expensive for London to solve alone. This had been recognised in the middle ages when the liberties were created, to bring into the city's control a potentially unruly and unhealthy outer belt. The process continued through the centuries, with a complementary opposition from the outer districts in danger of being absorbed; no sooner was new territory acquired, than the movement of Londoners continued beyond its borders. Relatively late in this process, the L.C.C. incorporated Middlesex and parts of Surrey and Kent, but was itself superseded by the still larger G.L.C. in 1965, in an attempt to include under London's administration all those areas most closely related to London.

With the G.L.C.'s creation, the urban concentration of London has been diluted. In the new outer boroughs people are more thinly spread; the borough of Bromley sprawls over Beckenham, Penge and Chislehurst, with a population of less than 10 to an acre, whereas the inner suburbs of Islington, Lambeth and Hackney all have a density of over 50 to the acre, which conceals very high densities indeed in certain sections. A glance at the one-inch map of Greater London reveals the contrast; in the grey built-up areas there are virtually no open spaces, and certainly no parks, between Bankside, Southwark and Herne Hill, nor between King's Cross and Bethnal Green, although east London is blessed with Victoria Park, thanks to the benevolence of Sir James Pennethorne, who created it as 'a rational and wholesome place of recreation similar to those enjoyed by the north and western districts'. It is easy for the fortunate residents of Richmond, Marylebone and Kensington to think smugly of the often-quoted praise for London's 'lungs', and forget those areas whose lack of appeal as hunting parks for royalty in the past now denies their inhabitants open spaces. (Pls. 30, 69)

Where east London meets Essex the Greater London Development Plan proposed the Lea Valley regional park, to run along either side of the river Lea between Stanstead Abbotts and Mill Meads, but this is merely to improve existing open space. Possibly the Bankside reconstruction, which is to remove redundant Victorian warehouses and replace them by hotels, shops and a business centre, will incorporate some public open space, but the potential commercial value of this derelict riverside area, the last in central London available to the developer, may preclude considerations of public amenity, unless the G.L.C. insists.

London's river frontage remains less attractive than it could be; as the Plan pointed out, only 12 of the 70 miles of river bank in the London area – between Chelsea and Blackfriars, and upstream towards Putney – are accessible to the general public. The imagination exercised over the plans for St. Katharine's Dock shows what could be achieved downstream when the entire dock system of the Pool of London finally closes down. Already the delightful Georgian houses of riverside Wapping are attracting the attention of Londoners.

Another of London's neglected pleasures clearly visible on the present-day map are the forgotten waterways which wind through the suburbs – the Wandle in Wandsworth, Beverley Brook in Wimbledon, the Pool in Lewisham. These neighbourhood-rivers disappear underground when they meet roads, and their existence behind the houses lining those roads is often further concealed behind hoardings to prevent children from falling in. Perhaps the London boroughs will rediscover them, clean them up and re-open them to the public.

Post-war planners recognised the need to retain diversity and colour, and to avoid the creation of a district entirely given over to banks and insurance companies. The Barbican scheme is an attempt to create a new residential area on the City's borders, which may succeed if the rents can be kept low enough to attract families, rather than the wealthy requiring a convenient pied-à-terre. The vitality of the City is due at least in part to the persistance of the ancient markets, for fish at Billingsgate and poultry at Leadenhall (although the former's existence is threatened by the popularity and convenience of quick-frozen fish).

Contemporary Maps

Two elements characterise the 20th-century map-field in London; one is the predominance of specialised maps, the province of the sociologist, the planner, the urban administrator. Efficient, impersonal and packed with statistical information, from traffic flow problems to the incidence of working wives, this class is best represented by the *Atlas of London* recently published under the direction of Professor Emrys Jones of the L.S.E. (Pl. 68) The other modern type of London map, meeting a continual and increasing need, is the simple map or street plan, used at one time or another by all visitors, and most Londoners, who know intimately only the urban 'village' in which they live and the few streets around their place of work. (Those who travel by Underground may not even acquire a sense of the relationship between the districts below which they daily pass, except in the limited and special sense that certain stations seem closer together than others – those on the Central Line, for example, being more frequent than those on the Circle. These variations may reflect a genuine difference in character between Bayswater and Kensington, a difference significantly influencing Victorian transport systems.) Such modern maps may be the raw materials for future urban historians, but neither type seems likely to become popular with collectors.

The Lure of Old Maps

As London, by the continuous renewal of its fabric, eats up the past, so nostalgia for the disappearing city grows. Local societies devoted to preserving and studying their own localities flourish in almost all the London boroughs; several local authorities actively encourage archaeological investigations, although the soaring land values of central London forbid preservation of more than a minute fraction of those discoveries. The lengths of Roman and medieval wall rediscovered since the war and protected intact are an outstanding exception, thanks to the City's preservation policies. The Greater London Council maintains a section devoted to the study of London's historic buildings and has also an active preserving policy, attempting to retain London's elusive charm by designating conservation areas.

For those interested in owning visual reminders of London's past, a flood of 18th- and 19th-century topographical engravings fills the print shops. Most of the famous old maps of London, however, cannot be so easily purchased. Whatever the size of the original editions printed of Rocque's, Horwood's and Ogilby's maps, few copies come on to the market, and those which do appear are bought by the collector or the specialised library. A clean copy of Rocque's 16-sheet map of London and its environs in the mid-18th century might cost £300; a copy of the far rarer map of Stuart London by William Morgan, considerably more. Even the maps published by Greenwood in the 1820's and 1830's can fetch up to £100, putting them beyond the reach of most interested amateurs.

For this reason, facsimiles of old maps are becoming increasingly popular. Reproductions of maps have sold well since George Vertue engraved a version of the so-called 'Agas' woodcut map of Tudor London for the Society of Antiquaries in 1738. In the 1860's and '70's Edward Stanford published lithographed editions of Rocque's and Faithorne's maps, soon to be followed by the London and Middlesex Archaeological Society with facsimiles of almost all the important early (Tudor and Stuart) maps of London.

In the present century the London Topographical Society, founded in 1898, has until recently almost monopolised the publication of facsimiles of historic maps. It has enlarged its scope for members by reproducing not only the well-known printed maps, but also unique manuscript plans, many of them Tudor and Jacobean surveys of properties in and around London. Without the minute detail given on such large-scale plans as those of the Clothworkers' Company estates, or the properties belonging to St. Bartholomew's Hospital, no true picture can be painted of the gradual changes in land-use in the city and its suburbs. These published facsimiles, of surveys inaccessible to the general public, give the basic information vital in tracing that process which has transformed the heart of London from a living organism, both home and place of work to thousands in the middle ages, to the present-day commercial centre, dead at night and at weekends.

The popularity of the Topographical Society's reproductions is undeniable; its membership grows every year. It has now been joined in the facsimile publishing field by the Greater London Council, whose Map Room has produced inexpensive, but good-quality, reproductions of many of the famous printed maps of London in the Council's collection.

The modern map, of whatever type, is far removed from the Tudor bird's-eye view which was the earliest map of London, not only by four centuries of technical improvement in cartographic and printing methods, but also in its expression of the human scale of the capital. The sheer size of London now demands simplification, and only on the large-scale Ordnance Survey sheets can those physical details be seen which go to create the environment of London's people.

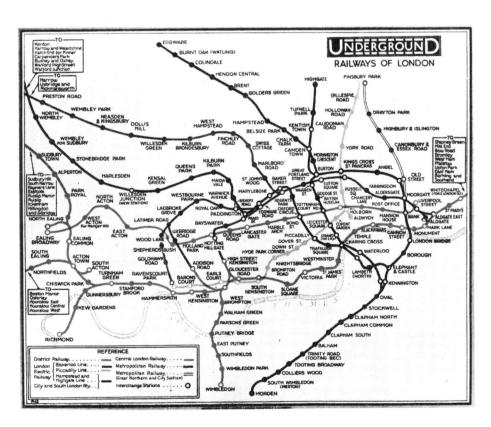

Underground railway map, printed in six colours, c. 1930

CHAPTER VII

Map-maker and Map Seller: the trade through four centuries

'Some, to beautify their Halls, Parlors, Chambers, Galeries, Studies or Libraries with . . . useth Maps'; to Dr. Dee in 1570 it seemed the Elizabethans regarded maps primarily as suitable ornament for the cultured home. This desire has persisted to the present day with, on the one hand, library editions of contemporary maps, and on the other, a continuous demand for reprints of old maps, but side by side with these has emerged a far larger market for cheap, simple, practical maps for everyday use. These two streams have run parallel for the best part of four centuries; the variety of maps published in that time reflects the continually renewed efforts of map-publishers to anticipate the demands of their market and to attract the public anew to each successive publication.

From the grand to the humble

In price, in size, in format, maps ranged right through the market spectrum. John Overton's description of his map of London, published in 1676, may stand for a whole class of advertisements, in which the publisher attempted to satisfy the potential customer's every possible need: it was available 'in one sheet of large Paper, price 1s.; with Descriptions, 1s. 6d. on Cloth, with roll and ledge, 4s. . . . you may have choice of all sorts of Maps large and small, black and white or on Cloth and coloured'. In spirit this differs very little from Sayer and Bennett's puffs for Rocque's map of London in their 1775 catalogue, a century later. They sold several versions of the map, the largest available at three guineas in loose sheets or bound in a volume, or at five guineas mounted on canvas with rollers. The advantages of the more expensive version were emphasised; it 'may be fixed on a Roller, with a Pulley to the Cornice of the Wainscot in such a Manner that it will not interfere with other Furniture, and it may be let down for Examination at Pleasure. It likewise makes a beautiful and useful screen'.

These expensive maps were never more than a relatively small proportion of the total map market. The need to satisfy the cheaper end of the market led to the publication not only of original one-sheet maps in large numbers, but also of reduced one-sheet versions of certain outstanding maps. Sayer and Bennett also sold both the eight-sheet version of Rocque's map 'for the conveniency of Rooms which will not commodiously admit the larger', at one guinea, and a smaller one still, in one sheet printed either on silk or paper. *The London Directory*, another map on their list, was also available in several formats for different purposes, the cheapest on paper and coloured at one shilling, another at two shillings in a pocket-case and the third on silk pasted on cloth, the lightest and most durable, but also the most expensive at three shillings.

The slip-case for folded maps was gradually adopted in the 18th century and had become universal for smaller maps by 1800. Attractively covered in green marbled paper and bearing an elaborate title, those produced by John Cary, for example, are a positive inducement to buy the map. The folded map had its drawbacks, however, and some map sellers supplying the popular market experimented to find an alternative format; C. F. Cruchley published with pride in 1830 his *New Plan of London in Miniature* in book-form. A delightful coloured copy is in the map collection at the Royal Geographical Society; it had, he claimed, 'decided advantages over all other methods, by avoiding the unpleasant necessity of unfolding the whole in the street'. Perhaps the public did not agree; few copies exist, and the slip-case maps continued to sell well. Improvements in format were made in the 19th century, notably with the addition of numbered references and pages listing street names, so that the whole folded together to form a small book; virtually imperative in view of the physical growth of London in that period. The *A to Z London Guide* and similar modern map-books are the ultimate descendants of this process.

Augmenting the Map

From almost the earliest days of the printed map, travellers had demanded more than a mere plan of London's streets. The lists of streets and place-names on the re-issues of Norden's and Dankerts' maps, entitled 'the Countreymans or Strangers ready helpe', have already been mentioned: once this element was established as a valuable addition to the map, publishers using it emphasised their forethought and initiative in supplying it. Faithorne, who managed to engrave extraordinarily few names on the face of his map, despite its large scale, gave a long numbered list of churches and street names at the bottom of the middle sheet 'By which allsoe the Eye may be partly guided to the Eminent Streets in or neere which they stand'. (Pl. 9) Thomas Porter repeated this method in his *Newest and Exactest Mapp of London*, published about 1655, which was numbered east to west in horizontal lines, starting with Blackfriars, a mere step from the shop of his publisher, Robert Walton, at the west end of St. Paul's. 'If you find 21, then 22 is not farre off'.

Ogilby's and Rocque's large-scale maps were published with explanatory booklets listing street and place-names running to several hundred entries, which are invaluable today for identifying on the ground many of the small alleys and yards that disappeared in the improvements of the 19th century. Fortunately, since the booklets are extremely rare, facsimiles of both have been published, one by the London and Middlesex Archaeological Society and the other by the London Topographical Society.

The continual increase of visitors to London, both from the provinces and from abroad, guaranteed a steady sale for pocket maps. In order to attract customers to their products in preference to any others, map publishers were continually trying fresh novelties, although caring little for the absolute topographical accuracy of the information on the face of the map. The practical value of street-guides was no doubt enormous, and the frequently-added lists of hackney and watermen's fares invaluable, but the map had to appeal visually as well. An obvious answer, since the map publishers were commonly also print sellers, was to employ the skill of their engravers in ornamenting the maps with 'appropriate Embelishments got up and introduced in the most tasteful and masterly style'.

Decorative Detail

London's famous buildings were a popular choice for such ornamental additions to attract the purchaser. On the early map-views of Braun and Hogenberg, Norden and Dankerts, all buildings were represented in perspective, so that no justification existed for adding extra engravings, but from the mid-17th century, as the true ground-plan map gradually emerged, pictorial representations of, for example, St. Paul's, Temple Bar or Whitehall Palace filled the borders or were printed on additional sheets and sold with the map. At the same period panoramas of London from the river were engraved and sold with maps, a fashion which flowered briefly under the later Stuarts and died in the 18th century, although some sheets of Horwood's map of the 1790's tentatively revive the style. The finest of these panoramas were those published by William Morgan as an adjunct to his great map and by De Ram. The Long Views of Hollar and Visscher were not originally sold in conjunction with the maps of London.

Ornamental engravings on maps continued to be popular well into the last century, though few later map publishers were able to insert their engravings of buildings on to the face of the map as Morgan had. Ingeniously he made good use of the empty land flanking Piccadilly to illustrate the great Restoration mansions standing there, the pride of contemporary Londoners. 'Having room on their own ground we have raised Berkly Albemarle and other great Houses, and given them their proper Front, desiring the beholder to suppose himself in the street before the house'. (Pl. 18) Two centuries later, to boast the commercial supremacy of London, a similar method was used by Collins, publishers of an illustrated map of the capital in 1854, to show the façade of the great metropolitan stores standing proud, quite out of scale with their surroundings. (Compare Pl. 64)

Most engravers were content to limit their perspective views to the margins of the map. To this rule the bridges were the main exception; for some reason they were frequently represented in elevation, especially in early 19th-century maps, as was the shipping in the river and docks, which ranged from the state barge illustrated by Braun and Hogenberg to the ubiquitous light skiffs which were London's taxis for many centuries and which appear clustered at the most commonly-used landing steps, Temple Stairs, Whitehall Stairs and Queenhythe. (Pls. 14, 24)

In the 19th century the traditional engravings of historic buildings were joined or replaced by such recent innovations as the new Houses of Parliament, the Thames Tunnel and, increasingly, the railway termini. Shury's map, first published in 1831, which went into at least seven editions, was

Churches in Westminster: from the map of St George's, Hanover Square parish by G. Bickham, 1757

perhaps the most heavily laden with views, 33 in all, to which the Crystal Palace was added in 1851. The charm of these little engravings is considerable, although they are not all necessarily to be relied on for absolute accuracy in either topography or architecture. The picturesque rural view near Willow Bridge, Canonbury, which Thomas Starling engraved for the corner of his map of Islington, can only convey a romanticised idea of that district.

Most of the maps sold must have been the cheap, small, popular ones which went into many editions, could be easily stuffed into the pocket and were soon worn out. These maps survive in considerable numbers in the national collections, and are those most frequently offered to museums by members of the public; creased into many folds and often grubby from much use, they have only been casually preserved. In contrast to these are the magnificent collections made by men of scholarly tastes in the past, as a fitting adjunct to a gentleman's library. Maps were purchased and treated as engravings, to be carefully pasted into folios, or bought already bound into a volume; in this way many rare maps have been preserved intact and clean by contemporary scholars with a lively interest in topography.

Map Collections

'A public Library is the safest port': thanks to such collectors, examples of most important maps are now safely in national institutions where they can be studied and enjoyed. Pepys's London collection is rightly famous, particularly so as it still remains in the large classified volumes which he assembled and which were later bequeathed with his library to Magdalene College, Cambridge. The collecting custom continued to appeal; the Royal topographical collection, nucleus of the British Museum Map Room, thanks to the generosity of George IV who presented it in 1828, contains many gems, including a rare map of Hyde Park published in 1764 by Joshua Rhodes. (Pl. 30) This group, and the unique collection of London topographical material formed in the 19th century by Frederick Crace, make the Map Room first port of call for any student of London maps.

Oxford is fortunate in possessing two great topographical collections with maps of London interest; Richard Gough's map and print collection at the Bodleian Library and, in the Print Room of the Ashmolean Museum, the grangerised copy of Clarendon's *History* assembled by Sutherland, containing Wyngaerde's topographical drawings and several London maps.

This literary interest which has resulted in the deliberate preservation of maps was not confined to English scholars. Several exceptional examples of early London maps and engravings are preserved in the Royal Libraries at Copenhagen and Stockholm, the Bibliothèque National, Paris, and the University Library, Utrecht. The group at Utrecht, a collection formed by a Dutch visitor to London in the 1620's, is unusual in that its history is known, but it must be typical of the souvenirs taken back by visitors to this country in the 16th and 17th centuries, especially those from Protestant countries: it includes a unique engraved panorama of London from the north, the only one to show the Theatre, an early place of dramatic entertainment in Finsbury. The list of European subscribers to Rocque's map of London's environs illustrates the extent of continental demand in the mid-18th century; many of the French names without addresses presumably belonged to his Huguenot compatriots living in London, but in addition his subscribers came from Paris, Lausanne, Amsterdam and 'The Publick Library of Geneva', not to speak of the Sardinian and Dutch ambassadors. This demand Rocque probably anticipated, as the printed titles to the map are in three languages, French and Latin as well as English.

Maps purchased by cultured people were not only pasted into volumes; they were regarded as decorative engravings and were hung on walls, but the hazards of time have resulted in few maps treated in this way surviving. At the Vyne, Hampshire, one room exists to illustrate a use to which many maps and prints were put – its walls are entirely lined with engravings, pasted edge to edge and varnished over. Memories only remain of others, similarly treated and long since vanished. Bagford referred sadly to Norden's map of English battles, formerly hanging in the picture gallery at the Bodleian: ''tis now destroyed' – the fate which had overcome another engraving of Norden's, the long view hanging on the stairs at Dulwich College which, Bagford commented, Pepys wanted to buy. 'But since it is decayed and quite destroyed by means of the moistness of the wall', this particular engraving is now only known to us from an example preserved in the Stockholm Royal Library.

Scattered references in inventories indicate the early demand for maps as ornament. The Sheldon tapestry map is a curiosity which reflects a wealthy man's fancy for Saxton's map as a unique wall hanging, but from the mid-16th century English stationers were selling cheap paper maps to be put on the wall. Sir William More's library at Loseley was hung with maps of England, Scotland and France when his inventory was taken in 1556. Another inventory, quoted by Halliwell, demonstrates that hanging in a London study in 1610 were seven maps, six of 'dyvers contreyes' and the seventh 'the great mappe of London'. Pepys's cousin noted in 1661 that in a 'taylor's lodgings' which he inspected the chamber was 'hung with stript hangings, with maps'. On Pepys's own library wall hung a large roller map, seen in a pen-and-wash drawing of his York House library now at Magdalene.

Finance and the Subscription System

Despite the undeniable demand for maps, publishers were reluctant to embark on the expense of engraving and printing maps without certain guaranteed sales. Their caution was justified; the costs of survey, engraving and colouring, not to speak of the materials involved, could be considerable. The first English engraved town-plan, Richard Lyne's single-sheet map of Cambridge, cost his patron, Archbishop Parker, nearly 50 shillings in contemporary money, which did not include any fee to Lyne to cover the costs of the initial surveyor's drawings. This represented a substantial sum, in an age when a labourer might receive as little as sixpence a day.

The subscription system of financing such ventures, once introduced, was common until the early 19th century. The map-buying public was familiar with it as a means of financing county histories and large, expensive publications of all sorts, and no doubt a comparison of names of subscribers would reveal a community of gentlemen subscribing to both forms of publication.

Few specific costings for map-publishing ventures have survived, but one prepared for John Seller's scheme to publish an English atlas shows the amount of capital required. His survey of the English counties, to be published on the three-inch scale, would cost one shilling a mile; each plate cost eight pounds to engrave, and he proposed to include 100 town plans at one pound each. He failed to gain many subscribers at 40 shillings a head, but this may not be a true reflection of potential public interest in his scheme, since at the time at least two other such atlases were in progress. William Morgan was responsible for one, his continuation of Ogilby's *Britannia*, but was not demanding subscriptions 'till he hath it in his power to assure the Adventurers when they shall receive what they subscribe for' – an obvious weakness of the system was that the publisher might fail to achieve sufficient support and disappoint his early subscribers. Morgan had used the method satisfactorily to help his London map on to the market in 1681–2: the subscribers, who had first been notified about the project and approached for their support seven years before, were given their copies several months before the map was on sale to the general public at Morgan's shop 'Next the Blew Boar in Ludgate Street'.

In Humphrey Wanley's diary we have a glimpse of how subscribers were recruited; Robert Harley, as a nobleman with a fine library, was an obvious target for the enterprising publisher with a map to support. On 17 November 1722, his librarian noted that a familiar bookseller called: 'Sparke brought a proof Map of the Fens as recently surveyed by Dr. Stukeley, with desire that my Lord would Subscribe for Six at the Rate of Half a Guinea'. There is no record of whether my lord obliged on this occasion. Rocque, to encourage potential subscribers living in the fashionable villages to the west of London, advertised that they could give their names to his brother Bartholomew, at Walham Green, conveniently close to the Brentford high road.

As an occasional additional attraction to solicit support for the publication, map-makers might include subscribers' coats of arms, or detailed plans of their rural estates. Warburton proposed publishing a map of Middlesex in 1721 to replace the 'bare copies of Saxton, and Norden's Superficial surveys, made near two hundred Years since'; he invited subscriptions at two rates, 10 shillings for separate sheets, 12s. 6d. for the map pasted on cloth and coloured; this 'makes them cheaper (even for Furniture) than the meanest prints', he claimed, but he urged the gentry to pay a guinea so that he could include their coats of arms. Despite this persuasive offer, he took 25 years to complete and publish the map. Subscribers' names were often listed on the map, as on Andrew's great map of the country 65 miles round London published on 20 sheets between 1774 and 1779, and Rocque not only noted subscribers but flattered the vanity of his intended customers by listing, with a location reference, all gentlemen's seats, parks and great houses in the environs of London.

The subscription system was no doubt responsible for the care with which subjects of interest to the largest section of the potential map-buying public, the gentry and upwards, were delineated. Maps of the environs of London, such as Rocque's, Andrew's, Chapman's in the 18th century, and Bryant's in the 19th, are lavish in their treatment of park and garden plans. Rocque's attention to these details of layout may be accounted for by his earlier career as a landscape gardener, but Bowles and Dury, for example, were merely gratifying the customer's vanity and ignoring what to us are more important changes when on the third edition of their map they changed very little from the first issue 14 years before except the name of the noble occupier of Wanstead House in Essex. The Earl of Tylney had died in 1784, a fact immediately acknowledged by the publishers in their edition that appeared in the following year, where his name is replaced beside Wanstead by that of his heir, Sir James Tylney Long.

Greenwood was explicit, in the *Explanation* to his Surrey map, that he was giving the public what it wanted. 'It has been a principal object, to introduce and describe individually the Palaces and all the numerous Noble-mens and Gentlemens Seats and Residences and their different Parks, Lawns, Pleasure Grounds and ornaments'. Cary in his road-books followed a similar principle; assuming that most of his potential customers would be carriage-folk, he recorded the names and addresses of those gentry living within sight of the main roads. (Pl. 40)

Advertising   Having successfully financed the engraving and printing of his map, the publisher had then to bring it to the attention of his public. Most of the early maps carry directions as to where they might be purchased, such as the picturesque description of his address given by George Willdey, 'the Great Toy Spectacle, China Ware and Print Shop the Corner of Ludgate Street near St. Paul's'. Before the Fire and for several years later most of the premises clustered around St. Paul's, in Blackfriars, Ludgate Street and Little Britain, the traditional home of printers and booksellers. The earliest true English print and map sellers, John Sudbury and George Humble, set up 'at the White Horse in Popes Head Alley' where their first imprint is dated in 1599.

This historic quarter missed the fruitful market in Westminster, where so many transients called on business connected with the Court, Parliament and the Law Courts, so that during the legal terms at least enterprising book and print sellers maintained agents in Westminster Hall, as William Morgan did. His main shop was in Ludgate.

Even in 1785, when Pendred's *Vade Mecum*, or directory of London shops and tradesmen, was published, only the enterprising Cary, of the seven firms described specifically as map sellers, had premises west of Ludgate Hill, at 188, Strand. By the mid-19th century, the reverse was true. Map sellers clustered around Trafalgar Square and along the Strand.

Advertising has played as important a part in the marketing of maps as of any other commodity. Magazines and newspapers, today's shop windows for publishers, only emerged late in the 17th century, so that early map-sellers were forced into other forms of advertisement. For expensive maps, printed handbills of proposals inviting subscriptions were prepared and distributed, perhaps stuck on a wall in some public thoroughfare or on the pillars of St. Pauls, and potential customers were invited to inspect specimen sheets. This was the system used by John Seller to promote his *English Atlas*, of which certain already-engraved pages were, according to the handbill, visible at his establishment in Wapping, home of many Stuart chart and instrument makers, and also at Oliver's shop on Ludgate Hill. A decade earlier, John Ogilby had appointed several book sellers to receive subscriptions for his abortive Atlas, including, as he claimed on his trade card, Robert Peake 'at the Stationers Armes and Ink Bottle, in Lombard St. . . . who selleth all Sorts of choice Mapps and Stationary Wares'.

Ogilby's partner, William Morgan, advertised his large-scale map of London lavishly and repeatedly, well before its final publication, in the *London Gazette*. After it went on the market, he continued to insert advertisements for six months or so, quoting favourable customer reactions.

A few years later, in 1718, Bowen published proposals for his revision of Ogilby's *Roads*, which was to appear two years later. Subscriptions were to be left with Bowles, Overton and 'The Printsellers of London & West'tr '.

One copy of the proposals carries a manuscript addition indicating that Members of Parliament were specially served, in that subscriptions would also be taken 'at the anchor Room over ag'st the Loby of the House of Commons'. Drawn as they inevitably were from all over England to London, M.P.'s might be expected to take a special interest in route maps converging on London.

Thomas Bowles was to turn Bowen's new edition of the road-book to good use as a vehicle for advertising his own publications. Pasted into a copy in the British Museum is a long list of maps 'available at his shop next ye Chapter House in Pauls Ch-Yard London' including 'Large Landskips proper for Chimney-peices . . . with large Maps upon Cloath for Halls'. Examples of such catalogues are rare, although many were presumably printed. Entries from Sayer and Bennett's catalogue of 1775 have been quoted earlier. Comparable is John Overton's, published in 1672, which demonstrates the crude commercial rivalry between competing print sellers. Since the 19th century it has not been considered good commercial form to criticise competitors, but Overton had no such reservations. He 'scorns to sell anything pittyfully done and he hath more than ten time the Choice and stock that R(obert) W(alton) hath, though he vapors that he is the oldest man'. Overton was a practised salesman; on the list of 20 places of interest in London to which he gives reference numbers on his 1706 map of the capital, the address of his own shop, 'the White Horse without Newgate' comes last.

Changes in map designing

During the second half of the 19th century the map publishing field was dominated by fewer firms, and their publications became increasingly more authoritative and similar in appearance, under the influence of the Ordnance Survey. Idiosyncracy and quirkiness gradually disappeared from both the content and the titles of maps, although the occasional oddity still came on to the market. A map entitled *The Modern Plague of London*, which the National Temperance League published in the 'nineties, marked all the public houses in central London clustered in the seamier districts of the West End and virtually absent from Kensington. (Pl. 59) Another, prepared perhaps by some Edwardian forebear of the Central Office of Information, whose job it is to promote the British image abroad, was 'under the Official Control of the British Consul, Paris'. It showed the large stores and manufactories which graced central London, from the vast United Horse Shoe and Nail Company Ltd. at Greenwich to Kilburn Brewery. (Pl. 64)

Since the earliest days of map-publishing, two main types have been popular, one the small-scale guide or street plan, simplified and emphasising only that information on public buildings, 'bus routes and the like which is necessary to the casual visitor. In this, the difference between Norden's map and the *A to Z Guide* is only one of technique. The other variety, the large, detailed survey, has always sold fewer copies; it has become increasingly elaborate, reflecting the complex network of services which lie below present-day London. William Morgan marked administrative boundaries, yet ignored the physical structure of London, but today a large-scale town map hints at the presence of sewers and cables. Fire hydrants and tube stations are other visible reminders of underground London.

John Ogilby presenting Charles II with the names of subscribers to his London map: from the map of London and Westminster by W. Morgan, 1682

Techniques of Map Reproduction

This book has inevitably touched only in passing on the changing techniques of map production. While it is impossible to give here a comprehensive account of a subject so specialised and complex, a brief historical comment on methods of reproduction may help to put into perspective the achievements of the London map-makers who have appeared in the foregoing chapters. However skilful and accurate their surveying and recording methods, the quality of their maps when reproduced was ultimately dependent on the abilities of contemporary engravers and printers.

Manuscript maps do not come within the strict terms of this discussion, since they were by their nature not the subject of mechanical reproduction. Several copies may exist of a particular map; thus, copies were frequently made for office use of the rough sketches made by surveyors in the field. The fine chart of the Thames prepared for the Navy Office (see end papers) is a version made at leisure after the actual survey had taken place – presumably for the purpose of display, as the watercolours of naval yards and the illuminated royal arms indicate. Fair copies might be made as a preliminary to engraving; the manuscript map of the Isle of Dogs (Pl. 38) is a clean and refined version of the surveyor's field drawings, worked up in the Board of Ordnance Drawing Office.

Such manuscript maps, whatever the format of the preliminary field sketches (and by its nature, such flimsy first-stage work rarely survives) were, at least before the 19th century, either copied into folio volumes or drawn out on sheets of parchment, as the most durable material available. The former method was used for the post-Fire surveys of the city. The Posting Books of the Chamberlain's Office consist of measured plans of the properties destroyed in the Fire, reduced from the sketch plans made on the spot and certified by the city's sworn surveyors. (Compare the survey for a lease in Pl. 16)

Surveys drawn onto parchment and intended as a permanent source of reference, such as John Ward's for the Goldsmiths' Company (Pl. 20) were often ornamented with elaborately floreated scale-bars and tricked out in gold with coat of arms; the ability to draw such ornaments, as much as sheer familiarity with surveying techniques, was required of the Tudor and Stuart surveyor.

Woodcut and Copper engraving

Since the 16th century three main methods (excluding photography) have been used to reproduce maps. The two earliest both originated on the Continent during the 15th century, woodcut prints in Germany and copperplate engraving in Italy. The former method of printing was introduced to England by Caxton for book illustrations about 1480; the view of London on page 16 of 1497 is an early example, but few English woodcuts are better than 'second-rate hack work'. (Hind, *Engraving in England*.) Woodcut could be printed in the same press with type, since the design, cut round with a burin on softwood, stood out in relief, whereas copper engraving in intaglio required a double roller press and therefore a separate printing operation; however, from the mid-17th century the latter entirely superseded woodcut in English map-printing and indeed in all illustrative printing, until Bewick revived the art of woodcut in the late 18th century. The so-called 'Agas' map is a rare example of an English woodcut map. (Pl. 8)

Engraving on copper plate was particularly appropriate for expressing the fine line and crowded detail required in town maps. The earliest known printed map of London – two of the copper plates for which survive (Pl. 2) – demonstrates one of the finest achievements of the technique; the late 16th century was a period of superb copper engraving. Some of the finest maps were produced under the patronage of Archbishop Matthew Parker by English and Netherlands engravers working at Lambeth.

Copper engraving remained the only technique for printing maps until the late 18th century – a period of printing experiments. Steel plates, capable of printing very many more impressions than the softer copper, were introduced from about 1820, and lithography at the same date.

Lithography

With the discovery of lithography there was introduced a completely new principle to printing; instead of engraving the design on metal, the lithographer drew in a greasy medium on a slab of porous stone. The stone was damped and then inked, but ink adhered only to the greasy surfaces, to which paper was then applied under great pressure. Its advantage, in that the lithographer was working in a flexible line on stone in a way comparable to drawing on paper, was soon realised by the War Office, which used lithography for preparing maps from the 1820's. The technique allowed the use of coloured inks and chromolithography was used to print surveys in official reports (Pl. 50) and estate maps from the 1840's. The commercial map publishers realised its possibilities after the Great Exhibition, where exhibits on colour printing attracted considerable attention; in this century lithography has been extensively used for printing popular maps such as the familiar folding Underground and 'bus routes published by London Transport (see page 54), although since about 1880 zinc plates have replaced the heavy and unwieldy stone.

Colour in maps   Until the 19th century colour-printing was virtually unknown in maps. Wooden hand stamps, carved with symbols representing trees and houses and dipped in coloured inks, were used on a few Tudor estate plans, now in the British Museum, but this primitive form apart, mechanical reproduction in colours was technically impossible before the introduction of lithography. However, only a relatively small proportion of surviving printed maps have not had some colour applied by hand.

While coloured county maps are the more familiar kind, town maps also received attention, whether as single lines of colour to mark boundaries (Pl. 25) or in a broad wash to differentiate between parishes or administrative districts (Pls. 31, 37). This colour was applied either before the map was sold, in the printer's workshop – Stuart and Georgian map sellers' lists and advertisements frequently differentiate between coloured and black-and-white versions, at appropriate prices – or by the purchaser or his family at home, as 'an amusement both extremely agreeable and of great advantage'. The earliest English handbook to deal with map-colouring by hand appeared after the Civil War, and the exercise was highly valued, as much because it imparted geographical knowledge as because the end result was a decorative effect.

Because of the current popularity of coloured copies of old maps, hand colouring cannot always be assumed to be original and to have been applied at the time of publication. The financial temptation to 'improve' a black-and-white map is obvious.

The conventions governing the colouring of town-maps in the era of hand-colouring, together with recipes for making the actual tints, were explained in numerous books published from the mid-17th to the 19th centuries, aimed at both the professional colourist and the amateur. It is clear from surviving specimens of London maps which have contemporary or near-contemporary colouring that these conventions were regarded only as guide-lines; there are enormous variations in the strength of the wash or line, the elements of the map chosen for differentiation and even in the colours used. (Compare the different approaches in, for example, Pls. 42 and 43). It is characteristic of Georgian maps of London that the capital's multitudinous administrative districts, wards, liberties and parishes, received the colourist's attention, while topographical features were ignored (Pl. 47).

With the introduction in the 19th century of lithographic colour, uniformity in the use of symbolic colour necessarily became the rule – at least within editions of particular maps. The 20th century has seen certain additional conventions recognised on virtually all maps of London, especially those of the street-guide type. Red dots or circles are generally used for the Underground stations, green wash for parks and open spaces and blue lines for small watercourses and for the banks of larger rivers such as the Thames, while increasingly in post-war maps dotted coloured lines indicate the network of motorways which are continuously superimposing themselves on the face of London (Pl. 69). These conventional colours are of course of enormous value in distinguishing between the crowded details of a London street-guide: the difference can best be appreciated when one compares the copy of a cheap monotone guide such as the *A–Z* with Bartholomew's or Philips' expensive colour atlases. (For German conventions, see Pl. 66.)

The Surveyor's Task

by D. J. Bryden

Curator of the Whipple Science Museum, Cambridge

'There are but two principall instruments fit indeede for the plotting of grounds, and that is this that hath the name of a *plaine table*, and the *Theodo-lite*', wrote John Norden in 1607; yet we cannot be sure exactly how and with what instruments Norden compiled the data for his panoramic map *Civitas Londini*. His text-book is concerned only with topographical surveying in rural areas. Indeed, from the Elizabethan age to the Victorian era the majority of instruction manuals on surveying technique gave scant attention to the particular problems of urban survey. Only the novice surveyor would need Abraham Crocker's advice, a couple of centuries later, 'to be at his street-work long ere the votaries of pleasure and dissipation are awake, or the bustle of commerce is begun; that neither the prying eye of idle curiosity, nor the busy hum of men may interrupt his progress'.

The basic geometric principles on which the surveyor's work was founded were all known by the time continental cartographic practice reached England in the 16th century. Standards of measurement for the purposes of geodetic and topographic survey improved as the ideal of precision led both to the design of better instruments and to careful attention to procedures in the field. Given good instruments, it was in these detailed procedures that the secret of accurate town surveying lay.

The 18th-century instrument-maker George Adams described the practice of surveying as comprising three parts: measuring straight lines, finding the position of those lines with respect to each other, and laying down these positions upon paper. Though the prolixity of text-book writers suggests otherwise, it really was as simple as that. Naturally it was vital that the techniques of manipulating the instruments be mastered, but until recent times the essential instruments were limited to three; the theodolite, the chain and the offset-staff.

The prototype of the theodolite was known in England by the later decades of the 16th century. Although substantial improvements in design and construction separate Leonard Digges' 'Instrument Topographicall' of 1571 and the 19th-century transit theodolite, they both serve the same purpose – that of measuring horizontal and vertical angles. Contemporary with the introduction of the theodolite, the wire chain superseded the knotted line for measurement of distance. Most land surveyors knew, and at times used, indirect geometric methods, but in practice they relied on the chain to measure distances on the ground. Various lengths of chain were used, normally based on the statute denomination of the Rod, Pole or Perch (16½ feet). Rathborne in 1616 recommended a two-pole chain with 100 links to each pole; Gunter in 1624 a four-pole chain with a total of 100 links, which became the chain of 66 feet. In 1653 Leybourne described both of these, with an additional mention of the Foot-Chain with links of 12 inches. For urban surveying the latter was more convenient, 'because the Ground-plots of the

Surveyors of 1701 with their instruments. On the left a plane table and on the right a circumferentor reading horizontal angles only

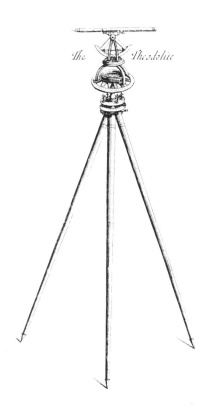

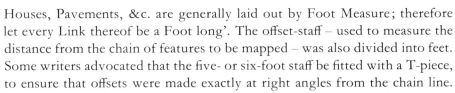

'Mr Jonathan Sisson's new Invented Theodolite' of 1723. Sisson was one of the earliest makers to replace the open sights traditionally used on land-surveying instruments with a telescope

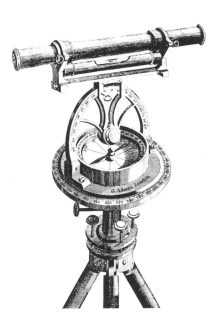

A 'common theodolite' of the late 18th century

Houses, Pavements, &c. are generally laid out by Foot Measure; therefore let every Link thereof be a Foot long'. The offset-staff – used to measure the distance from the chain of features to be mapped – was also divided into feet. Some writers advocated that the five- or six-foot staff be fitted with a T-piece, to ensure that offsets were made exactly at right angles from the chain line.

Before proceeding, the surveyor would walk over the area to be mapped, possibly drawing an 'eye-draught' of the principal streets to assist in planning the sequence of the field work. Armed with his tools, and with an outline knowledge of the street pattern, the surveyor was ready to proceed, with two chain-men, the 'leader' and the 'follower', as his assistants.

Where to begin the survey offered almost limitless choice. The single essential was for the theodolite to be set on its tripod at the intersection of two streets, in order to command a vista down each to some junction with another street. At these intersections in the city's network of thoroughfares the assistants set up marker poles, 'making', as William Gardner said in 1737, 'holes for them between the pebbles with a pointed iron of six or seven inches long'. Now the surveyor's work begins in earnest. After carefully levelling the theodolite, he turns it to view one of the markers, adjusting the horizontal scale to read zero. Then he rotates the sights to view the other marker and records in his fieldbook the horizontal scale reading. This indicates the angular separation of the two sight-lines.

At a word from the surveyor, the chain men begin their task. The leader drags the chain out to its fullest extent, with the 'follower' holding his end against a short marker post hammered into the ground between the tripod legs and exactly under the centre of the theodolite. Looking through the sights, the surveyor signals the 'leader' to left or right until the extended chain is exactly on the sight-line from the theodolite at station one to the distant marker at station two. The surveyor now leaves his theodolite and walks along the chain line. With the offset-staff he measures off to both left and right of the chain the distances of all the features he intends to incorporate in his map. 'Take notice of all manner of *Breaks, Courts, Alleys, Houses* of note, and other publick *Remarks*, with their true Perpendicular distance from your Chain', recommended William Leybourne, one of the surveyors responsible for Ogilby and Morgan's 1677 map of London. It was vital that this mass of information be recorded in the field-book. By the 18th century this book would normally be arranged so that offsets were logged to left or right of a central column in which the respective chain distances were recorded. Further columns were used to note or sketch the features measured, so that the field book became a linear strip map recording topographical detail on either side of the sight line.

On reaching the end of the chain the surveyor returns to his theodolite. The 'leader' drags the chain out again, having first knocked a small metal arrow in the ground to record the end point for the 'follower'. The surveyor ensures that the chain lies on the sight-line, and the whole procedure is repeated as before, until the marker at station two is reached. The follower may be instructed to use the offset-staff to measure distances indicated by the surveyor, leaving the latter free to concentrate on recording. 'The Performance of this Work', wrote Samuel Wyld in 1725, 'is very laborious, and you must be careful to keep the Field-book in a plain and regular Manner, otherwise the Multitude of Observations and offsets will be apt to breed Confusion'. On reaching station two the theodolite can be moved and set up at that point. The surveyor then sights back to station one, recording the slope and setting the horizontal scale to zero. Meanwhile, one of the assistants will have walked down the intersection and hammered in a marker pole at station three, and so the process continues. As part of his initial planning the surveyor will have chosen the sequence of his stations in order to return to or 'close on' the starting point in four or five legs, surveying along the sides of a trapezium or irregular pentagon of chain lines. Within this circuit there will still be detail to be recorded, for example cul de sacs and lanes to be surveyed with the chain. The surveyor's work does not end there, for he must also explore behind the façade and, include, to quote Laurence, in *The Young Surveyor's Guide* of 1716, 'the Yard or Gardens that are behind the Houses; with the turnings and windings thereof . . .'.

A circuit of streets once completed, the whole town is mapped in the same manner, each closed trapezium being linked to the next by a common side. For a city the size of London, who can possibly doubt Samuel Wyld when in his 'General Directions for taking the Ground-plot of a City or other Town', he characterises it as 'a work that will take up a great deal of Time'.

Some surveyors saved time at the expense of accuracy by dispensing with the theodolite and relying on compass bearings of the sight-lines. They 'chained' from station to station, but paid little attention to careful offset measurements, relying on the 'eye-draught' sketch for detail. Such practices were less objectionable as the scale of the finished map decreased. There was little point in recording detail that would not appear, and on this matter the surveyor had to exercise his professional judgment as the field work proceeded.

The final stage of the surveyor's work was also the first stage for the cartographic draughtsman: transferring the data recorded in the field-book. In principle this process was remarkably simple. It required only a ruler and a protractor to draw in the chain-lines to scale, a single compass-bearing down a principal street being sufficient to fix the orientation. In practice there were many cross-checks and data corrections that the mathematically sophisticated surveyor could apply. The simplest example is to scale down chain distances to true horizontal distances, by incorporating an adjustment for slope; and there are many others. Once the surveyor began to plot detail from the field-book onto the network of chain lines the map visibly grew, until at last the finishing touches were added. 'I write the names of the Streets, Lanes and Alleys in them', said William Gardner: a finishing touch indeed, when cartography becomes calligraphy.

Surveyors of 1788 with their instruments – note the chain, offset staffs, and the compass with open sights

BOWLES's
ONE-SHEET PLAN
of the CITIES of
LONDON
AND
WESTMINSTER
WITH THE
BOROUGH OF SOUTHWARK;
comprehending their Outſkirts
and Extent of the Thames
from Chelſea to Deptford.
EXHIBITING ALSO
THE NEW BUILDINGS, ROADS,
and other Alterations
1800

Printed for the Proprietors,
No 69 BOWLES & CARVER, London.
St. Paul's Church Yard, London.

Bibliography

Since this book sprang from historic maps of London, it seems useful to preface the formal bibliography with a brief note of the major collections of London maps accessible to the interested public. For further details, and an invaluable location list of individual printed maps, see the *Catalogue* compiled by J. Howgego and I. Darlington.

No one library has copies of all the important maps, although the British Museum comes close, with copies, facsimiles or photographs of almost all the outstanding ones. The collection is divided between the Map Room, which contains the fine series of printed maps collected by Frederick Crace and those from the Royal Library, and the Manuscript Room, in which considerable numbers of manuscript maps of London are held, especially estate surveys and plans prepared in connection with canal and railway schemes.

In the Guildhall Library and the Greater London Record Office at County Hall, the large collections are similarly split between general printed maps and manuscript plans originating in various administrative purposes, such as the post-Fire surveys of the city at the Guildhall, and the large-scale surveys prepared for the Georgian and Victorian Commissions of Sewers. Manuscript maps relating to Middlesex are in the Middlesex Record Office in Westminster, and maps of those sections of London that were once part of Surrey and Essex are in the relevant county record offices. Collections of maps relating to particular localities are held in most of the London borough reference libraries, with especially rich collections at Kensington and Westminster.

Much of the material about London maps is scattered in articles in learned journals and in a wide range of books which deal only incidentally with the subject. Those relating to the individual maps illustrated in this book are listed in the relevant captions. The following book-list contains not only those which I have found generally useful, but also some suggestions for further reading.

History and Topography of London

T. Baker, *Medieval London*, 1970.
T. C. Baker and M. Robbins, *A History of London Transport, Vol. I.* 1963.
W. Bardell, *Westminster Improvements*, 1839.
N. G. Brett-James, *The Growth of Stuart London*, 1935.
R. Clayton, *The Geography of Greater London*, 1964.
H. Clunn, *London Rebuilt, 1897–1927*, 1927.
H. Clunn, *The Face of London*, 1951.
Committee on the Improvement of the Port of London, *Reports 1793–1802*, 1803.
ed. J. T. Coppock and H. C. Prince, *Greater London*, 1964.
E. Course, *London Railways*, 1962.
H. J. Dyos, *Victorian Suburb: a study of Camberwell*, 1961.
H. J. Dyos and D. H. Aldcroft, *British Transport*, 1969.
P. J. Edwards, *History of London Street Improvements*, 1898.
W. F. Grimes, *The Excavation of Roman and Medieval London*, 1968.
H. A. Harben, *A Dictionary of London*, 1918.
E. Hatton, *A New View of London*, 1708.
C. H. Holden and W. G. Holford, *Reconstruction in the City of London*, 1947.
M. R. Holmes, *Elizabethan London*, 1969.
M. R. Holmes, *Moorfields in 1559*, 1963.
M. Honeybourne, 'The Reconstructed Map of London under Richard II' in *London Topographical Record 22*, 1965.
ed. C. L. Kingsford, *Stow's Survey of London, 1603*, 1908.
ed. R. C. Latham and W. Matthews, *Diary of Samuel Pepys 1660–2*, 3 vols. 1970.
L.C.C., *Survey of London*, 18 parts, 1900–1971.
L.C.C., *Names of Streets and Places in London*, 3rd ed. 1927.
D. Lysons, *The Environs of London*, 10 vols. 1811.
W. Maitland, *History of London*, 1756.
R. Merrifield, *The Roman City of London*, 1965.
R. Merrifield, *Roman London*, 1969.
D. J. Olsen, *Town Planning in London*, 1964.
N. Pevsner, *Buildings of England: London and Westminster*, 1952.
N. Pevsner, *Buildings of England: London except the City and Westminster*, 1957.

H. Philips, *Mid-Georgian London*, 1964.

S. E. Rasmussen, *London: the Unique City*, 1934.

T. F. Reddaway, *The Rebuilding of London after the Fire*, 1940.

M. Rose, *The East End of London*, 1951.

Royal Commission on Historic Monuments, *West London*, 1925; *The City*, 1929; *East London*, 1930.

G. Rudé, *Hanoverian London*, 1971.

F. Shepherd, *London 1808–1870, The Infernal Wen*, 1971.

S. Smirke, *Suggestions for the Architectural Improvement of London*, 1834.

J. Summerson, *Georgian London*, 1947.

ed. J. Strype, *Stow's Survey of London 1598*, 1720.

ed. C. W. Sturge, *Diary of John Allen 1777*, 1905.

H. B. Wheatley and P. Cunningham, *London Past and Present*, 3 vols. 1891.

C. C. Willatts, *Middlesex and the London Region* in *Report of the Land Utilisation Survey of Great Britain*, 1937.

History of Cartography

British Museum, *Catalogue of Exhibition: Mapping of the British Isles*, 1964 (typescript, Map Room, British Museum).

C. Close, *The Early Years of the Ordnance Survey*, 1969.

E. Croft-Murray and P. Hutton, *Catalogue of British Drawings in the British Museum, Vol. I, 16th and 17th centuries*, 1960.

H. G. Fordham, *The Roadbooks and Itineraries of Great Britain*, 1924.

H. G. Fordham, *Some Notable Surveyors of the 16th, 17th, and 18th Centuries*, 1929.

A. M. Hind, *Engraving in England, Vol. I: The Tudor Period*, 1952.

W. Martin, 'The Early Maps of London', in *Transactions of the London and Middlesex Archaeological Society new series, 3*, 1917.

G. E. Mitton, *Maps of Old London*, 1908.

J. Norden, *A Preparative to the Speculum Britanniae*, 1695.

R. A. Skelton, 'Tudor Town Plans' in *Journal of the Royal Archaeological Institute*, 1952.

R. A. Skelton, *Decorative Printed Maps of the 15th to 18th Centuries*, 1965.

R. A. Skelton, 'The Map Trade in the 16th and 17th Centuries', in *Map-Collectors' Circle, 34*, 1967.

E. G. R. Taylor, *The Mathematical Practitioners of Tudor and Stuart England*, 1954.

R. V. Tooley, 'A Dictionary of Mapmakers', in *Map-Collectors' Circle, 16, 28, 40, 50, 67*, 1965–70.

F. M. L. Thompson, *Chartered Surveyors: the growth of a profession*, 1968.

Catalogues of Maps

British Museum, *London: excerpt from the Catalogue of Printed Maps*, 1967.

British Museum, *Catalogue of Exhibition: the Surveyor's Craft*, 1968 (typescript, Map Room, British Museum).

T. Chubb, *The Printed Maps in the Atlases of Great Britain*, 1927.

ed. T. G. Crace, *Catalogue of Maps . . . collected by F. Crace*, 1878.

I. Darlington and J. Howgego, *Printed Maps of London, c. 1553–1850*, 1964

ed. F. G. Emmison, *Catalogue of Maps in the Essex Record Office*, 1947.

R. Gough, *British Topography*, 1780.

R. Hyde, 'Ward Maps of the City of London', in *Map-Collectors' Circle, 38*, 1967.

R. Hyde, *Printed Maps of London 1851–1900* (forthcoming).

Middlesex Record Office, *Middlesex in Maps and Surveys: exhibition catalogue*, 1957.

Public Record Office, *Catalogue of Maps and Plans, Vol. I: British Isles*, 1967.

I. Scouloudi, *Panoramic Views of London 1600–1660*, 1953.

R. A. Skelton, *County Atlases of the British Isles, Vol. I: 1579–1703*, 1970.

Catalogue of Manuscript Maps of Surrey (typescript, Map Room, British Museum).

P. Walne, *Catalogue of Manuscript Maps in the Hertfordshire Record Office*, 1969.

Individual Map-makers and their work

M. Beresford, *History on the Ground*, 1957 [Norden].

I. Darlington, 'E. Chadwick and the First Large-Scale Ordnance Survey of London' in *Trans. London & Middlesex Arch. Soc., 22*, 1969.

H. G. Fordham, 'John Ogilby and his *Britannia*' in *The Library new series, 6*, 1925.

H. G. Fordham, *John Cary . . . engraver, map, chart & printseller*, 1925.

P. J. Glanville, 'William Morgan's Map' in *London Topographical Record* (forthcoming).

J. B. Harley, *Christopher Greenwood, County Mapmaker*, 1962.

J. H. Harvey, 'Four fifteenth-century London plans' in *London Topographical Record*, 20, 1952.

A. M. Hind, *Wenceslaus Hollar & His Views of London*, 1922.

M. R. Holmes, 'An Unrecorded Map of London' in *Archaeologia 100*, 1966 [copper-plate map].

M. R. Holmes, 'A seventeenth-century map of London and the Thames' in *London Topographical Record*, 20, 1952.

W. Hooper, 'Rocque's Map of Surrey' in *Surrey Archaeological Collections*, 40, 1932.

E. Jones, 'The London Atlas' in *Geographical Journal 131*, 1965.

G. Kish, 'The Correspondence of Continental Mapmakers . . . with a London firm (Jefferys & Faden)' in *Imago Mundi 4*, 1947.

London Topographical Society, *Mills' & Oliver's Survey of Building Sites after the Fire*, 5 vols. 1900–67.

S. N. P. Marks, *The Map of 16th century London*, 1964 [copper-plate map].

W. Martin, 'Note on Vertue's edition of Agas' in *Proceedings of the Society of Antiquaries 22*, 1907.

W. H. Overall, Notes on early maps of London in *Proceedings of the Society of Antiquaries 6*, 1870.

H. Phillips, 'John Rocque's Career' in *London Topographical Record*, 20, 1952.

I. Scouloudi, 'A Discovery at the Public Record Office' in *Guildhall Miscellany 4*, 1955 [Agas map].

R. A. Skelton, 'The Ordnance Survey 1791–1825' in *British Museum Quarterly*, 21, 1958.

W. C. Snowden, *London 200 Years Ago*, 1948 [Rocque].

J. K. Stanford, *The House of Edward Stanford*, 1952.

E. G. R. Taylor, 'Robert Hooke and the Cartographic Projects of the 17th century' in *Geographical Journal 90*, 1937.

J. Varley, 'John Rocque' in *Imago Mundi 5*, 1948.

H. B. Wheatley, 'Norden and his Map of London' in *London Topographical Record 2*, 1914.

ed. H. B. Wheatley and E. A. Ashbee, *William Smith's Description of England 1588*, 1879.

Index

Acton, *42, 52*

Adams, George, *38, 63*

Administration of London, *29–30, 41, 46, 47, 52, 208*

Agar Town, *42*

Agas, Ralph, *20, 22, 31, 54, 61, 86*

Agriculture, horticulture, around London, *14, 39, 41, 114, 118, 130, 146, 150, 154, 160, 170, 172*

Air raids, *202, 204, 206*

Aldersgate, *78, 82*

Aldgate, *51, 82, 104*

Aldwych, *50, 158*

Alehouses, inns, public houses, *15, 17, 60, 78, 112, 118, 140, 190*

All Hallows, Barking, *14, 86*
Hallows in the Wall, *72*
Souls Church, *122*

Alsatia, *118*

André's map, *35*

Andrews' map, *59*

Anerley, *184*

Anglo-Saxon London, *13*

Archers' map, *46*

Art Galleries, *30, 39, 48, 106*

Arundel House, *24, 30, 90*

Atlases, *18, 19, 20, 21, 37, 53, 58, 59*

Augustinian Priory, *72*

Austin Friars, *19*

A-Z London Guide, *55, 60, 62*

Bacon, G. W., *200*

Bacon's maps, *45*

Baker St., *167*

Bakers' map, *40, 146*

Balloon Ascents, View, *128, 174*

Balsover St., *122*

Bank, *48, 52, 134, 138, 186*

Bankside, *11, 17, 38, 52, 53*

Barbican scheme, *53*

Barbon, Nicholas, *30, 90, 106*

Bardwell, William, *41, 42*

Barge(s): see Boats, river

Barge, royal, *20, 24, 56, 81*

Barking, *46*

Bars, City, *14, 15, 37*

Bartholomew's Atlas, Guide, *42, 62*

Battersea, *11, 39, 48, 150, 162, 172, 178*
Park, Gardens, *178, 210*

Battle Bridge, *112, 146, 154*

Baynard's Castle, *14, 81*

Bayswater, *53, 156*

Bazalgette, Joseph, *154*

Bear-baiting grounds, *17, 78*

Beaumont St., *37*

Beckenham, *52*

Becklow Rd., *51*

Becontree estate, *50*

Bedford estate, *9, 37, 43, 48, 90, 106, 170, 176, 190*

Bedlam Hospital: see Bethlem

Belgrave House, Belgravia, *30, 41, 42, 118, 156, 166*

Bethlem (Bedlam) Hospital, *72, 104, 134*

Bethnal Green, *49, 52*

Bett's map, *44*

Bickham, George, *130*

Billingsgate, *14, 53, 104*

Bills of Mortality, *35, 130*

Bingley House, *122*

Bird's eye view-maps, *17, 21, 22, 54, 78, 81*

Bishopsgate, Bishopsgate St., *19, 51, 72, 78, 104, 110*

Blackfriars, Blackfriars Bridge, *12, 14, 23, 33, 35, 52, 53, 56, 81, 98, 118, 134*

Blackheath, *35, 202*

Blome, Richard, *32, 118*

Bloomsbury, *25, 30, 37, 48, 170, 176, 190*

Blow Bladder St., *27, 102*

Bluecoat School, *51, 86, 210*

Board of Works, *42, 44, 45, 51, 130, 156, 166, 172*

Boats, river, *24, 28, 38, 56, 78, 98, 114*

Bond St., *118*

Booth, Charles, *47, 196, 198*

Borough, The, *78, 134, 140*

Boroughs, *46, 51, 52, 186, 208*

Boundaries, *9, 17, 26, 27, 35, 40, 46–7, 60, 62, 98, 102, 106, 146, 160, 162, 186, 208, 210*

Bow, Bow Church, *19, 35, 36, 42 St., 90*
St. patrols, runners, *42*

Bowen's maps, *33, 59, 60*

Bowles family's maps, *33, 36, 38, 59, 60, 134, 138, 154*

Bowling alley, *18, 24*

Braun and Hogenberg map, *17, 19, 20, 23, 24, 31, 56, 78, 88*

Brentford, *138*

Bridewell, *78*

Bridges, *12, 14, 24, 28, 30, 41, 42, 47, 52, 56, 108, 174*

British Museum, *146, 170, 176*

Brixton, *49*

Broad St. and Station, *43, 104, 110*

Bromley, *52*
by Bow, *146*

Brompton *38, 130, 154, 156*

Bryant's maps, *39, 59, 156, 162*

Buckingham Palace, *42, 166, 174, 204, 210*
Palace Rd., *48*

Bucklersbury House, *13*

Buildings on maps, *17, 22, 45, 56, 104, 118*

Bull Inn Yard, *51*

Bull-baiting grounds, *17, 78*

Bunhill Row, *142*

Burial grounds, cemeteries, *30, 49, 94*

Burlington House, *166*

Burying Ground Passage, *51*

Bus maps, routes; see Omnibuses

Camberwell, *37, 41, 42, 174*

Camden Town, *37*
William, *16, 20*

Canals, *41, 98, 114, 146, 162, 167*

Cannon St. and Station, *12, 13, 43*

Canonbury, *56, 57, 146, 198*

Canon's Row, *82*

Carnaby St., *30*

Cars, car parks, etc., *50, 52, 122, 160, 208*

Carteret St., *82*

Cartographic conventions, etc., *16, 17, 18–23, 26, 28, 33–4, 35, 37, 38, 45, 46, 60, 62, 63, 65, 78, 81, 100, 108, 120, 126, 138, 146, 150, 156, 162, 166, 180, 210*

Carver & Bowles' maps, *38*

Cary Brothers' maps, *34, 37, 38, 39, 46, 55, 59, 96, 150, 156, 170*

Cattle, Stock, *28, 36, 37, 112, 146*

Cavendish Sq., *33, 122*

Cemeteries; see Burial grounds

Central London, *19, 35, 37, 42, 45–53, 60, 72–94, 98, 106, 112, 118–124, 130, 134, 138, 154, 156, 158, 160, 166, 176, 180, 190, 194, 196, 200, 210*

Chapman's maps, *59*

Charing Cross, Charing Cross Road *14, 24, 39, 42, 43, 78, 106, 118, 120, 140, 166, 174, 178, 180, 194*
Cross Station, Hotel, *24, 43, 140, 200*

Charities, etc., *72, 78*

Charterhouse, *17, 23, 88*

Cheapside, *13, 18, 26, 52, 86, 88, 102, 110*

Chelsea, *15, 36, 39, 41, 53, 118, 130, 154, 160, 166, 172, 178, 208*
Bridge, *172*
Embankment, *42, 45, 104, 172*
Hospital: see Royal Hospital

Chislehurst, *34, 52*

Chiswell's map, *31*

Chiswick, *52*

Christ Church, Lambeth, *134*

Christ's Hospital, *51, 78, 82, 86, 88, 102*

Churches, Chapels, *28, 30, 35, 36, 39–40, 100, 104*

City Companies, *27, 54, 82, 110, 114*
of London, *9, 12, 13, 14–15 29, 35, 47, 50, 52, 53, 78, 86, 94, 166, 186, 206*
Road, *86, 142*

Clare Market, *50*

Clerkenwell, Clerkenwell Road, *86, 88, 112*

Coach services, roads, *23, 30, 96, 130, 162*

Cole, Benjamin, *32*
Humphrey, *18*

Collins' maps, *56*

Colour printing, *62*

Colouring by hand, *30, 38, 62, 166*

Commercial Road, *114, 152*

Commissioners for Improving the Metropolis, *172*

Commons, *51, 128, 150*

Conduits, conduit fields, *29, 86, 96, 112, 118*

Continental maps of London, *17, 18, 19–20, 31, 32, 86, 94*

Copenhagen Fields, *146*

Copperplate maps, *19–20, 61, 72, 78, 88, 110*

Cornhill, *12, 14*

County Hall, *51, 194*
maps, *20, 21, 34, 46, 162*
of London Plan, *48*

Court of Assistants, *110*
of Burgesses, *41, 78*
suburbs, *24, 78, 106, 120*

Covent Garden, *23, 50, 90, 158, 190*

Craven Hill Gardens, *30*

Cremorne Gardens, *178*

Cripplegate, *12, 13, 78, 88*

Cromwell Road, *44, 48, 180*

Crooms Hill, *126*

Crosby Hall, *15, 104*

Croydon, *51, 108, 162, 167*

Cruchley's maps, *39, 46, 55, 156*

Crutched Friars, *78, 104*

Crystal Palace, *45, 57, 184*

Cubitt, Thomas, *42, 126, 166*

Custom House, *14, 104*

Cut, The, *134*

Cyclist's maps, *44*

Dagenham, *50*

Dalston, *49*

Dankerts' maps, *21, 23, 55, 56, 86*

Darlington and Howgego, *10*

Davies' maps, *46, 167*

Dawson's maps, *42, 46*

De Ram's panorama, *31, 56*

Deadman's Place, *17, 140*

Dean St., *106*

Decorations, map, *17, 31, 56–7, 61, 120*

Deptford, *36, 126*

Devonshire St., *37*

Digges, Leonard, *21, 63*

Directories, *55, 59*

Dirty Lane, *106*

District Railway and maps, *44, 45, 190*

Ditch, City, *19, 37, 86*

Docks, *11, 14, 25, 38, 41, 45, 53, 56, 104, 114, 126, 130, 146, 150, 152, 162, 192, 202, 204*

Dowager's Bottom, *35*

Dowgate, *14*

Downing St., *78*

Drainage, *41, 60, 154, 192*

Drury Lane, *50, 86*

Dulwich, *184*

Dutch community, churches, *36, 72* maps, map sellers, *19, 26, 31, 32, 86, 94*

Duty on maps, *32*

Ealing, *51, 52*

Earl's Court, *45, 48, 178*
Terrace, *160*

East and West India Docks, *152*

East Cheap, *14*
London [East End], *11, 23, 38, 49, 52, 53, 86, 114, 118, 130, 146, 150, 152, 186, 192, 204*
Sheen, *47*

Economic life, *47, 196, 198, 208*

Edgware, *36, 50*
Road, *13, 50, 154, 156, 167, 182*

Edmonton, *44, 51*

Eel Brook Common, *178*

Egham, *210*

Eleanor Crosses, *14, 86*

Elephant and Castle, *134*

Ely Place, *186*

Embankment(s), *42, 45, 140, 172, 180*

Endell St., *176*

Engraved maps, *18, 53–4, 61, 62*

Epidemics, *30, 41, 42, 47, 192*

Epping, Epping Forest, *11, 52, 96*

Ermine St., *13*

Essex, *29, 35, 44, 53, 146*
Road, *198*
St., *28*

Estate maps, surveys, *17, 18, 22, 24, 26–7, 61, 82, 102, 110*

Euston, *43, 45, 48, 170*
Road, *35, 42, 52, 156, 167*

Evelyn, John, *26, 94*

Exeter Exchange, *158*
Road, *118*

Facsimiles of maps, etc., *54, 56*

Factories, *60, 78, 118, 152, 162, 172*

Faden's maps, *138, 150, 156, 158, 178*

Fairburn, *38, 152*

Faithorne's maps, *23, 26, 54, 56, 88, 94*

Farming: see Agriculture

Farringdon, *78, 118*

Fenchurch St. and Station, *104, 204*

Fig's Mead, *43*

Finchley, *96, 150*

Finsbury, *19, 46, 51, 72, 110, 142*

Fitzherbert, *17, 22*

FitzStephen, William, *13, 14*

Fleet Conduit, River, Bridge, *14, 28, 43, 86, 98, 112, 118, 166*
Prison, *15, 98, 138*
St., *48, 88*

Floods, flooding, *11, 41, 154, 172*

Forts, fortifications, *12, 25*

Foster family's maps, *33, 120*
Lane, *102*

Foundling Hospital, *37, 112*

French community, churches, *106, 142*
maps, *32*

Friern Barnet, *96*

Frith St., *106*

Fulham, Fulham Palace, *11, 15, 35, 48, 150, 170, 178, 208*

Gascoyne's map, *114*

Gates, gateways, city, *13, 19, 26, 72*

General Enclosure Act, *51, 150*
Post Office, *88*

Geography, geology, of London, *11*

Georgian London, *9, 118–158*

German churches, *36*
maps, *17*

Glasshouse St., *28*

G.L.C., *52, 54*

Golders Green, *51*

Gordon, Gordon Riots, *128, 138*

Gosling, John, *22*

Goswell St., *23, 86*

Gough, Richard, *33, 57*

Gower St., *48, 170*

Gracechurch St., *28*

Gravel pits, *36, 160*

Gray's Inn Road, Lane, *36, 112*

Great Exhibition, *45, 62, 174*
Fire, *9, 25–7, 86, 88, 98, 104, 110, 118*
New St., *110*
Peter St., *196*
Turnstile, *36*

Greater London Council: see GLC London Development Plan, *51, 53*

Greek Church, *106*

Green Belt, *51*

Greenford, *52*

Greenwich, *25, 30, 42, 43, 118, 126, 150, 154, 170, 202*
  Palace, *25, 81, 126*

Greenwoods' maps, *34, 39, 41, 46, 47, 54, 59, 156, 162, 166*

Gresham College, *104*

Grey Friars, *82, 86, 88*

Grosvenor Canal, *48, 166*
  Crescent, *36*
  Estates, *9, 30, 41, 178, 190*
  Place, *166, 174*
  Square, *124*

Ground plans, plots, *56, 81, 94*

Guildford Road, *138*

Guildhall, *27, 94*

Guy's Hospital, *140*

Hackney, *38, 47, 52, 130*
  carriages, *30, 56, 112, 120, 162, 170*
  Haggerstown, *49*

Hammersmith, *40, 43, 52*

Hampstead, *49, 51*
  Road, *118*

Hampton Court, *108*

Hanover Square, *30, 118*

Hanwell, *46*

Harley Estates, St., *9, 120, 167*

Harrison, William, *21*

Harrow, *34, 43*
  Road, *167*

Hatton's maps, *31*

Haymarket, *14, 106*

Hayward's plan of Tower, *22*

Heathrow, *12*

Hèbert, Louis, *150*

Hedge Lane, *106*

Hendon, *150*

Herne Hill, *52*

Highbury, *35*

Highgate, *36, 49, 51, 96, 146*

Holborn, *23, 36, 52, 88, 118, 134, 158, 180, 198, 206*
  Bridge, *28, 118*
  Viaduct, *26*

Holborne river, *112*

Hollar's maps, *9, 23, 25, 26-27, 28, 56, 90, 94,* also endpapers

Home Counties, *108, 130, 138, 210*
  Office, *78*

Hondius, Jodocus, *21, 81*

Hooke, Robert, *26, 27, 28, 94, 100, 104*

Horse Guards, *24, 78, 124*
  traffic, etc., *24, 34, 39, 41, 44, 122, 124, 170*

Horwood's maps, *33, 34, 37, 38, 54, 56, 140, 142, 158*

Hospitals, *15, 49, 78, 82, 86, 134, 140, 142, 154*

Hounslow Heath, *38, 150*
  Road, *138*

Houses of Parliament; see Parliament

Howgego and Darlington *10*

Hurlingham, *48*

Hyde Park, *57, 108, 120, 124, 130, 156, 166, 210*
  Park Corner, *35, 52, 130, 138, 150, 174*

Imperial Institute, *200*
  War Museum, *72*

Industrial London, *47, 94, 104, 126, 140, 162, 200*

Inns: see Alehouses, etc.
  of Court, *118*

Irving St., *106*

Isle of Dogs, *38, 61, 126, 146, 152, 186, 192*

Isleworth, *138*

Islington, *29, 32, 33, 40, 46, 52, 57, 86, 96, 108, 112, 118, 130, 146, 160, 170, 186, 208*

Jefferys' maps, *30, 33, 34, 37, 134*

Jewel Tower, *15*

Jones, Emrys, *53*
  Inigo, *106*

Kennington, *35, 49, 78*

Kensal Green, *35, 49*

Kensington, *35, 40, 41, 49, 52, 53, 60, 120, 138, 160, 208*
  High St., *44, 50*
  Palace, Gardens, *130, 160*

Kent, *12, 13, 29, 47, 52, 146, 150*

Kentish Town, *170*

Kew, *172*

Kilburn, *44, 182*

King, Gregory, *28, 106, 110*
  St., *15, 24, 42*
  William St., *48*

King's College, *158*
  Cross, *52, 146, 178*
  Printing House, *98*
  Roads, *14, 138, 156, 166*

Kingsland, *146*
  Road, *13*

Kingston, *24, 43, 108*

Kingsway, *48, 50, 158*

Knightsbridge, *52, 124, 130. 154*

Ladbroke, *49, 160*

Lambeth, *15, 24, 36, 46, 49, 52, 61, 78, 128, 130, 134, 162*
  Marsh Road, *134*
  Palace, *15*

Lamb's Conduit St., *112*

Land Use, *34, 38, 54, 130, 138, 150*

Laurie and Whittle, *33*

Law Courts, *48, 158*

L.C.C. *46, 47, 50, 51, 52, 186, 194*

Lea, Lea and Glynne, *33, 34, 112*

Lea River, *35, 38, 53, 114, 130, 146, 152*

Leadenhall Market, *12, 53, 104*

Leake, John, *27*

Legal London, *78, 118*

Leicester Fields, Square, *106, 174*
  House, *78*

Leland, John, *15-16*

Lewisham, *35, 53*
  St., *196*

Leybourne, William, *27, 28, 63, 64, 100, 110*

Liberties, City, etc., *14, 15, 28, 41, 52, 186*

Lime Kiln Dock, *114*

Limehouse, *23, 30, 36, 38, 114, 130, 152*
  Cut, Docks, Reach, *38, 114, 146*

Lincoln's Inn Fields, *25, 37, 49, 90, 176*

Lisson Green, Grove, *43, 156, 167*

Lithography, *46, 61, 172*

Little Britain, *59, 86*
  Turnstile, *36*
  Venice, *167*

Liverpool St. and Station, *19, 44, 52, 72, 110, 206*

Lombard St., *13*

London Bridge, *9, 11, 24, 52, 81, 86, 100, 104, 140, 206*

London Bridge and Station, *11, 86, 140, 170*
  County Council: see L.C.C.
  Hospital, *142*
  Passenger Transport Board, *51, 62*
  Topographical Society, *54*
  University, *170*
  Wall: see Wall, London

Long Acre, *86, 90*

Ludgate, Ludgate Hill, *14, 23, 26, 88, 98*

Maida Hill, *182*

Maiden Lane [Maid Lane], *17, 18*

Mall, *50, 194*

Manuscript maps, plans, surveys, *18, 21, 24, 25, 27, 54, 61*

Map(s) as decoration, *57-8*
  catalogues, *67*
  collections, collecting, *31, 54, 57-8, 66*
  facsimiles, etc., *54, 56*
  printing, reproduction, *18-19, 27, 45, 46, 55-62*
  sellers, *33, 58-60*

Map-making: see Cartography

Map-publishing, *18-19, 21, 27, 30-32, 33, 37, 39, 40, 44-47, 53, 55, 58-60, 134, 182*

Map-views, *17, 23, 25, 56, 81, 86, 88, 130*

Marble Arch, *13, 36*
  Hill, *34*

Market(s), *26, 53, 86, 94*
  gardens, etc.: see Agriculture

Market St., *122*

Marlborough House, *120*

Marylebone, *23, 35, 36, 37, 40, 46, 49, 52, 120, 154, 167, 170, 182*
  Basin, *33, 122*
  roads, *35, 36, 39, 156, 167, 182*
  Station, *43*

Mayfair, *33, 118, 120, 124, 190*

Medieval London, *11, 13-15, 24, 28, 72, 100*

Metropolitan Board of Health, *47, 192*
  Board of Works, *42, 46, 130, 186, 194*
  Boroughs map, *42*
  Commission for Sewers, *45, 46, 47, 182*
  London, *41-42, 46-48, 50-53, 172, 180, 186, 206, 208*
  Police: see Police

Mews, *78, 106, 122, 166*

Middle Row, *36*

Middlesex, *12, 14, 15, 20, 24, 29, 30, 34, 35, 37, 39, 52, 58, 78, 130, 146, 150, 152, 182, 210*

Middleton, John, *150*

Middleton, Sir Hugh, and New River, *29, 90, 146*

Mile End, *118, 192*

Mile, value of, *21*

Mileages, *11, 31, 35, 138*

Millbank, *24, 41, 48, 78, 196*

Mills, *108, 126, 128, 138, 146, 152, 162*

Mills, Peter, *27, 94*

Millwall, *126*

Millward, *31*

Milne, Thomas, *38-9, 150, 156*

Minories, *78*

Mint, *204*

Modern Plague of London, *60, 190*

Moggs' map, *44, 45*

Molesey, *34*

Moll, Herman, *31, 112*

Moore, Jonas, *26, 27*

Moorfields, *17, 24, 72*

Moorgate, *19, 134*

Morden and Lea's map, *29, 33, 34, 112*

Morden, Robert, *108, 112*

Morgan's maps, *9, 28, 29, 31, 32, 33, 34, 54, 56, 58, 59, 60, 98, 100, 104-8, 118, 120*

Mortality returns, *130*

Motorways, etc., *50, 52, 210*

Mount St., *25*

National Trust, *210*

Naval Yards, Navy, *126*

Neat Houses, *154*

New Bond St., *118, 180*
  Bridge St., *98*
  Brompton, *178*
  Fish St., *104*
  Oxford St., *42, 106, 190*
  Queen St., *94*
  River, etc., *29, 90, 96, 112, 146*
  Road, *23, 39, 134, 167*

Newcourt's maps, *23, 26, 88, 94*

Newgate, *50, 88, 112*
  St., *13, 26, 51, 82, 86, 98*

Newington, *108, 118*

Nineteenth-century London, *38-49, 150-198*

Noble St., *13*

Norden's maps, etc., *16, 20, 21, 27, 31, 38, 55, 56, 57, 58, 60, 63, 78, 81, 146*

Norman London, *14*

North and South Circular Roads, *52*
  London, *19, 72, 86, 88, 112, 120, 142, 146*

Northeast Surrey, *162*

Northwest London, *86, 88*

Northumberland Avenue, *15, 24, 180*
  House, *24, 48, 166, 174*
  St., *48*

Norwich Road, *118*

Norwood, *49, 150*

Notting Hill, *49, 160*

Office of Works, *194*

Ogilby's maps, *9, 27, 28, 31, 32, 34, 54, 56, 58, 59, 64, 96, 98, 100, 104, 108, 150*

Ogle St., *122*

Old Bailey, *51, 98*
  Brentford, *138*
  Broad St., *206*
  Cottages, *51*
  Ford, *152*
  St., *88*

Omnibuses, omnibus routes, maps, *41, 44, 45, 51, 62, 190*

Open spaces, *11, 24, 51, 52, 53, 142*

Ordnance Survey, maps, *9, 28, 34, 37, 38-9, 44, 45-6, 54, 60, 138, 146, 150, 154, 156, 162, 178, 182, 192, 204, 210*

Overton, Henry, *33*
  John, *55, 60, 94*

Oxford Circus, Market, *122*
  St. [Road], *36, 50, 118, 120, 122, 124, 176*

Paddington, *36, 41, 49, 154, 156, 178, 182, 210*

Palace Yard, *24*

Palaces, Royal, *9, 24, 78*

Palmer's Village, *41*

Panoramas, *18, 31, 56, 57, 81*

Paris Garden, *134*

Paris's road map, *11, 15, 72*

Parish(es), *35, 94, 100, 114, 162, 166*
  Bills of Mortality, *35, 130*
  maps, surveys, *39-40, 160*

Park(s), *11, 17, 52, 108, 120, 156, 166, 170, 178*
  Lane, *124*
  Royal, *52*
  St., *140*

Parker, Archbishop, *18, 58, 61*

Parliament, Houses of, etc., *9, 11, 15, 42, 56*
  Boroughs, *46*
  St., *42*

Paternoster Row, *98*

Paul's Wharf, *14*

Peckham Rye, *47*

Penge, *44, 52, 184*

Pentonville Road, *35*

Pepys' map collection, *18, 20, 25, 57, 58*

Perspective view maps, *17, 45, 56;* see also Bird's eye view maps

Petty, William, *30*

Philips' maps, *44, 62*

Phillimore Place, *160*

Phoenix Fire Office Survey, *34, 37*

Physic Garden, *172*

Piccadilly, Piccadilly Circus, *30, 50, 56, 106, 118, 120*

Picture maps: see Map-views

Pimlico, *11, 43, 154, 156*

Pine, John, *35, 37*

Plague of London, Modern, *60, 190*

Planetarium, *167*

Plats, *17, 18*

Play House Yard, *98*

Pocket maps, *30, 39, 56*

Police, police stations, etc., *42, 167, 186*

Pool in Lewisham, *53*
  of London, *38, 53*

Poor Law Commissioners, *46, 186*

Pope's Gardens, *34*

Popham St., *198*

Poplar, *152, 186*

Population, *9, 17, 24, 26, 29, 30, 41, 42, 43, 44, 47, 48, 50, 51, 52, 78, 110*

Port of London Authority, *50*

Porter's map, *21, 23, 56*

Portland Estate, *122, 167*

Portsoken, *78*

Post-Fire London, maps, etc., *26-8, 61, 94, 98, 100, 102, 104*

Post-roads, *96, 108*

Postal services, *37-8, 170*

Poverty map, Booth's, *47, 196, 198*

Prehistoric sites, *12*

Primrose Alley (now Road), *110*
  Hill, *166, 170*

Print and book sellers, *33, 56, 59*

Printed maps, *9, 18-9, 61-2, 72*

Printing House Yard, *23*

Prisons, penitentiaries, *41, 48, 50, 118, 134, 138, 140, 196*

Privy Garden, *78, 166*

Profile maps, *17, 21, 22, 81, 82*

Public health, *41-2, 47, 192*

Public houses, 60, 190
  transport, 9, 41, 52, 162, 174, 178, 180, 184, 190, 206; see also Hackney carriages, Coaches, Omnibuses, Trams, Cars, Railways, Boats
Pudding Lane, 94
Putney, 52, 53

Quays, 14, 28, 38; see also Docks
Queen St., 90
  Victoria St., 13
Queenhythe, 14, 56, 206

Railway(s), 39, 41, 43–5, 47, 48, 49, 50, 51, 54, 56, 170, 174, 178, 180, 182, 184, 190, 204
Ratcliff(e), 146, 186
Rathborne, Aaron, 18, 22, 63
Red Lion Square, 112
Regency St., 48
Regent St., 50, 106, 156, 166, 180
Regent's Canal, 38, 114, 152, 167
  Park, 156, 167, 170
Religious houses, 23, 72
Restoration London, 9, 25–30, 56, 94–106
Rhodes, Joshua, 57, 130
Richmond, 11, 34, 52
River(s), minor, 53, 110, 138; see also Fleet, Holborne, Lea
  steamers, 41, 174
  Thames: see Thames
  traffic; see Traffic, river, 14, 24, 28, 38, 41, 56, 78, 112, 120, 125, 146, 152, 174
Road(s), roadworks, etc., 9, 12, 13, 26, 27, 35, 36, 41–4, 47, 48, 50, 52, 94, 96, 128, 130, 134, 150, 156, 180, 194, 210
  maps, books, 11, 15, 31, 32, 59–60, 72, 96, 100, 150
Rocque's maps, 32, 33, 34–7, 38, 54, 55, 56, 57, 58, 59, 108, 122–7, 130, 138
Roman Bath, 210
  London, 11, 12, 13, 14, 53
  roads, 152
Ropemaker's Field, 114
Rose Lane, 114
Rother, 126
Rotherhithe, 23, 150, 162
Route maps: see Road maps
Roy, Gen., 37, 38, 138, 146, 150
Royal Academy, 39, 158, 166
  Arcade, 180
  barge, 20, 24, 56, 81
  Exchange, 19, 20, 94, 100
  Hospital, 36, 160, 172
  Mews (stables), 78, 106, 166
  Palaces, 9, 15, 24, 78
  Society, 25, 27, 28, 94, 104
Ruff, E., 39, 166
Ruislip, 52

Sadler's Wells, 112
Saffron Hill, 43
St. Albans, 13, 210
  Alban's Road, 96
  Alphage, 13, 19
  Andrew, Holborn, 118
  Anne, Limehouse, 114
  Bartholomew's Hospital, 18, 19, 23, 54, 86, 88,
  Botolph, 19
  Bride, Fleet St., 13, 118
  Christopher le Stocks, 186
  Clement Danes, 146
  George's Chapel, 156
  George's Circus, 128, 134
  George's Fields, 35, 128, 130, 134
  Giles, 23, 36, 42, 43, 90, 146, 176, 198
  Giles Church, Camberwell, 37
  Helen, 104
  James, Piccadilly, 30, 106
  James's Palace, 78, 200
  James's Park, 24, 41, 42, 78, 82
  James's Square, 118
  John, Clerkenwell, 88
  John, Watling St., 86
  John's St., 23
  John's Wood, 39, 118, 167, 182, 210
  John's Wood Chapel, 182

St. Leonard, Shoreditch, 29
  Margaret, Westminister, 160, 196
  Martin in the Fields, 28, 30, 106, 176
  Martin-le-Grand, 102
  Martin's Lane, 49, 176, 190
  Mary Abbot, 35, 160
  Mary Spital, 72
  Mary-le-Strand, 30
  Mary on the Bourne, 167
  Mary-Rounceval, 15
  Marylebone; see Marylebone
  Matthew, Friday St., 86
  Michael Bassishaw, 19
  Michael le Querne, 27
  Olave's St., 140
  Pancras, 35, 38, 86, 112, 118, 130
  Paul, Covent Garden, 106, 176
  Paul's Cathedral, 12, 14, 19, 20, 72, 81, 98, 146, 166, 206
  Thomas' Hospital, 78, 140
Salisbury Court, 118
Salway, Joseph, 130, 150
Sands End, 48
Saxon London, 13, 14
Saxton's Maps, 20, 21, 34, 58
Sayer's maps, 33, 55, 60, 134
Schools, 47, 49, 51, 81, 82, 186
Scotland Yard, 24
Seller, John, 58, 59, 120
Sessions House, 98
Seven Dials, 50, 106, 118
Sewers Commissioners, 45, 46, 47
Shaftesbury Avenue, 42, 106
Sheldon tapestry map, 58
Shepherd Market, 190
Shepherd's Bush, 35, 48, 49, 52
Ship-building, 114, 146, 152, 186
Shipping, 38, 56, 98, 104
Shoe Lane, 43
Shops, stores, 44, 50, 56, 60, 122, 200
Shoreditch, 29, 72
Shug Lane, 106
Shury's map, 56
Sketch maps, plans, 17
Sloane's Physic Garden, 172
Smyrke, Sydney, 42
Smith, C., 45
Smith, William, 9, 17, 21, 81
Smithfield, 23, 36, 52, 86, 88, 112, 118, 146, 206
Snow Hill, 88, 112
Snow, John, 47
Societies of Antiquaries, 26, 54, 158
Sociological maps, 47, 190, 192, 196, 198, 208
Soho, 9, 29, 30, 42, 90, 106, 112, 190
Somers Town, 37, 42
Somerset House, 24, 28, 39, 78, 90, 158, 166
South Kensington, 45
  London, South Bank, 37, 118, 128, 134, 138, 140, 150, 162, 174, 178, 186, 190
Southwest London, 138
Southampton Buildings, 25
Southwark, 12, 17, 18, 25, 28, 30, 35, 38, 47, 48, 52, 78, 86, 128, 140, 162
Spas, wells, 112, 146
Specialized maps, 44–45, 53
Speed's county maps, 21, 27
Spring Gardens Passage, 194
Spitalfields, 19, 72
Squares, 29, 33, 51, 118, 166, 176
Stairs, Thames-side, 24, 56, 78, 120, 134
Stanford's maps, 44, 46, 47, 48, 49, 54, 180, 184, 186
Staple Inn, 14, 36, 118
Starch Green Road, 51
Starling's maps, 40, 57, 160
Stationers' Hall, 98
Steamers, river, 41, 174
Stepney, 29, 114, 146, 192
Stock; see Cattle
Stockwell, 48
Stow's Survey, 9, 16, 19, 24, 31, 142
Strand, 9, 15, 21, 23, 24, 30, 48, 59, 78, 158, 190
Stratford le Bow, 146
  Place, 118
Streatham, 42
Street markets, 26, 86, 94
  names, 51, 55–6, 160
  numbers, 37

Strype, John, 9, 31, 32, 36, 106, 118
Stuart London, 9, 22–3, 25–32, 82–115
Suburbs, estates, new, 9, 37, 43–44, 52
Surrey, 12, 29, 30, 34, 35, 44, 47, 52, 108, 138, 162
Survey(s), estate and property, etc. 17–18, 24, 25, 33, 54, 61, 82, 102, 110
  of London: see Stow
  Post-Fire, 25–8
Surveying, surveyors, 17–8, 19, 20–2, 25–8, 33, 34, 35, 37, 38–9, 45, 63–5, 82, 96, 102, 110, 120, 138, 150, 162, 172, 182
Sydenham, 45, 184
Symbols, map, 21, 38, 45, 46, 62, 81, 120, 126, 150, 154, 162, 210

Tallis's London Street Views, 200
Tea gardens, 37, 172
Teddington, 11, 39, 48
Temple Bar, 14, 15, 48, 56, 88, 90
Tenements, 17, 23, 24, 42, 43, 78, 82, 86, 102, 196
Tennis courts, royal, 24, 78
Thames, 11, 12, 21, 25, 38, 47, 48, 56, 61, 72, 78, 81, 98, 104, 112, 120, 126, 134, 146, 150, 154, 172, 174, 186, 192, 204; endpapers
  Quay, 28, 100
  St., 12, 94
  Tunnels, 42, 56
Theatres, etc., 18, 57, 72, 86, 118, 167
Threadneedle St., 94
Three Colt Lane, St., 114
Tilbury, 210
Tiltyard, 24, 78
Tolls, toll-gates; see Turnpikes
Tooley St., 140
Tooting, 46, 202
Topographical collections, 57
Tothill Fields, St., 25, 41, 82
Tottenham, 44, 46
  Court Road, 36, 106, 174
Tower Hamlets, 114
  of London, 13, 14, 22, 47, 72, 104, 114, 204
Trafalgar Square, 39, 48, 50, 59, 106, 166, 174, 194
Traffic, road, 24, 36, 52, 112, 152
  river, 14, 24, 28, 38, 41, 56, 78, 112, 120, 126, 146, 152, 174
Trams, 50, 190
Transport maps, 44, 45, 62
Treswell family's maps, 18, 22, 82
Troops in London, 124, 138
Tube; see Underground
Tudor London, 9, 11, 15, 17, 18, 19, 23–4, 72, 78, 81, 82, 86
Turnmill Brook, 9
Turnpikes, toll-gates, etc.: 36, 41, 42, 96, 128, 130, 138, 150
Twentieth-century London, 50–3, 200–11
Twickenham, 34
Tyburn, Tyburnia, 13, 24, 122, 124, 156, 167

Underground, 48–9, 51, 53, 60, 62, 190
University College, 48, 170
Uxbridge, 48, 122

Vauxhall, Vauxhall Bridge Road, 25, 27, 42, 47, 48, 172
Vertue's maps, 20, 25, 26, 31, 35, 54
Victoria Embankment, 42
  Park, 52
  Station and St., 42, 43, 48, 178, 196
Victorian London; see Nineteenth-century London
Villages of London, 24, 29, 34, 36, 108, 134
Villiers St., 24
Visscher's Long Views, 56

Walbrook river, valley, 12, 13, 14, St., 12
Wall, London, 9, 11, 13, 14, 19, 26, 37, 53, 72, 78, 86, 94, 104, 134
  Roman, 13, 14, 53
Wallis and Cary's maps, 38
Walworth, 27, 38
Wanstead House, 59

Wandsworth, 51, 162, 174, 208
Wapping, 36, 38, 53, 59
Ward, John, 61, 110
  maps, 32, 118
Wardour St., 106, 176
Water power, mills, 24, 108, 152
  supply, 9, 18, 29, 36, 46, 47, 48, 86, 90, 96, 112, 118, 124, 152, 166, 186
Watercourses, 29, 35, 53
Watergate, 24
Waterloo, Waterloo Bridge, 43, 158, 174
Watermen, 24, 30, 56, 120
Watling St., 13, 182
Wellclose Square, 118
Weller, Edward, 47, 176
Wellington St., 158
Wells: see Spas, Wells
West Bourn, 130, 154
  Central London, 23, 90
  Cheap, 14
  End, 26, 30, 60, 106
  Ham, 192
  London, 24, 48, 106, 118, 120, 130, 156, 178, 180
Western Avenue, 52
Westminster, 9, 13, 14, 21, 23, 24, 25, 28, 29, 30, 31, 32, 36, 41, 42, 59, 78, 120, 128, 154, 166, 172, 178, 190, 196
  Abbey, Hall, 13, 15, 23, 72, 78
  Bridge, 24, 30, 33, 36, 120, 134, 138
  Palace, 13, 15, 78
Westway, 210
Whitcomb St., 106
White Friars, 15, 118
Whitechapel, 96
Whitehall, 13, 14, 15, 21, 24, 29, 42, 78, 90, 96, 166, 174, 176
  Palace, 24, 56, 78, 81, 166
Willesden, 47
William of Worcester, 15
Wimbledon, 11, 12, 44, 53, 202
Wimpole St., 167
Windmill(s), 86, 128
  Fields, St., 29, 106
Wood Lane, 48
  St., 13
Woodcut maps, 18, 20, 54, 61, 86
Woodford, 34
Woolwich, 38, 51, 204
Workhouses, 47, 167
Wormwood Scrubs, 48
Wren, Christopher, 24, 26, 94, 96, 98
Wyld, James, 39, 178
Wyngaerde, Anthony van den, 18, 19–20, 57

York Gate, 167
  House, 15, 24

Zarah Buildings, 51
Zoological Gardens, 167

PLATE 1 (*opposite*)

Section of an itinerary from London to Rome

by Matthew Paris, *c* 1252

British Museum, Royal MS. 14 c vii f.2

R. Vaughan, *Matthew Paris*, 1958
H. G. Fordham, *Roadbooks and Itineraries of Great Britain*, 1924
J. B. Mitchell, 'Maps by Matthew Paris,' *Geographical Journal* 81, 1939

In this early road map, which includes the first view of London, the artist has been concerned merely to give a thumbnail sketch of the city, emphasising its major features and thus identifying for the traveller the end of his day's journey. Six of the gates are named, and Westminster Abbey, St. Paul's, the Tower and the river identified.

The conventions of the modern route-map are already established, in embryo at least, in this drawing. All bends and deviations are ignored and only the basic information required by the traveller is given, that is, the distance between stopping-places on the route. Matthew Paris expressed this in terms of a comfortable day's travelling, or 'journee', a convenient traditional measure before the introduction of a standard mile. Paris, a monk of St. Alban's Abbey, must have known London well, since he frequently visited the Court at Westminster on business for the King. Although other maps of England prepared by Paris demonstrate his detailed knowledge of the country's geography and of the points of the compass and the need for a scale, he has chosen here to omit all detail irrelevant to his purpose, so that this view of London is not a true indication of the state of contemporary cartographic technique, but a unique reminder of London's significance in medieval routes.

The itinerary was prepared to illustrate Paris's account of the papal offer of the Sicilian crown to Richard of Cornwall in 1252. It is reproduced from the *Chronica Majora*.

PLATE 2 (*pages 74–75*)

Finsbury from a lost map of London

by an unknown cartographer, *c* 1553–1559

Howgego and Darlington, no. 1.

This lively Tudor view is engraved in reverse on a copper plate (prepared for printing). It was one of twenty such sheets which together made up the earliest map of London, but unfortunately no copies of the complete map exist to-day, and only one other copper plate of the set is known, in a private collection.

Finsbury and Moorfields were used by Tudor Londoners for drying clothes, marketing, pasturing cattle, archery and other semi-rural pleasures. All these activities can be seen on the copper plate, which covers an area north of the wall, including the site of Liverpool Street Station. The marsh of Moorfields was unsuitable for building, so it remained an open space close to the wall until the 18th century, although to the north houses were spreading along Bishopsgate Street to house Londoners who wished to move out of the crowded city.

This, the first printed map of any part of London, recaptures the medieval city, its walls intact and its gates – bedecked with traitors' limbs – closed every night. The charities and religious houses of the pre-Reformation city have left their mark even in this small quarter of London; Spitalfields, part of the estate formerly attached to the dissolved Hospital of St. Mary Spital, is the most familiar name today. Opposite All Hallows in the Wall is a large and elaborate complex of buildings, with a vaguely ecclesiastical crenellated tower and roof. This, the dissolved priory of the Augustinians, had been taken over by Sir William Paulet, Marquis of Winchester, who built himself a fine house in the priory; part of the church he granted to the Dutch community in London as a church, but the tower he retained as a storehouse. The precinct outline persists today, but only by footways.

Half a century after the map was made the first public theatres in London, the Theatre and the Curtain, were to open in Shoreditch, just to the north of the map's edge. Another more brutal form of entertainment was offered by the lunatics in Bedlam Hospital, which stood by Bishopsgate Street (burnt in 1666 and rebuilt) until its removal in the 19th century to the asylum in Lambeth now housing the Imperial War Museum.

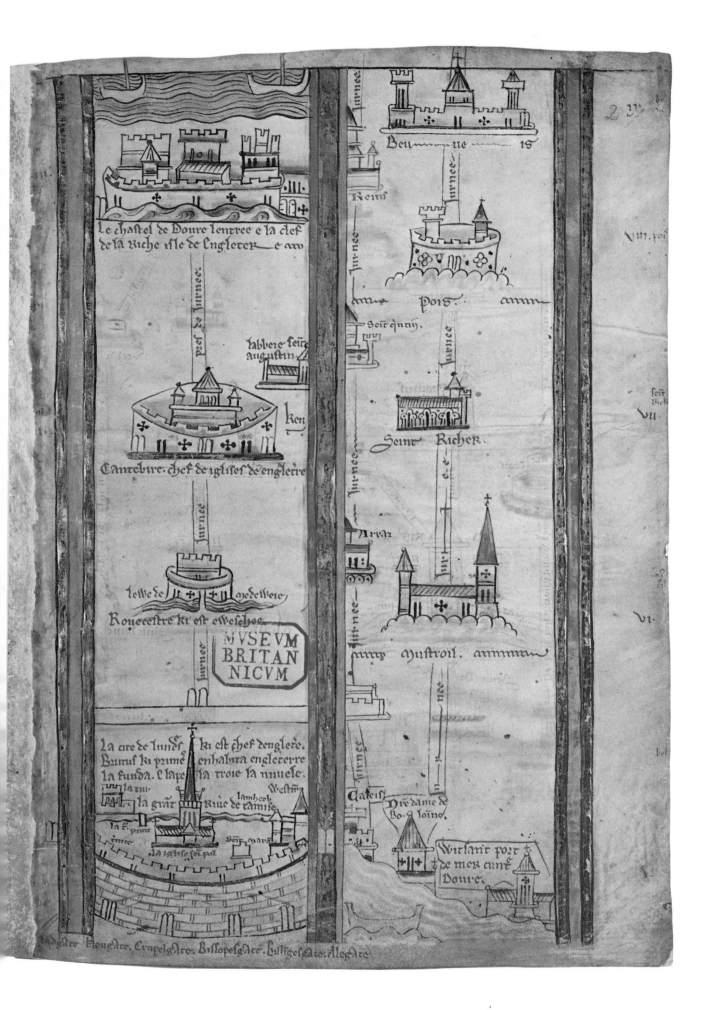

FYNNESBVRIE FIELD.

Fynnesb Courte.

Dogge hows.

MOOR FIELD.

S. Thaphins.

MOOR GATE.

All holyes ni the wall.

Bury

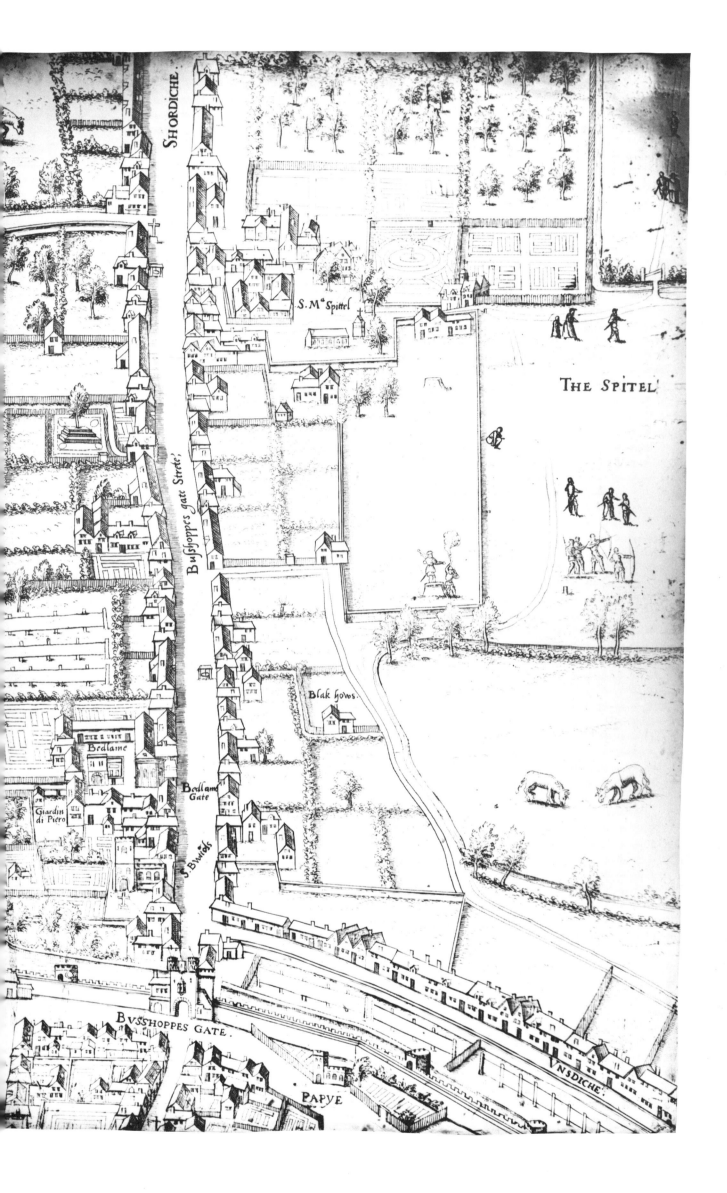

SHORDICHE.

S. M⁺ Spittel

THE SPITEL

Busshoppes gate Strete

Blak hows.

Bedlame

Bedlam Gate

Giardin di Piero

S. Bwtofs

BVSSHOPPES GATE.

PAPYE

VNSDICHE.

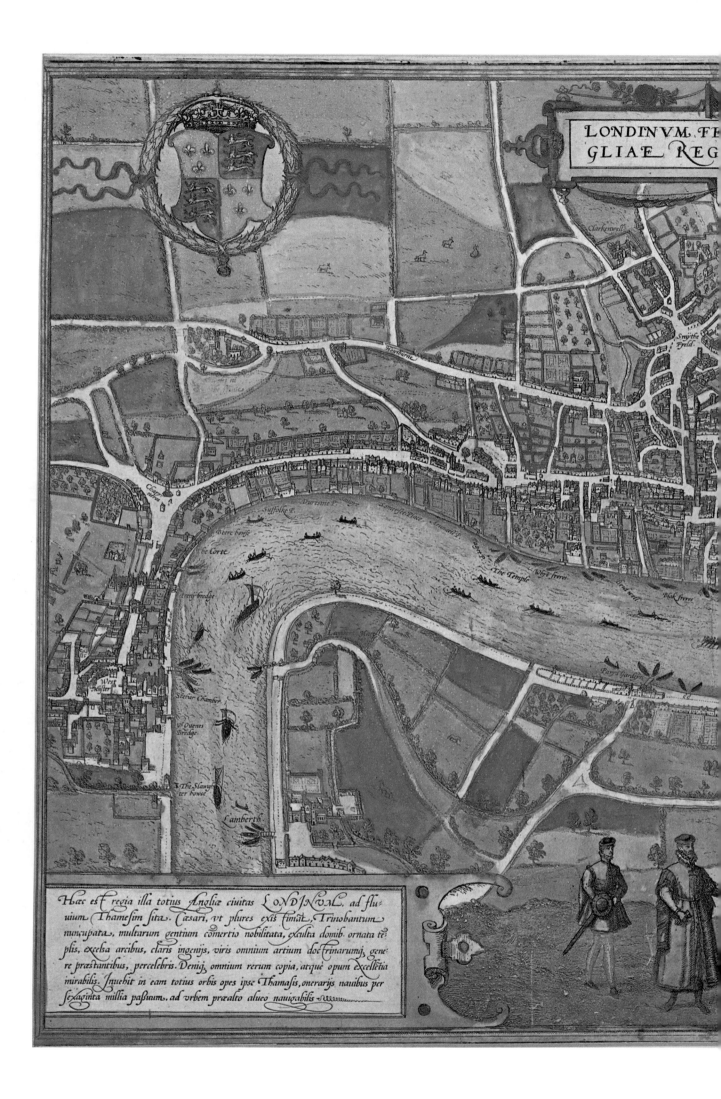

LONDINVM, FE
GLIAE REG

Clarkenwell

Smythe Fyeld.

Holburne

Clerken well

Suffolke P. *Duresme P.* *Savoye* *Somerset Place* *Arundel P.* *The Temple* *Whyt frere.* *Blak frere.*

Beere house

The Corte

Arrey breche

Lambeth Marsh *Parys Garden*

West Minster

Ferris Chamber

yt Quenes Bredge

The Slaughter howes

Lamberth

Hæc est regia illa totius Angliæ ciuitas LONDINVM, ad flu-
uium Thamesin sita. Cæsari, vt plures exis timât, Trinobantum
nuncupata, multarum gentium comertio nobilitata, exculta domib. ornata té=
plis, excelsa arcibus, claris ingenijs, viris omnium artium doctrinarumq, gene=
re præstantibus, percelebris. Deniq, omnium rerum copia, atque opum excellétia
mirabilis. Inuehit in eam totius orbis opes ipse Thamasis, onerarijs nauibus per
sexaginta millia passuum, ad vrbem præalto alueo nauigabilis.

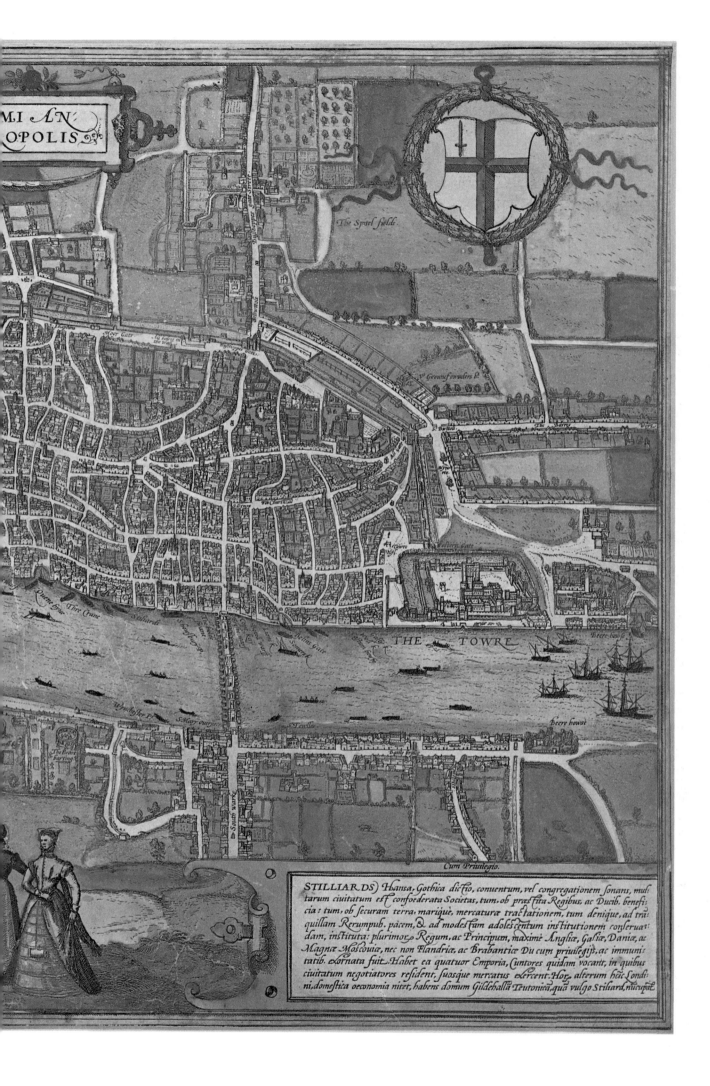

STILLIARDS) Hansa, Gothica dictio, conuentum, vel congregationem sonans, multarum ciuitatum est confoederata Societas, tum ob praesita Regibus, ac Ducib. benefi-
cia: tum, ob securam terra, marique, mercaturae tractationem, tum denique, ad tra-
quillam Rerumpub. pacem, & ad modestam adolescentum institutionem conseruan-
dam, instituta: plurimorum Regum, ac Principum, maximè Angliae, Galliae, Daniae, ac
Magnae Moscouiae, nec non Flandriae, ac Brabantiae Du cum priuilegijs, ac immuni-
tatib. Cornata fuit. Habet ea quatuor Emporia, Cuntores quidam vocant, in quibus
ciuitatum negotiatores resident, suosque mercatus exercent. Hor, alterum hîc Londini, domestica oeconomia nitet, habens domum Gildehallâ Teutonica, quâ vulgo Stiliard, nucupat.

PLATE 3 (*overleaf*)

Londinum Feracissimi Angliae Regni Metropolis

by G. Braun and F. Hogenberg, 1574

Howgego and Darlington, no. 2.

This, the most familiar of all the maps of Tudor London, represents the city substantially as it had been in the 1550's, two decades before the map was published. It appeared in a German atlas of European cities, the *Civitates Orbis Terrarum*, first published in 1572. Its similarity in detail to the copperplate map indicates that the (presumably German) engraver reduced it from a copy of the latter map.

The map gives a fascinating picture of the capital before Elizabeth came to the throne. The walls no longer confined the city; to the east Portsoken lay entirely outside, and Bishopsgate, Cripplegate and Aldersgate wards each extended beyond the wall, as did Farringdon, the massive western ward which had been subdivided into an inner and outer section in 1394. Houses lined each of the roads out of London, and the suburb of great palaces and inns along the Strand to Charing Cross linked London with the Court at Westminster.

Across the river Southwark had nominally become part of London in 1550, when the city purchased three royal manors there, but its later disorderly reputation as the home of public entertainment was to resist all the city's attempts at control. The bull- and bear-baiting grounds, with the dogs set to leap from their kennels, can be seen to the west of the Borough.

London's population at this time can only be guessed at, but was perhaps in the region of 90,000. It had grown since the beginning of the century and was to grow even more rapidly before its close, but this expansion was slow to influence the broad outline of the city's limits.

The dissolution of the monasteries gave unprecedented opportunities for re-using their vast precincts in and around London; some were subdivided into tenements, others used as factories – notably Crutched Friars which housed glass kilns, and the Minories, conveniently accessible from the Tower, which became a gunpowder factory.

London's pressing need for charitable institutions to cope with the urban poor and handicapped was temporarily satisfied by taking over and refounding Christ's Hospital, St. Thomas's Hospital and Henry VIII's palace of Bridewell, so that massive institutional building was rendered unnecessary for another century.

The map is a true plan, although this is obscured by the cartographer's preference for a bird's eye view of all standing buildings; the scale, about 6 inches to a mile, is only approximately a quarter of that of the copperplate map.

PLATE 4 (*opposite*)

Westminster in 1593

by John Norden

John Norden, *Speculum Britanniae: Pars Middlesex*, 1593
E. G. R. Taylor, *Tudor and Stuart Geography*, 1934

Westminster stretched from Millbank to Temple Bar, a separate entity outside the City of London's jurisdiction and home of four royal palaces – Westminster, Whitehall, St. James and Somerset House. Royal influence pervaded the area; between the old palace on the riverside opposite Lambeth, and the royal mews at Charing Cross, 'the farthest building west on the north side of the High Street', court interest controlled both sides of Whitehall, the royal tennis courts and tiltyard lying towards St. James's Park (under Downing Street, the Home Office and the Horse Guards), and the privy garden and royal lodgings along the river.

The Strand was lined with great noble houses whose owners were drawn to London by the lure of Elizabeth's court. Her most famous servant, Burleigh, owned a large and elaborate house, seen on the map south of the old convent garden. Another, Leicester House, had changed its name and owner several times in half a century of political vicissitudes; at the Reformation it had been Paget Place. It was then renamed for Robert Dudley until 1588, and then briefly for the ill-fated Earl of Essex.

Westminster was not only the haunt of royalty and noblemen. To it flocked lawyers and their clients during the four legal terms, to hear their suits in Westminster Hall. This army of transient visitors required refreshment, and Westminster was notorious for its alehouses 'harbouring all sorts of lewde and badde people.' For the sake of public order the Court of Burgesses was established in 1585 to cope with the particular problems of an area densely populated but with a shifting population, 'many of them wholly given to vice and idleness, living in contempt of all manner of officers', and the number of alehouses was limited to 100. Norden gives a vivid impression of the busy traffic by river to and from Westminster and the wherries clustering at the Thames-side stairs.

Norden's map is neither signed nor dated, but was published, together with others of the City and of Middlesex, in the Middlesex volume of his *Speculum Britanniae* in 1593. The London map was signed 'John Norden Anglus,' and although the engraving of both was probably by Pieter van den Keere, it is fairly certain that the surveys were, as he claimed on the title page, 'By the Travaile and View of John Norden', putting him among the earliest English map publishers. He worked professionally as a surveyor in the London area and elsewhere; a plan of lands in Kennington prepared by him for the Common Council is in the Guildhall Record Office.

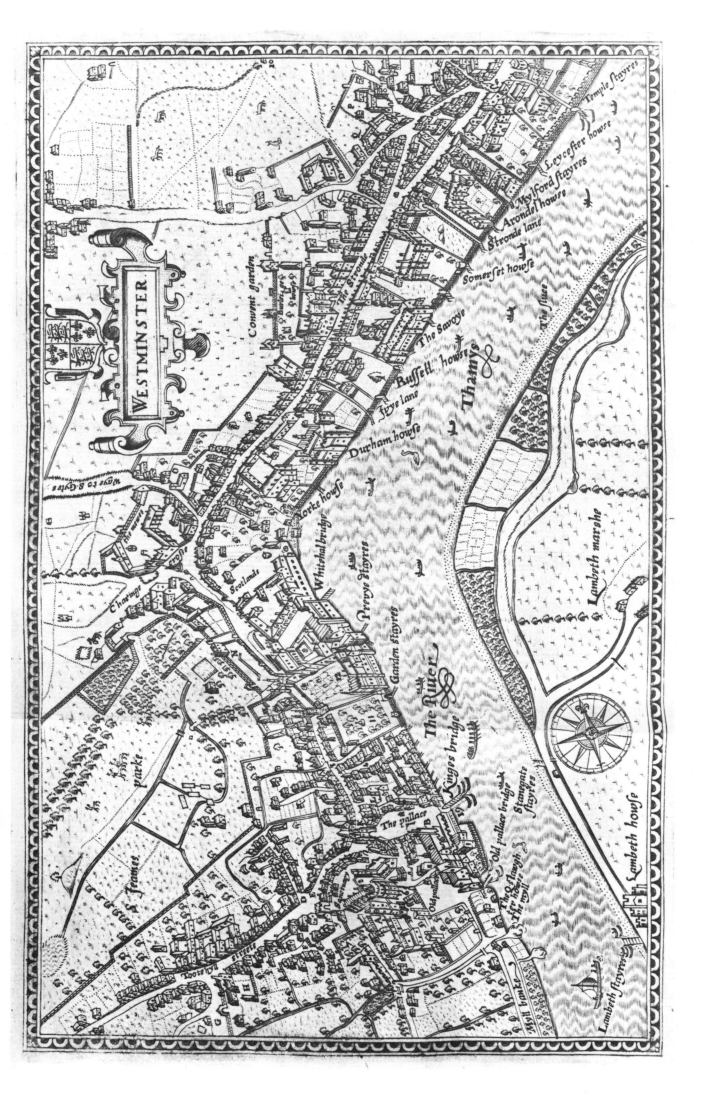

WESTMINSTER.

Covent garden

Temple stayres

Leycester howse

Mylford stayres

Arundell howse

Stronde lane

Somerset howse

The Stronde

The Savoye

The Sluse

Russell howse

Fryye lane

Durham howse

Thamys

Yorke howse

Whitehall bridge

Preiye stayres

Garden stayres

Lambeth marshe

Scotland

Charinge

Waye to S. Gyles

The River

Kinges bridge

parke

The pallace

Old pallace bridge

Stangate stayres

St James

Olde

The Q. Almery

The hedge

The mill

Lambeth howse

Myll banke

Lambeth stayres

LONDON.

PLATE 5

Bird's eye view of
London from the
*Particular Description of
England*

by William Smith, 1588

British Museum,
Sloane MS. 2596, f.52

This view comes from a volume prepared by a famous Elizabethan herald and topographical artist, which included 'Portratures of Certaine of the Chieffest Citties' of the country. Others in the volume, such as the map-views of Norwich and Bristol, were closer to true maps, in the sense of being related to a ground plan, but Smith found the panoramic form more convenient to express the grandeur of London.

William Smith had lived for 10 years in Germany and learnt there certain well-established cartographic conventions, such as the use of a numbered grid for references and a table of symbols, both of which he probably passed on to John Norden. The maps and 'profiles' in his *Particular Description* were presumably drawn originally for his own interest, although four, not including London, were later redrawn and engraved in the Netherlands by Jodocus Hondius as part of the preparatory work for an atlas of English town and country maps.

The method used to represent London, the 'profile', was apparently felt to be as suitable for towns as the more familiar map-view, though Smith uses the latter technique to show Bristol, with a note as to the exact date on which he made the original sketches. Both techniques were popular with topographers until well into the 17th century. Indeed, the concept of the flat ground plan was alien to contemporary taste, which preferred to stress the splendour of the subject, the height of the spires and 'the fayre buildings . . . the greate substance of rychesse conteyned in them'.

For William Smith, London Bridge and St. Paul's Cathedral were two of the eight wonders of England and neither could appear to its true advantage except in his chosen technique. This view illustrates both, and other sights familiar to Tudor Londoners but now long vanished, such as the late 15th-century river-front palace called Baynard's Castle, which stood east of Blackfriars and was destroyed in the Fire of 1666. Its foundations were uncovered in 1972 in groundwork for the new City of London School. On the Thames floats Queen Elizabeth's royal barge, a frequent traveller between the riverside palaces of Greenwich, Whitehall and Richmond.

PLATE 6

An estate in Tothill Street, Westminster, surveyed for Christ's Hospital

by Ralph Treswell, *c* 1612

Guildhall Library,
Christ's Hospital MSS.

The later 16th century saw a massive shift of property in London into the hands of such institutions as the new post-Reformation hospitals and schools and the livery companies. These bodies took an active interest in estate management, and as a corollary to this had surveys made of their properties, giving work to a new generation of estate surveyors, among which the Treswell family were prominent.

On its foundation Christ's Hospital had been granted the old Grey Friars precinct on Newgate Street, and a portion of this was let out in tenements and shops, the bulk being retained for the school's own use. To provide an adequate income further rentable properties were needed, and over the years were generously gifted by charitably-minded Londoners. These estates, scattered piecemeal through the City and Westminster, might consist of one tenement only, or of a considerable block, depending on the wealth of the donor, so the need for efficient registration of boundaries was obvious. To this end, a Jacobean steward of the Hospital compiled a register of properties, bound up with plans of the separate estates, surveyed and drawn by Ralph Treswell.

The properties covered the then extent of London, from Canon's Row, Westminster, to Aldgate High Street, and included Treswell's own premises rented from the Hospital, a large and comfortable house off Aldersgate Street consisting of a study, buttery and kitchen, parlour and three other rooms, together with stairs to the upper floor and a well and 'cestern to the newe cunditt' shared with other houses in the yard. The complex interweaving of property boundaries and access rights in the overcrowded city that is apparent from these plans must have given rise to innumerable disputes. In many cases the pumps, privies and baking ovens were communal, shared by 10 or 15 households.

The property illustrated, lying between Tothill Street and St. James's Park, was only partly in the Hospital's ownership; it consisted of a close of ground against the park wall, 'an orcharde and gardeine and . . . Barne' willed to the Hospital by Richard Castell, shoemaker of St. Margarets, Westminster. It remained a garden and stable for a century after his death, when Carteret Street was laid out across the site.

This plan is typical of its period in that although full measurements, abuttals and alignments are given, the surveyor has seen fit to add the 'profiles' of the houses in Tothill Street, so giving a glimpse of the typical late-Tudor London house.

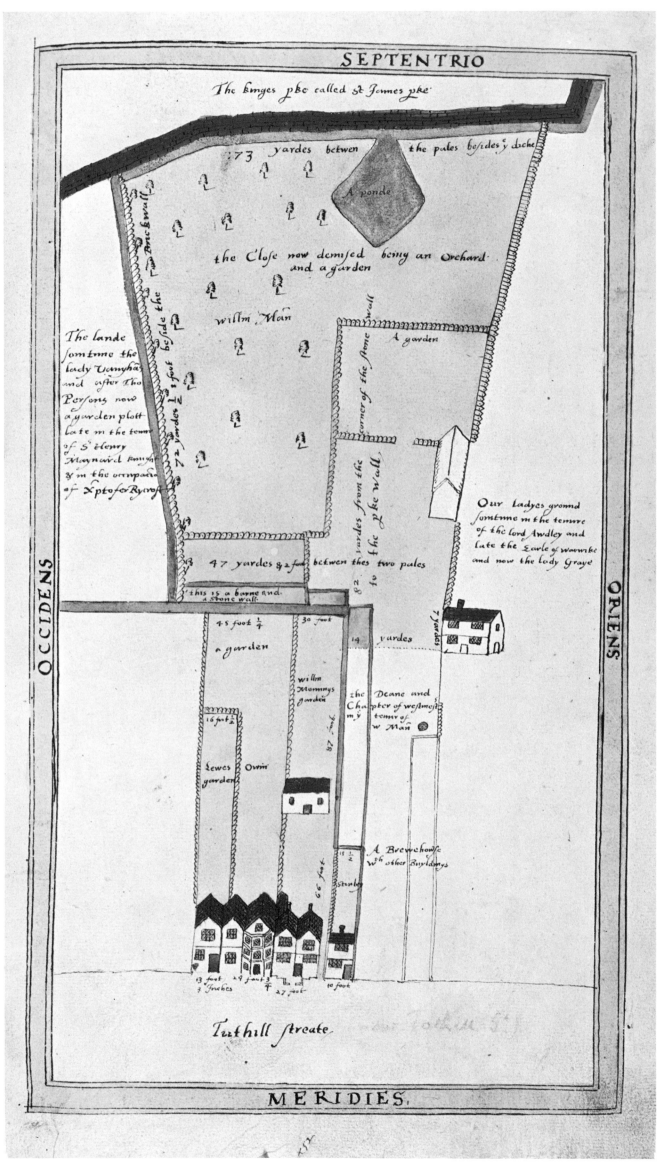

SEPTENTRIO

The kinges pke called St Iames pke

73 yardes betwen the pales besides y̆ diche

A ponde

the Close now demised being an Orchard
and a garden

willm Man

A garden

The lande
somtime the
lady Tamyhā
and after Thō
Persons now
a garden plott
late m the tenur
of Sr Henry
Maynard knight
& m the ocupac
of Xptofer Rycrof

corner of the stone wall

72 yardes 2 1/2 foot beside the Bricke wall

82 yardes from the
to the pke wall

Our ladyes ground
somtime m the tenure
of the lord Awdley and
late the Earle of warwike
and now the lady Graye

OCCIDENS

ORIENS

47 yardes & 2 foot betwen thes two pales

this is a barne and
a stone wall

45 foot 1/4   30 foot   14 yardes   7 yardes

a garden

16 foot 1/2

willm
Mannys
garden

87 foot

the Deane and
Chapter of westmest
m y̆ tenur of
w Man

Lewes Owin
garden

A Brewehowse
wth other Buyldyngs

66 foot

15 1/2
Stable

13 foot   29 foot 3   10 foot
3 Inches   27 foot

Tuthill streate

MERIDIES.

the c
LON

Islington

THE   RIUER

The   Banke   side

Are to be sould at Amsterdam by Cornelis Dankerts grauer of Maps

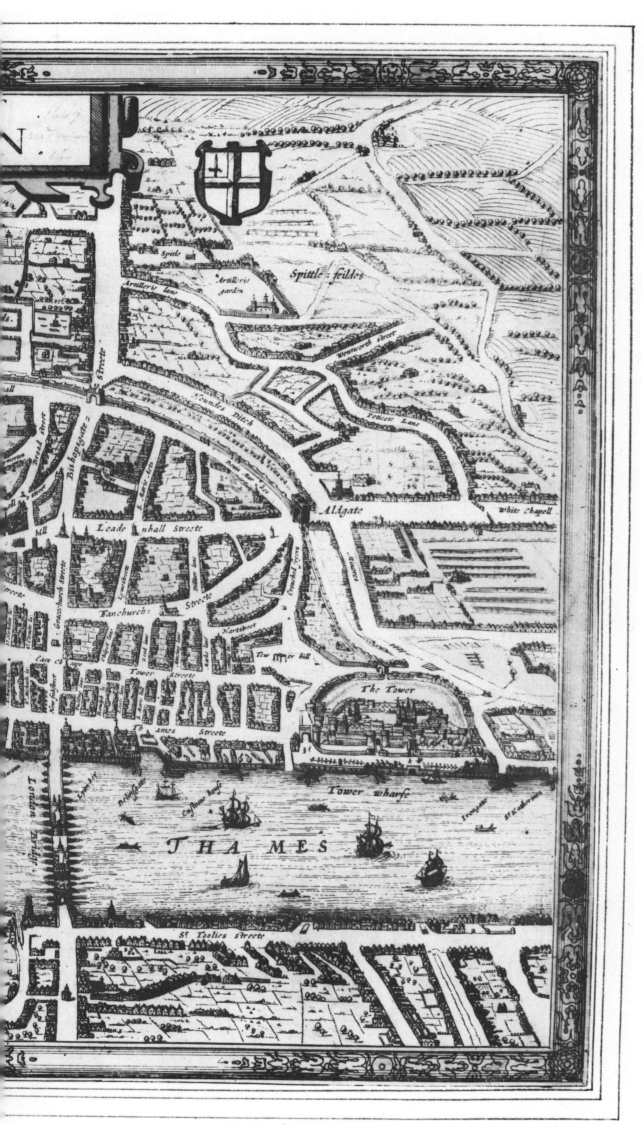

N.

Spitle

Spittle-feildes

Artillerie lane

Artillerie garden

Wentworth street

Leonardes Ditch

Pellicot Lane

Streete

Bishopsgate

Broad street

S. Marie Axe

Brick layers lane

Aldgate

white chapell

Leade nhall Streete

Fenchurch

Gracechurch streete

Lymestrete

Philpot lane

Pillior lane

Streete

Crutched fryers

Hart streete

hill

East cheape

New fishstreet

Tower Streete

S. Marie

Tower hill

The Tower

Thames Streete

London Bridge

Lymestrete

Pellinshate

Engham harfe

Tower wharfe

Ironygate

St Katherines

THAMES

St Toolies streete

PLATE 7 (*overleaf*)

The Cittie of London

by Cornelis Dankerts, *c* 1633

Howgego and Darlington, no. 9.
T. C. Dale, *The inhabitants of London in 1638*,
1934

This simplified and decorative map-view of the city was perhaps prepared and engraved in Holland, as well as being sold there, to satisfy a European market. It is hard to imagine any self-respecting Londoner or anyone with even the slightest personal knowledge buying this map in preference, say, to Braun and Hogenberg's or even to Norden's, reprinted at about the same time; however, the scarcity of London maps led to this misleading example also being reprinted at least twice, with only slight changes. These included the provision of a compass rose effectively blocking out the Bankside theatres. In one respect the map-maker did have local knowledge; he shows the gap on London Bridge cleared by a disastrous fire the year before, which acted as a fire-gap in 1666 and prevented the Great Fire from spreading to the bridge itself.

The cartographer, presumably to insert the names, has made all the streets ludicrously wide and assumed that behind the frontages lay lavish gardens – vanished from the city for at least two centuries. The map is interesting in showing the conduit near Fleet Bridge, an important link in the water supply line from St. Pancras. At this time the population of the city and liberties was probably about 130,000 and growing rapidly, particularly in the out-parishes. The lists prepared for the Lord Mayor in 1638 of the 1300 or so new houses built since 1603 (payment of a composition fee protected the builder against the penalties for new building) indicated the areas of expansion, although they are misleading in that old properties in Southwark and the east end parishes were sub-divided into tenements rather than new houses being built, so that the growth of population in these areas is concealed.

Over 600 houses had been compounded for to the west of the city in Drury Lane, Long Acre and elsewhere, and 400 to the north, around Clerkenwell. A return of communicants in 1638 revealed the contrast in size and over-crowding between some of the tiny city parishes and those beyond the walls; St. Matthew Friday Street had 24 houses, St. John Watling Street the same, with 140 communicants, whereas All Hallows Barking contained 300 houses.

The Stuarts recognised the problems created by an outer belt beyond the City's control, and the Council offered in 1633 'whether they woulde accept of parte of the suburbs into their jurisdiction and liberty for better government,' but the City rejected the offer and it was not repeated.

PLATE 8 (*opposite*)

Northwest of the city
from the woodcut
Civitas Londinum

attributed to Ralph Agas,
published *c* 1633

Howgego and Darlington, no. 8

This map-view, though published in the 17th century, shows London unchanged from the 1550's, when the cartographer was originally at work. Although it was brought up-to-date in one respect, the substitution of the Stuart for the Tudor royal arms, it gives otherwise a fascinating picture of the mid-Tudor capital, taking no account of later topographical developments and so creating an invaluable backward look at London just after the Reformation, a period of dramatic change for which there are virtually no maps.

The outskirts of London are dominated by a windmill-topped hill and a limekiln between the modern Goswell Street and the City Road; to the north stands the village of Islington on the road to St. Albans. Between the open countryside and the bastions of the city wall lies a belt of large houses set in gardens and ex-religious precincts adapted to some secular use. St. Bartholomew's, its gatehouse facing the cowherds depicted standing in Smithfield, was refounded as a hospital under the City's auspices in 1547.

Beyond Little Britain, the traditional pre-Fire home of printers and booksellers, lay the city ditch and Grey Friars, refounded as Christ's Hospital 'For the Innocent & Fatherless . . . where poor Children are to be trained up to the overthrow of Beggary.' The blue-coat children were originally brought in from the streets as being in need of shelter; the school's later academic development is a far cry from its initial purpose. The city ditch presented such a risk to the health of the children that it was partially covered over in 1552, but the hospital privies continued to drain into it and the writing-school stood directly above it.

Outside the hospital gate Newgate Street was blocked by market stalls, which remained a nuisance to traffic until Charles II insisted on a permanent market site to the south after the Fire. Further to the east Cheapside is noticeably wider than the other thoroughfares of the city, befitting its use as a processional and major shopping street, but it also was impeded by the Eleanor cross, much mutilated, and the Standard, both visible in this detail.

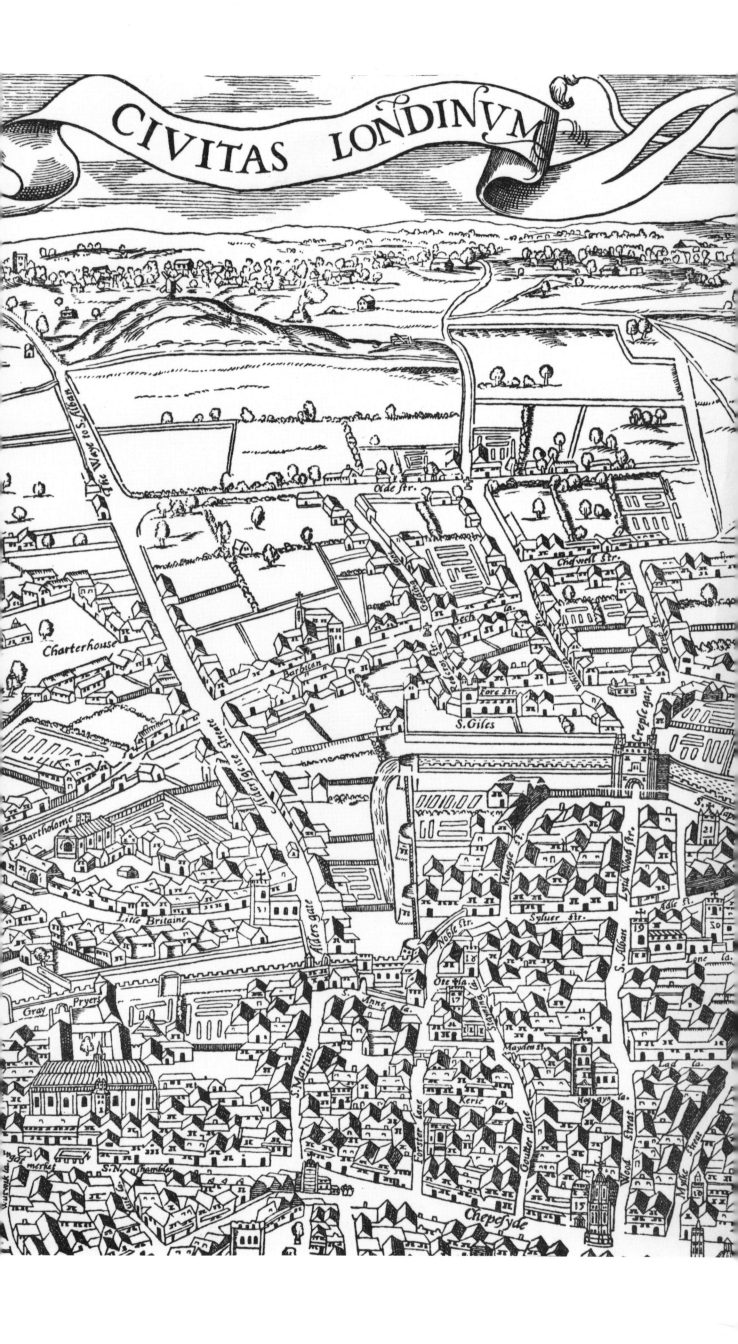

PLATE 9

Northwest of the city from *London*

by Richard Newcourt, 1658

Howgego and Darlington, no. 12

Newcourt's map is not strictly a plan but a map-view, an older form of cartographic expression. The value of the form lies in its ability to express the human scale of a town and to indicate the activities of its inhabitants; the copperplate map and Braun and Hogenberg's are fine Tudor examples of the genre. This, engraved by Faithorne, is far cruder, although on a larger scale, with the coarseness of a woodcut rather than the delicate and precise line of copper-engraving, and he omits the human detail which gives such vitality to the earlier maps, but his is of interest in showing the extent of building to the north-west of the city by the mid-17th century (compare with the woodcut map showing the same area, plate 8) and the way in which the precincts of the Grey Friars (Christ's Hospital), St. Bartholomew's Hospital, Smithfield and the Charterhouse have become filled up with miscellaneous buildings. These monolithic precincts, long since divided into multiple occupancy, still influence the topography of this part of London. The G.P.O. took over the Christ's Hospital estate almost entire, and the Charterhouse is still intact, with no through roads. St. John's Clerkenwell now stands in a quiet backwater north of the Clerkenwell Road, which today is the westward extension of Old Street (not Golden Lane, as Faithorne's misplacing of the name suggests).

In spite of the schematic and repetitive nature of the map, in which any one building is indistinguishable from any other, unless it be a church, which can be identified by its reference number, it does convey the densely-crowded nature of this section of London even before the Fire, which by destroying their traditional homes within the walls, drove Londoners out to the west and north from that 'vast unwieldy and disorderly Babel of buildings.' It also vividly illustrates the inconvenient approaches to the city along Fleet Street through the double bottleneck of Temple Bar and Ludgate, and from Holborn the awkward swing south along narrow Snow Hill (not abolished till 1867) and through Newgate. The approach from the north through Cripplegate was even more straitened, but at least the way ran reasonably clear from the gate to Cheapside.

LONDON.

Clarkin Well

St John Street

Charter house

Smith Feild

Holborne

Fleete Street

Saint court

Black Friers Pudle Wharfe

Chea[p]

PLATE 10

Gray's Inn to the river from *West Central London*

by Wenceslaus Hollar, *c* 1658

A. M. Hind, *Wenceslaus Hollar and his views of London*, 1922

This is an incomplete sheet from an intended large-scale map of London; the street lines are in plan, but the buildings and other standing features are seen in isometric projection, to give a vivid three-dimensional view of this bustling and fashionable district.

Most of the houses shown had been newly built or much altered since the beginning of the century, in an unprecedented building boom: the streets around Covent Garden as part of the Bedford town-planning schemes of the 1630's, when Bow Street was described as 'large and open, with good houses well inhabited and resorted unto by gentry for lodgings', and Long Acre a decade or so earlier, with the first houses around Lincoln's Inn Fields appearing in 1638.

James I had taken some interest in the development of the district, which lay astride his route from Whitehall to the hunting at Theobalds Park, and in particular in the quality of the houses in Queen Street and Long Acre. Those lining Queen Street were substantial, with gardens 200 feet long, but a proposal to erect two-roomed cottages in an alley off Long Acre was rejected. 'Pestering with alleys of mean houses' would rapidly create a slum atmosphere out of keeping with this aristocratic enclave.

Within a few years of the Restoration Nicholas Barbon was to begin building houses in St. Giles's Fields, eventually to become the homes of French and other immigrants, giving Soho its traditional cosmopolitan flavour.

This populous area required new sources of fresh water; the pipes of Sir Hugh Middleton's New River Company stretched outside the city only to Temple Bar, and in 1656 the enterprising Sir Edward Foorde, having failed in his project to bring water from the river Colne to St. Giles in the Fields, erected a waterhouse on the water front by Arundel House. Unfortunately it was too good a vantage point for Somerset House, and on Henrietta Maria's request the king ordered its demolition in 1665.

Clarkenwell greene

Hatton garden

Long lane
Smith: field

Holborn hill
Holborn bridge

Shoe lane

Fetter lane

Harp alley

Part of Lin colne ius fields

Fleet River

White Fryars

THE · RIVER

A. Westminster Abby
B. S Pauls Cathedrall
C. White hall
D. S Iames
E. Southampton house
F. Grayes Inn
G. Lincolns Inn

H. The Temple
I. The Tower
K. Lambeth march

A GENERALL
of the whole Citty
with Westminster
Suburbs, by which
computed the prope
that which is burnt,
the other parts sta

a Tuttle Fields
b S Iames Fielde
c S Martins Fields
d S Giles Fields
e Lincolns Inn F.
f Grayes Inn Fields
g Hatton garden
h Moore fielde
i Spittle Fields
k East Smithfield

S Iames Parke
Westminster

South warke

S Georges fields

Lambeth

W Hollar fecit 1666

A MAP or GROVNDPLOT of the Citty of London and the Suburbes thereof, that is to say, all which is within the Iurisdiction of the Lord Mayor or properlie called London by which is exactly demonstrated the present condition thereof, since the last sad accident of fire. The blanke space signifeing the burnt part & where the houses are exprest, those places yet standig.

Sould by Iohn Overton at the White horse in little Brittaine, next doore to little S. Bartholomew gate. 1666.

Bunhill
Finsbury Fields
Artillery ground
Moore Fields
Spittle Fields
Thames Street
Tower hill
East Smith field
the Bulwarke
The Tower
Part of Southwarke
THAMES

Annotations of the Churches, and other remarkable places in this Map.

Goodſall of S. Paul	21. S. Steven Colmanſtreet	42. Bow Church,
...Church,	22. S. Mildred,	43. S. Matthew,
...chaell	23. S. Margaret,	44. S. Auſtins,
...ers by Woodſtreet	24. S. Chriſtopher,	45. S. Gregory,
...ter,	25. S. Bartholomew	46. S. Martins by Ludgate,
...onard,	26. French Church,	47. S. Andrew,
...n by Aldeꝛſgate	27. S. Benet,	48. S. Benet in Thamſtreet,
...chaell in Woodſtreet	28. Auguſtine Fryars,	49. S. Peters,
...n Zachary	29. S. Martins Outwich,	50. S. Mary,
...aues,	30. S. Michaell in Cornhill,	51. S. Nicholas,
...ry Stayning,	31. S. Peters,	52. S. Nicholas Olaues,
...ury Aldermanbery,	32. Allhallowes	53. S. Mary Somerſet,
...chaell Baſhaw,	33. S. Edmunds,	54. S. Iohn Evangeliſt,
...aurence,	34. S. Nicholas,	55. S. Mildred
...audlins,	35. S. Mary Wolnoth,	56. Allhallowes
...hallowes,	36. S. Mary Wolnoth,	57. S. Mary,
...Martins in Irenmon...	37. S. Mary in Canwike ſtreet,	58. S. Thomas Apoſtle,
...s lane,	38. S. Stevens in Walbrooke,	59. S. Iohn Baptiſt,
...Olaues,	39. S. Bennet,	60. S. Michaell,
...ary Colechurch,	40. S. Pancras,	61. S. Olaues,
	41. S. Antholins,	62. S. Martins

63. S. Mary Buttolfs lane,	84. S. Catharin Colemans,	93. Temple Church.
64. S. Swithens,	85. S. Cath: Creed Church,	94. S. Dunſtans Weſt,
65. S. Mary in Bushlane,	86. S. Andrew Vnderſhaft,	95. S. Andrew in Holborne
66. Allhallowes great,	87. S. Hellins,	96. S. Pulchers
67. Allhallowes the leſſer,	88. Ethelborough,	97. S. Bartholomew great
68. S. Laurence Poultney,	89. Allhallowes in the Wall,	98. S. Bartholomew the leſſe
69. S. Mich: by Crooked lane,	90. S. Bottolphs Biſh: gate	99. S. Bottolphs by Aldeꝛſgate
70. S. Magnus,	91. S. Bottolphs Aldgate	100. S. Giles by Cripplegate.
71. S. Margaret,	92. S. Brides,	
72. S. Leonard,		
73. S. Bennet,		
74. S. Dennis,		
75. S. Margaret Pattens,		
76. S. Andrew Hubart,		
77. S. Georges,		
78. S. Bottolphs,		
79. S. Mary hill,		
80. S. Dunſtan Eaſt,		
81. Allhallowes Barking,		
82. S. Olaues,		
83. Allhallowes Fanch: St		

A Ludgate	O Hoſp: S. Barth:	c Black fryars Staires
B Newgate	P Charterhouſe	d Puddle dock
C Aldeꝛſgate	Q Guildhall,	e Paulos wharfe
D Cripple gate	R the Stokes	f Broken wharfe
E Moore gate	S Royall Exchange	g Quene Hythe
F Biſhopsgate	T Greſham Colledge	h 3 Cranes
G Aldgate	V Leadenhall	i Stilliard
H Eſtcheap	W Dukes Palace	k Coldharbour
I the Temple	X Cuſtome houſe	l Old Swan
K Dorſet houſe	Y Bedlane	m Belins gate
L Bridewell	Z Sion Colledge	n Tower wharfe
M Barnards Caſtle	a Temple Staires	o Artillery Yard
N Chriſt Ch: Cloyſt:	b Whi fryars Stayres	

This length is one English mile from one end to the other.

PLATE 11 (*overleaf*)

A Map or Ground-plot of the Citty of London . . . after the Fire of 1666

by Wenceslaus Hollar, 1666

Howgego and Darlington, no. 19

The Fire of London started in a baker's chimney in Pudding Lane, just east of London Bridge, and spread outwards in all directions, fanned by the wind. It destroyed an estimated 1300 houses, churches and many other institutions, including the city's administrative and commercial centres, the Guildhall and the Royal Exchange.

Although London had always been vulnerable (the earliest historic fire is recorded in the *Anglo-Saxon Chronicle*), so great a catastrophe far outshone all earlier fires, and the public interest, both in England and abroad, was relatively greater. Engravers were quick to recognise a potential market, so a flood of maps and engravings purporting to show the extent of the damage and the drama of the flames at their destructive height soon appeared in print, both in London and in Holland, with which country England was then at variance.

Hollar's map, engraved by John Overton, has at least the virtue that he was on the spot, knew London well and was an experienced topographical artist, so that the details have a strong claim to accuracy. Hollar was to be employed in the preparation of surveys for rebuilding the city and was in close touch with the cartographic élite of his day, whose standards at their highest were not surpassed until much later in the 18th century, and even in so simple a production as the map of burnt London the quality of his work is apparent. (Compare for example Plate 10.)

PLATE 12 (*opposite*)

Rebuilding scheme

by Richard Newcourt, 1666

Guildhall Library, Print Room

T. F. Reddaway, 'Rebuilding plans for London,' *Town Planning Review,* July 1937, December 1937, July 1939

The opportunity apparently offered by the Fire to rebuild London wholesale to an ideal plan and on the most modern town-planning principles was not ignored by Stuart urban enthusiasts. Within a few days of the Fire two men with the entrée, Wren and Evelyn, had presented plans to the king (although Evelyn had an advantage in that he had been thinking and writing about London improvements for several years). A third plan, the work of the fertile Robert Hooke, was presented to the Royal Society on 19th September, a fourth, by Peter Mills, city surveyor, is lost, a fifth, by Captain Valentine Knight, is little more than a sketch and the sixth, of which three versions exist in manuscript, is reproduced here. The author was apparently living in Somerset at the time, but was associated with an earlier essay in London cartography, the large map published by Faithorne in 1658 (Plate 9).

Newcourt's suggestions, in the text which explains the map, have much in common with those of the other planners and with the king's expressed requirements – over, for example, street-widening and the removal of markets from the streets – although he went considerably further in postulating a city wall moved outward by three furlongs to gain ground (the old wall line is marked with a dotted line and the gates named) and a wholesale realignment of parishes, cutting the number from over 100 to 39. He also agreed with Evelyn in banishing burial grounds, 'those abhorred dormitories in the very heart of the cities', beyond the walls, as the Romans had, and moving out noisome industries such as brew-houses, soap and sugar boilers and slaughter-houses.

None of the planners' dreams could be realised; the cost in both money and time was too great for the City, lacking the resources of modern banking and without effective financial support from the Crown, apart from the coal dues. As it was, the most notorious streets, such as Thames Street and Threadneedle Street, each only 11 feet wide between their house-fronts, were widened, steep approach roads eased and New Queen Street laid out as a fine 24-foot-wide route from the river to the Guildhall (Plate 15).

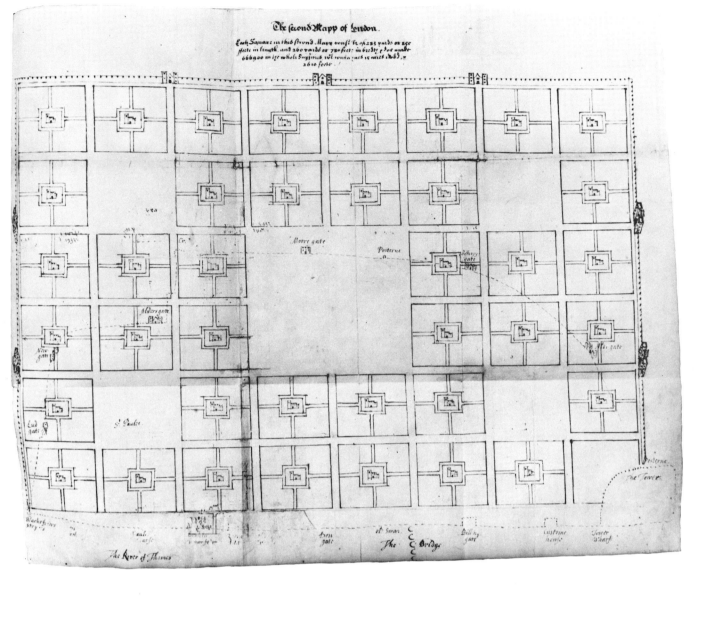

The second Mapp of London.

Each Square in this second Mapp const. to of 225 yards or 200 feete in length, and 200 yards or 720 feet: in bredth e doe make 666900 in the whole Square, the whole square is next 1663, v 2610 feete.

Moore gate

Posterne

Aldersgate

New gate

Lud gate

St Paules

Blackefriers stayers

Paules wharfe

Ebbgate

Bishopsgate

Ald gate

Posterne

The Tower

Fresh gate

ol Swan

The Bridge

Billing gate

Custome howse

Tower wharfe

The River of Thames

PLATE 13

The road from London to St. Albans from *Britannia . . . Principal Roads Thereof*

by John Ogilby, 1675

John Ogilby, *Britannia*, 1675
H. G. Fordham, *Road Books & Itineraries of Great Britain*, 1924

This, one of the seven main post-roads out of London on which Ogilby based his *Book of Roads*, was an ancient and hilly route. Its continuing importance can be gauged from the fact that the section between the capital and St. Albans was the earliest to have a regular weekly coach service in England, first mentioned in 1637.

Ogilby's chosen scale of one inch to the mile allowed the indication of such necessary details as wooden bridges and the steep descent of Ridgehill, site of a windmill. Notable features of the landscape visible from the road, by which the traveller might plot his progress, were the 'Diall' at Highgate, Friern Barnet Chapel, and Brown's Well near the eight-mile stone at Finchley. Where the road was hedged on either side, the engraver indicated it with a continuous line; when, as across Finchley Common, there were no hedges – and therefore presumably as in the New Forest today, the risk of meeting straying animals – a dotted line was used.

London's influence on the immediate countryside is clear even on the relatively small scale of Ogilby's engraving. In Islington the New River Head and by Jack Straw's Castle the Conduit emphasise the perpetually growing demand for piped water in London, which only the streams and springs of the northern heights, from St. Pancras to the Essex border, were able to satisfy.

Later road-books, such as Cary's, went further than Ogilby in distinguishing specifically the quality of the road surface. Maintenance of the roads outside London (where most major streets had been paved in the 16th century) was a haphazard business, and before turnpike companies took over substantially in the 18th century, was the responsibility of surveyors from each parish. In spite of Cromwell's Ordinance tightening up standards, repair of the roads often fell by default to some energetic local man with a special interest. Charles II's Lieutenant of the Tower, Sir John Robinson, liked to hunt in Epping Forest 'but the ways without White-Chappell were very bad and troublesome to him. . . . Upon this were laid across the ways, Trees earth and then Gravel, and Ditches were made . . . & in the middle is laid a high Row of large Gravel . . . to throw off the water . . . & thus is likely to last for ever.' A few years later Wren as Royal Surveyor was forced to dig out the road surface of Whitehall, a notoriously soft route because of the streams draining from St. James's Park into the Thames; he pitched and rammed it twice 'and it remains firm to this day.' (For travellers using a road-book, see page 32.)

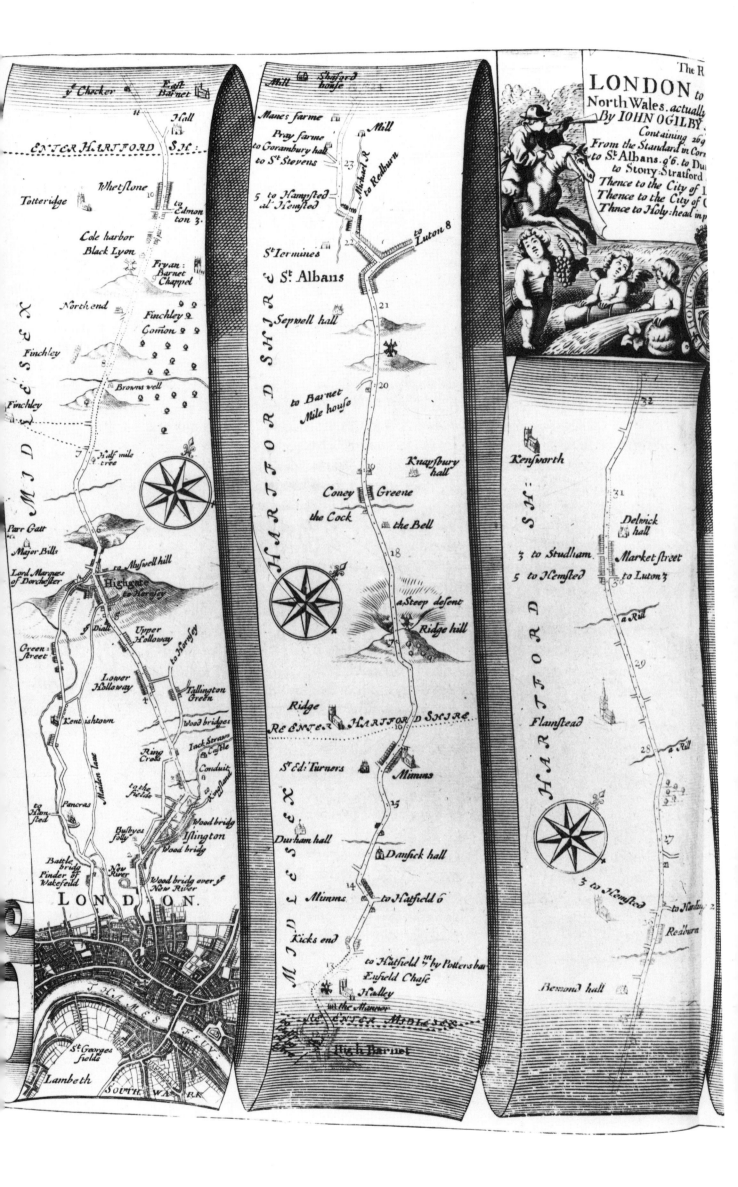

PLATE 14

Blackfriars from *A Large & Accurate Map of the City of London*

by John Ogilby and William Morgan, 1676

Howgego and Darlington, no. 28

This is a true map, with no perspective details apart from the boats on the river, and those by the bank at least are seen as though from directly above. In the section reproduced, Ogilby shows the traditional literary and judicial enclave of the City, with the booksellers along Paternoster Row and Old Bailey convenient for Stationers' Hall where all publications were licensed, and the King's Printing House in Play House Yard, now the home of *The Times*. The Sessions House on Old Bailey (its modern equivalent is the Central Criminal Court) disappeared long since, as has the Fleet Prison on the bank of Wren's New Canal, destroyed in the riots of 1780, then rebuilt and finally replaced by railway lines in the 1860s.

The Fleet itself was to disappear underground within 70 years and is now the site of New Bridge Street, leading to Blackfriars Bridge.

Ogilby has indicated along the two main thoroughfares, Ludgate and Newgate Streets, the line of posts erected to protect foot passengers from passing traffic. The lines of larger dots denote ward and parish boundaries, and the system of lettered and numbered references, more elaborate than on any earlier map, enabled the smallest alleys and courts to be identified, making this map the starting-point for any look backward into the topography and place names of the vanishing city. The Fire devastated this area but did not destroy traditional boundaries, and in the rebuilding both old plans and old names were retained – the major exception being St. Paul's, which was shifted slightly from its medieval axis, to provide a finer vista from Ludgate Hill.

Bishopshead Court

Little

Old Baily

Fleet Lane

FLEET

B.77

i.21

i.22

i.23

i.28

81

i.30

11

Sessions House Yard

Phisitians

College B.37

Warwick Court

B.78

B

C

AMEN CORNER

Stationers Hall

18

i.38

S:t Martin Ludgate Church & Yard

B.36

B.35

B.38

82 108

Newgate

Market

Warwick Lane

Ave mary Lane

C

PATER B NOSTER

C

124

82

St PA

STREET

LVDGATE HILL A Ludgate B LVDGATE STREET

A

B

FLEET DITCH

NEW CANAL

A

79

street

ELL

i.19

78

k.60

k.60

Black Fryers

Shoomaker Row 80

80

C.1

C.2

k.76

k.62 B

k.80

k.61

The Kings Printinghouse

B

k.11

m.8

Black Friers

Charles Street

Bridget Street

Samsers Lane

Holliday Court

81 k.70

k.60

k.70

Church yard

S. Ann Black Fryare Church

k.67

k.71

k.73

k.74

k.75

m.12

Duke Humphrys

m.8

m.8

m.11

Greedo Lane

B

C

Puddle Dock

C

83

the King's Wardrobe was here

S. Andrew Wardrobe Church & Yard

St PAULS

C.6

C.6

C.7

CARTER C LANE

C.8

C.9

Addle Hill

Knight

82

Rider

C.10

m.12

m.16

m.35

m.15

THAMES

Wharfe

Black Friers Staires

Wharfe

Wharfe

Baynards Castle

VER OF

PLATE 15

London Bridge to the Royal Exchange from *A Large & Accurate Map of the City of London*

by John Ogilby and William Morgan, 1676

Howgego and Darlington, no. 28
ed. H. W. Robinson. *Diary of Robert Hooke 1672–80*, 1935

This, the heart of the city, epitomises the traditional features of urban life within the walls. The small and narrow house-plots, the churches and halls set back from the street-line and embedded in buildings, the lack of open ground, the many churches side by side, each in its own tiny parish, and the strong flow of routes angled east to west across the city, following the contour lines, all are characteristic of the medieval city, unaffected by the Fire and the subsequent rebuilding. Ogilby has indicated the interior plans of those churches already rebuilt and the blank sites of those still in ruins and included the widened Thames quay and the improved roads uphill from the river, but in essence the ground-plan is that of the medieval city.

In preparing this map Ogilby had almost daily meetings at Garraway's coffee-house with Robert Hooke, Curator of Experiments to the Royal Society, who recommended the scale finally used (100 foot to 1 inch) when on 19th July 1673 he saw the first draft sheet prepared by William Leybourne. Six months later he approved the first engraved sheet to the new scale. He invented the style of lettering used for the many references on the map and no doubt his knowledge of French cartographic method was invaluable to Ogilby, whose varied career as dancing master and theatre manager had included no formal training in map-making, although he had the services of several of the city surveyors in making the map.

Hooke contributed also to Ogilby's road-book, published in 1675, although he was unable to persuade him to use his unique waywiser, a covered carriage for measuring the road in comfort reminiscent of an 18th-century velocipede. Ogilby's footwheel is depicted in the frontispiece to the *Britannia*.

PLATE 16

Plan of tenements in Cheapside owned by Christ's Hospital

1676

Guildhall Library, Print Room

A. Hall, 'The Estates of the Corporation of London', *Guildhall Miscellany* 17, 1956

This plot at the corner of Cheapside and Blow Bladder Street still exists today, in an angle between Foster Lane and St. Martin-le-Grand. The plan was prepared to accompany and illustrate a lease of Christ's Hospital land, a precaution which was an innovation of the late 17th century, after the Fire had given an impetus to the establishing of exact boundary lines. The traditional method of recording boundaries (by reciting abuttals and measurements in the lease) was retained, but the plan provided a new and valuable supplement.

Some indication of the utter confusion of property-ownership in the city appears in this plan, where in two areas of a single relatively small plot the Hospital owned only the structures above ground 'built upon Christ Hospitall Land intire from the shopp to the Topp of the Same'. The cellars below, 'since stopped upp by Tennants, belonged to the Grocers' Company.' In all, seven separate occupiers divided the narrow site between them, sharing the access passages to Cheapside and Foster Lane (A & I on the plan).

Two of the surveyors attesting to the truth of the plan, John Oliver and Robert Hooke, had been employed by the City as sworn surveyors after the Fire, to establish property boundaries which might otherwise have been in dispute when rebuilding began. Their official survey drawings, comparable in technique to this example, but of individual house sites only, have been preserved in fair copy in the Guildhall and published in their entirety by the London Topographical Society.

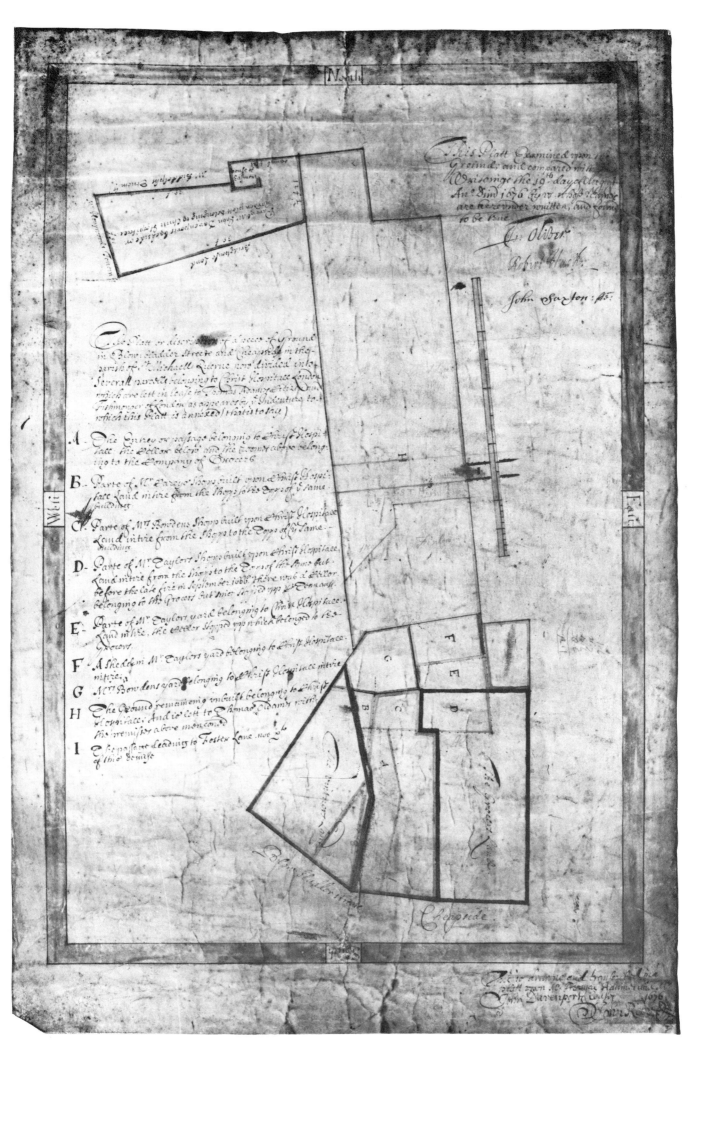

PLATE 17

East of London Bridge
from *London etc.*
Actually Survey'd

by William Morgan, 1681–2

Howgego and Darlington, no. 33

This section may be compared with Ogilby's version of the same area (plate 15). In spite of the close professional and family relationship between the two men, Morgan's map shows considerable differences in approach and technique. He has raised the prominent buildings in elevation, to add to the beauty of the map, and gives tiny but recognisable views of the Pillar commemorating the Fire on New Fish Street, Bethlem Hospital (recently rebuilt to the design of Robert Hooke) and the turrets and storehouses of the Tower, together with each church in the area rebuilt after the Fire.

In 1666 the Fire did not sweep right up to the city wall in the east, and two important buildings survived, Gresham College and the medieval priory church of St. Helens off Bishopsgate Street. Adjoining the latter was the fine stone house built by Sir John Crosby, the only domestic building to survive from the medieval city, whose hall now stands on Chelsea Embankment. Gresham College, founded by Sir Thomas Gresham in his house in Broad Street, was used for lectures under his will until 1768, and the earliest meetings of the Royal Society were held there.

With the shift of residents westward during the 17th century, the city's rôle as a financial and marketing centre became more marked. The great ships moored by Billingsgate Dock are a reminder that London's wealth depended on seaborne trade; until the dock system was created a century later, merchantmen were forced to crowd upstream near the Custom House. Within the city walls the spires of Leadenhall, principal market for leather, remained a major attraction for traders from the country, a vital element in its prosperity, as it had been since the 15th century. They were still forced to use the narrow routes through Aldgate and Bishopsgate, unchanged from the middle ages, although within 25 years came the first breach in the wall, when a section by Bishopsgate was demolished.

The influence of the old precincts is still apparent on the map; the irregular plot between Fenchurch Street and 'Crouched Friers', site of a pre-Reformation religious house, was not yet fully built over.

PLATE 18

The West End from
London etc. Actually Survey'd

by William Morgan, 1681–2

Howgego and Darlington, no. 33
C. L. Kingsford, *Piccadilly, Leicester Square and Soho*, 1925

The familiar section of London from Tottenham Court Road to Trafalgar Square is hard to recognise on this 300-year-old map. The wide sweep of Regent Street, New Oxford Street, Shaftesbury Avenue, Charing Cross Road and Trafalgar Square itself were all improvements of the 19th century.

Tortuous routes from north to south still followed the lines of old field boundaries, the close rural past recalled by Hedge Lane (Whitcomb Street), Dirty Lane (Irving Street), Windmill Street and Shug Lane (under Piccadilly Circus). The Haymarket retained its original function as a fodder and cattle market three times a week, until 1834 and its removal to Regent's Park. The irregular shape of Leicester Fields is still reflected in the trapezium of Leicester Square. Fifteen years after the map was published Seven Dials was laid out in the marshland of Cock and Pye Fields. The royal stables remained at Charing Cross until 1830; the entrance to the National Gallery now stands on the north wall of the mews yard.

The Stuart expansion of the area is reflected in its churches. St. Martin in the Fields was rebuilt in 1607 and again in 1722, acquiring a new churchyard behind the royal mews in 1668; St. Pauls Covent Garden, Inigo Jones's 'barn', was opened in 1638, St. James's Piccadilly in 1684 for 'noblemen and persons of quality' attracted by the new court suburb, and the newly-built Greek Church in Hog Lane (Charing Cross Road) was to be taken over by the fast-growing French community in Soho a year after this map was published.

Around Gregory King's as yet unnamed square – now Soho Square – well-known streets were not as yet entirely built up. Frith Street was 'graced with good buildings especially towards Soho', but Dean Street remained merely a dotted line on the map and there was still waste ground between Dean Street and Wardour Street when Strype's account was published in 1720. The area saw the earliest attempts at speculative development in London, first by the Bedfords, then after the Civil War by the Earl of St. Albans, Colonel Thomas, Panton, and Nicholas Barbon.

PLATE 19

Western section of the home counties from *A Map .. Twenty Miles Round London*

by Robert Morden, 1686

Howgego and Darlington, no. 36

The earliest map to show London in its surrounding countryside had been published two years before, under the imprint of Ogilby and Morgan. (A unique copy is in the Royal Library at Windsor.) The subject was to become increasingly popular in the 18th and 19th centuries, as the demand for printed maps increased. (Compare plates 28, 34.) The county map was inappropriate as a vehicle to demonstrate the growing streets of London in relation to the country homes of her prosperous inhabitants; Morden was well aware of his potential market when he claimed that the map contained 'Gentlemens Houses around London'. They are carefully differentiated in the key from 'Ordinary Houses' by a miniature castle.

The rural character of the home counties was already disappearing; the river valleys in Surrey and Middlesex are dotted with mills, using water-power in the manufacture of gunpowder, paper, iron, and copper and to grind corn for the London food market. Great enpaled parks still dominated the map, however – some noble, some royal game preserves, with at Nonsuch the remains of Henry VIII's Renaissance masterpiece slowly slipping into ruin.

London stopped short to the west at Hyde Park, with 'Lising Green' and Newington separate hamlets, but country villages such as Kingston and Croydon within a comfortable day's ride of London, i.e., something over 10 miles, were filling up with gentlemen's houses, in the gradual process whereby they have now become mere place-names in the mass of Greater London. The bridging point at Kingston was a natural area of growth, since there were as yet no other bridges connecting Surrey and Middlesex, and traffic to the royal palace at Hampton Court and along the post-roads to the west was always busy.

Morden was careful to provide the apparatus of a key and numbered grid for references, which at the time were not standard, but he includes some information irrelevant today, such as the names and boundaries of the 'hundreds' into which counties were divided. His picturesque delineation of hills is also strange to the modern eye; the problem of showing contours was not satisfactorily solved in English cartography until Rocque introduced the French method of hatching in the mid-18th century.

PLATE 20

An estate off
Bishopsgate Street,
from the Survey taken
for the Goldsmiths'
Company

by John Ward, 1692

Goldsmiths' Company MSS.

The Goldsmiths', like other great city companies, owned extensive properties in and around London. Some, such as certain shops and houses in Cheapside, had traditionally been reserved for working goldsmiths free of the company, whose work was thereby subject to control and supervision. Others, like the cottages shown in this survey, were let out at commercial rents, to contribute to the ever-increasing wealth of the company.

Primrose Alley, now Primrose Road, still exists today, bisecting the network of railway lines into Broad Street and Liverpool Street stations. The area was relatively damp and insalubrious; the Shore indicated on the map was one of the rivulets draining out of Finsbury Fields which can be seen on the Tudor copperplate map (plate 2). Few of the two-storey cottages are more than 15 feet wide, and most have workshops in their backyards, indicating that the inhabitants were principally then, as they remained until the mid-20th century, small craftsmen. The pressure on Stuart London of its growing population is clear in this maze of crowded buildings, gardens and yards, each with its privy at the bottom of the garden.

Until the late 17th century the company was content to rely on the medieval method of estate surveys, where properties were listed and their bounds and abuttals given verbally, but no permanent visual record was made. The Fire of 1666 demonstrated the inadequacies of this ancient system, and the City's lead in employing professional surveyors to make plans was followed by many institutions and large private owners. Unfortunately the methods used by Leybourne, King and the rest in their surveys were far in advance of those adopted by John Ward, whose results were less accomplished than Elizabethan estate plans of a century earlier.

The survey, on massive sheets of parchment, is legible, decorative and highly coloured, but as an example of accurate surveying utterly unconvincing. Its inadequacy was recognised within half a century. In 1738 the Court of Assistants graciously accepted and approved a report from the then clerk to the company, criticising 'the plans drawne at a large expense in 1692'; they 'are very imperfect and in particular do not shew Six houses standing in a court in Great New Street demised in 1666 to Ferdenando Gorges'. The clerk, Thomas Bankes, then revealed that he had at great pains and at a cost of £300 filled the gap with a new survey, made by himself during the previous nine years. This second survey, also still retained by the company, is far less gaudy than Ward's, but neat, workmanlike and apparently accurate.

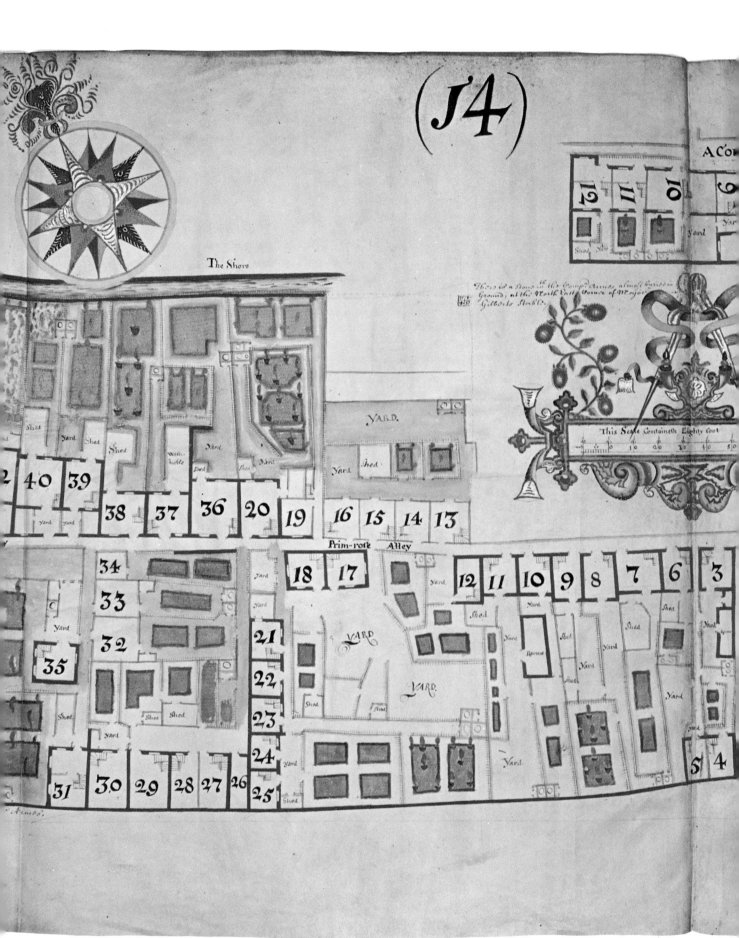

(J4)

The Shore

A Co[...]

12 11 10 9

Yard Yar[d]

Shed Sho[...]

There is a Stone w.th the Comp.ys Armes almost buried in
Ground, at the North East Corner of M.r. John
Gilbert's Stable

This Scale Containeth Eighty foot

Yard

Shed

Yard

Shed

Shed Yard Shed Shed
Shed
Wash-house Shed Yard Shed

40 39
38 37 36 20 19 16 15 14 13

Yard Yard

Prim-rose Alley

34
33
32
35

31 30 29 28 27 26

Yard

Yard

Yard

Shed Shed

Yard

18 17
21
22
23
24
25

Yard
Yard
Yard
Yard
Shed

YARD
YARD

Shed Shed

Shed

Shed

12 11 10 9 8 7 6 3

Shed
Roome
Yard
Shed
Yard

Yard

Yard Shed

Yard
Yard

Yard

Yard
Yard

Yard

5 4

PLATE 21

Central London from
the *Actuall Survey of
London, Westminster and
Southwark*

by Robert Morden and
Philip Lea, 1700

Howgego and Darlington, no. 42

This popular map, first published about 1690, was from its size (22½ × 38 inches) suitable to be included in the collection of maps published by Herman Moll in 1709, the form in which many copies have survived in gentlemen's libraries. This copy is from the royal topographical collections in the British Museum.

The late-Stuart building boom had affected this area less dramatically than Soho, further to the west, but the town was spreading northwards continually towards the New River Head and Sadler's Wells, and the taverns and bowling greens of Islington increased in popularity among Londoners anxious to escape the 'Cathars, Phthisicks, Coughs and Consumptions' of the city. London Spa, the chalybeate springs north of Clerkenwell, and the tavern called the 'Pinder of Wakefield' on Gray's Inn Road, were to disappear in the following century.

Islington was linked to the city by a busy road; cattle and sheep from the north-west rested in the pens there overnight before the last stage of their journey to Smithfield. Further west St. Pancras was an isolated village, north of Battle Bridge, under which the Fleet or Holborne river ran. Its church 'standeth alone as utterly forsaken old and weather-beaten.'

Lamb's Conduit Street recalls the former site of the conduit built by William Lamb, master of the Clothworkers' Company, in 1577 to supply water in lead pipes to the Snow Hill district, near Newgate and the Fleet. The conduit was moved to Red Lion Square when the Foundling Hospital was built in the 1740's.

The conflict between river and road traffic continued at this time. At the foot of each narrow alley running down to the river boats clustered for hire, while in the wide street running east to west hackney carriages and sedan chairs awaited customers. Von Uffenbach, who visited London in 1710, preferred a wherry or skiff to 'the Heckney-Coaches, which jolt most terribly'.

Wells

Battle Bridg

Rinder of Wakefield

White Conduit

Sheep Penns

Prospect house

Bowling

Part of Islington

Sadlers Well

New River Pond

Black Marys Well

Londons Spaw

Dr Newtons

Words close

St John Oldcastles

Ducking Pond

The Road to Kenwish Tow *Hampstead*

Lambs Conduit

The Long Walk

Grays Inn

44

15

T

Smith Hall

HIGH HOLBORN

HOLBORN

14

Lincolns Inne Fields

LUDG

FLEET STREET

Temple Bar

Temple

S

Covent Garden

STRAND

Temple Stairs

Arundel Stairs

Part

T

C

S

5

RIVE

R *I* *V* *E*

PLATE 22

*An Actual Survey of the
Hamlet of Lime-House*

by Joel Gascoyne, 1703

This, part of a larger survey of the vast parish of Stepney, is the first reliable map of Lime-house. It lay well outside the city's limit and therefore beyond the scope of maps of London before the 19th century, and as the hamlet was divided among many owners there is no comprehensive estate plan in manuscript, although the Haberdashers' Company has surveys of some parts of the parish.

The hamlet was an ancient one: the limekilns were first mentioned in the 15th century, and the surrounding market gardens continued to supply London's markets until the building of the docks a century after this survey was taken. Parts of the hamlet are still recognisable on the modern map; Limehouse Dock, now called Lime Kiln Dock, the Causeway, Three Colt Lane and Ropemaker's Field still exist, although Rose Lane has been swallowed up in the Commercial Road, which meets Three Colt Street to the east of Limehouse Cut. The Cut was the earliest of the canals which bisected the east end of London; it was opened in 1770 to bypass the crowded curve of the Thames between Limehouse and the mouth of the river Lea. The Regent's Canal had its easterly outlet here, disgorging barges conveniently close to the new docks.

Limehouse was part of the Tower Hamlets, the 21 settlements which together provided a night-watch of 500-odd as part of their service to the Lieutenant of the Tower. The custom was still exacted in 1641, but late Stuart and Georgian separatism and the influx of immigrants led to the creation of new parishes here. Limehouse became a separate parish in 1730. Hawksmoor's St. Anne's Church stands proudly at the corner of Three Colt Lane and Rose Lane.

Gascoyne's map brings out the predominance of market gardens in the hamlet; these, together with ship-building and its attendant crafts such as rope-making, dominated the area until the 19th century.

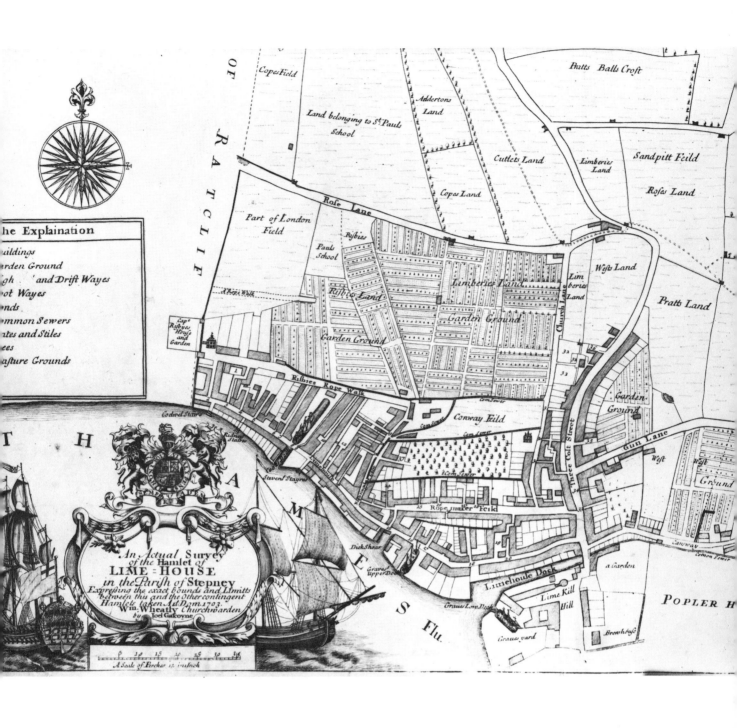

OF RATCLIF

Copes Field

Pratts Balls Croft

Adderttons Land

Land belonging to St Pauls School

Cutlets Land

Limberies Land

Sandpitt Feild

Copes Land

Roses Land

Rose Lane

The Explaination

uildings
arden Ground
gh ' and Drift Wayes
ot Wayes
nds
mmon Sewers
tes and Stiles
es
asture Grounds

Part of London Feild

Pauls School

Risbies

Limberies Land

West Land

Risbies Land

Lim beries Land

Pratts Land

Capt Risbyes House and Garden

Garden Ground

Garden Ground

Church Lane

Garden Ground

H

T

Codwels Stayrs

Risbies Rope Walk

Conway Feild

Garden Ground

Gun Lane

West

Ground

A

Steven Stayrs

Three Colt Street

M

Dick Shoar

Rope maker Feild

West

Canway

E

Graves upper Dock

Limehoule Dock

a Garden

S Flu.

Graues Lane Dock

Lime Kill Hill

An Actual Survey
of the Hamlet of
LIME=HOUSE
in the Parish of Stepney
Expressing the exact bounds and Limitts
between this and the other contingent
Hamlets taken A.st Dom.1703.
Wm. Wheatly Churchwarden
by Joel Gascoyne

Graues yard

Brewhoule

POPLER H

A Scale of Perches 12 in Inch

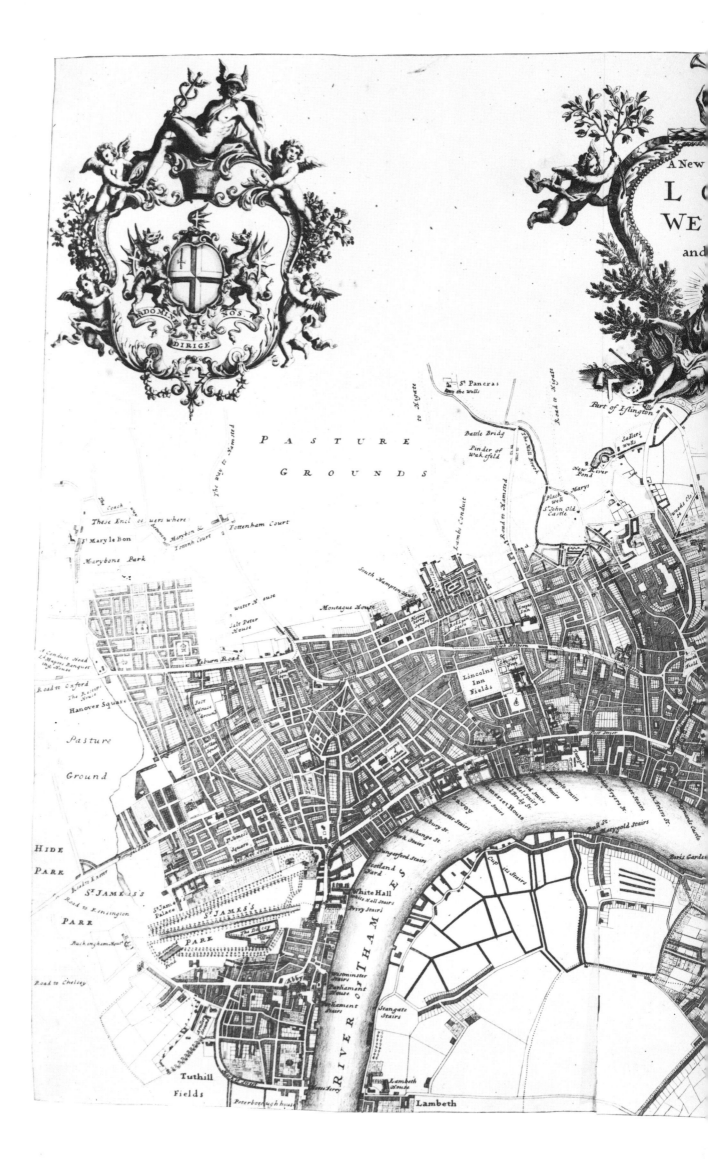

CITY of
ON,
STER,
WARK.

PART OF HACKNEY

Cambridge
Heath

Bishops Hall

Hoxton

Reed to Newington

Habberdashers
Hospitall

Cold Harbour

Nags Head

Taylor Row

way to Old Ford

Bun Hill
Fields

City Church
Yard

Artillery
Ground

Upper
Moore
Fields

Ivie Close

Bednal Green

Bednal Row

Norwich Road

Mile End

Mile End
Green

Stepney

Salmon L.

White Horse Lane

Hangmans
Acre

Rose Lane

Redmans
field

Gun
Clos

St. Paul Shadwell

Garden
Grounds

RIVER of THAMES

New Cran

King Edward St.

Execution Dock

London
Bridg

Kent Stairs

Battle Bridg

Kent St.

Wind Mill St.

Marriners St.
Salisbury St.
Fountain St.
Cherry Garden St.
Gold St.

Wapping Stairs

High Street

A Scale of ¼ Mile containing 2640 Feet

PLATE 23 *(overleaf)*

*A New Plan of the City
of London, Westminster
& Southwark*

by John Strype, 1720

Howgego and Darlington, no. 66
ed. John Strype, *Survey of the Cities of
London & Westminster, by John Stow,* 1720

Strype's map catches London in the aftermath of its Restoration building boom and before the dramatic physical extensions of the later 18th-century estate developers.

Chelsea, Kensington and Greenwich were all excluded, being royal villages outside the immediate orbit of London. Familiar inner London suburbs, Islington and St. Pancras, remain outlying settlements, supplying water, hay and pasture land for the capital. Bond Street was already open, and New Bond Street, completing the link across the fields between Piccadilly and the road to Oxford, was to be opened in 1721, as the neat squares spread into west London, forerunners of the great 18th- and 19th-century estates in Mayfair, Belgravia and St. John's Wood. The Lord Mayor's rural banqueting-house, now Stratford Place north of Oxford Street, scene of feasts after hunting parties, was gradually being surrounded, as was the ancient conduit which stood by Piccadilly and supplied water to the city via St. James's, Charing Cross and Fleet Street.

Long, narrow house-plots behind the street frontages, characteristic of an urban plan, mark developments on the outskirts of south and east London. To the north and west, more deliberate planning was possible, resulting in the regular outlines of Seven Dials, Lincoln's Inn Fields, St. James's Square and Hanover Square, with Wellclose Square, as yet unnamed, a solitary neatness in east London. On the map Mile End is seen for what it was, the first hamlet the traveller met on his journey outward from London, a mile east of the wall along the Norwich road. Each of the main roads is named for its ultimate destination – Oxford, Exeter, Norwich, Newington, Hampstead and Chelsea.

PLATE 24 *(opposite)*

Farringdon Ward Without

by John Strype, 1720

ed. J. Strype, *A Survey of the Cities of London
& Westminster, by John Stow,* 1720
R. Hyde, 'Ward Maps of the City of London,'
Map-Collectors' Circle 38, 1967

The large ward of Farringdon stretched from Smithfield market to the Temple and lay astride two major routes into the city, Holborn and Fleet Street. For this reason it was from early in the middle ages a fashionable and populous area, crammed with episcopal inns and legal houses. The ward was divided into sections within and without the wall as early as 1394, evidence of pressure of population, and the two medieval churches, St. Andrews Holborn and St. Bride's, Fleet Street, had each to be enlarged in the 15th century.

By the date of Strype's map, hints of a decline in the residential status of the area were apparent. Sanctuary for criminals in 'Alsatia', Whitefriars had finally been abolished in 1697, but a lead-glass factory, the earliest in England, was by then working in the old monastic precinct, where it was to remain for two and a half centuries, while the Duke's Theatre in Salisbury Court was a further indication of the shift of fashionable entertainment westward, away from Blackfriars. The prison and reformatory in Bridewell Palace founded by Edward VI had been burnt in the Great Fire, but was rebuilt and continued on the site until 1863. The Fleet river, newly canalised as part of the badly needed improvements in this area, was already threatened. North of Holborn Bridge a block of buildings straddled the stream – ominous sign of its disappearance underground.

The legal flavour of the area, firmly set in the middle ages and still persisting today, is clear on the map in the lawyers' houses flanking Holborn, Fleet Street and Chancery Lane, some, like Lincoln's Inn and the Temple, still the homes of lawyers, others, the Chancery Inns called Thavies', Clifford's and Barnard's, swept away in the legal reforms of the 19th century.

The scale of the map does not permit the marking of wells and conduits, but already by this date much of the water supply to houses in the ward was carried under the roads from St. Pancras and Islington in elm pipes, which frequently turn up today in diggings in the area.

The map-maker has used the technique of elevating significant buildings, a trick already old-fashioned by the date when the map was published; this may be understandable since it has been suggested that the map was originally taken by Richard Blome from William Morgan's map of 40 years earlier. (Morgan had advertised his willingness to supply ward maps, a new departure in London cartography.)

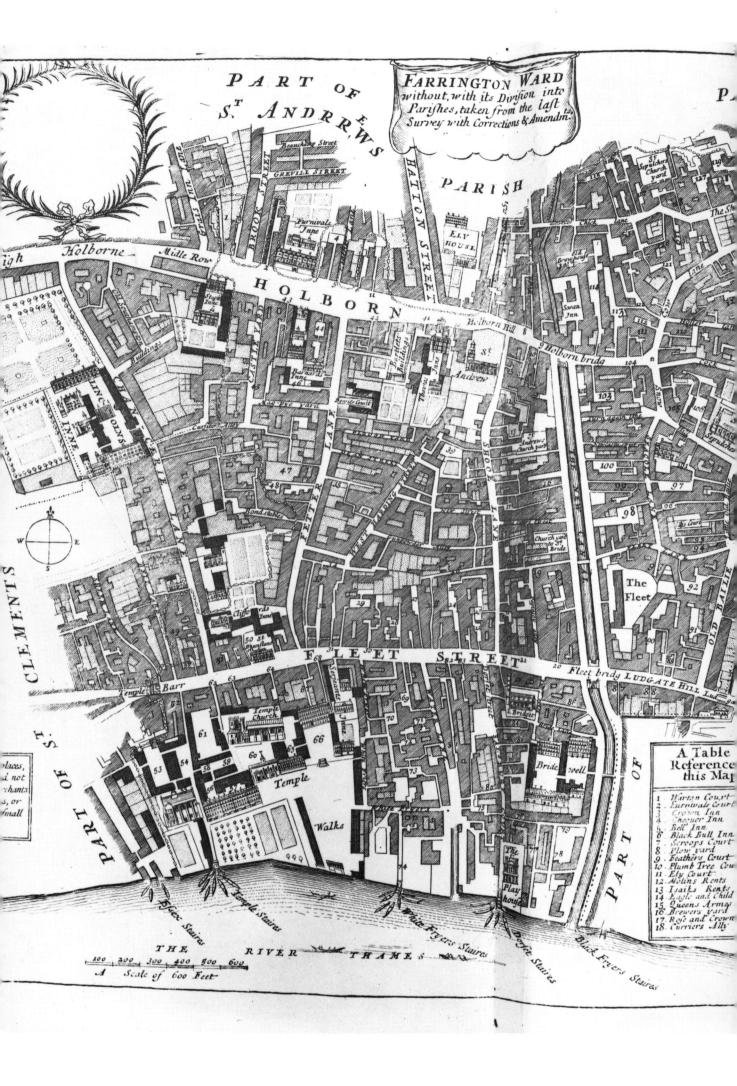

PLATE 25

Westminster from *A New and Exact Plan of the Cities of London and Westminster*

by George Foster, 1738

Howgego and Darlington, no. 82

Foster's map is typical of those published in large numbers in the early 18th century, showing little awareness of the surveying and cartographic innovations of Restoration map-makers such as Morgan and Seller (compare plates 17 and 18). He uses pictorial symbols for churches, hospitals and market houses and gives little sketches of public statues, such as those in Grosvenor Square and the garden of Marlborough House, but omits others, presumably from lack of space – notably the famous equestrian statue of Charles I at Charing Cross.

The map demonstrates the rapid growth of Westminster, in both area and population, which had taken place in the previous half-century. Some streets remained unfinished in Mayfair, but otherwise the block of land between Piccadilly and Oxford Street was entirely built over, with further fashionable development on the Harley estate in Marylebone.

The new streets were concentrated in the north and west of London because of the royal parks, which impeded building to the south-west. The village of Kensington lay two miles to the west, beyond Hyde Park, and although it had acquired a palace and a square, was not yet the court suburb it was to become in the following century. The ancient city of Westminster was by no means an aristocratic enclave, in spite of the royal and noble houses in St. James's. A poll book of the following decade, which gives the occupations of nine and a half thousand ratepayers, lists almost 400 different trades, of which 'victualling' was the most common.

The new bridge at Westminster, shown by Foster in elevation, the first to be built since the middle ages, had not yet been completed and was not to be opened for 12 years. Water transport predominated, as the numerous stairs along the Thames in Westminster imply, and Foster furnished purchasers of his map with additional information in the form of official tables of watermen's fares and hackney coach rates.

The elaborate dedicatory cartouches and the arms of the city companies are typical 18th-century embellishments, as is Foster's claim to 'show more than any map hitherto published'!

PLATE 26

North of Oxford Street
from a *Plan of the Cities
of London & Westminster*

by John Rocque, 1746

Howgego and Darlington, no. 96

Oxford Street, formerly the Tyburn Road or the way to Uxbridge, was already acquiring by this period some aspects of its modern character – wide, busy and thronged with people enjoying the shops. In 1786 the German tourist, Sophie von la Roche, commented favourably on the window displays ('some goods look more attractive by artificial light') and on the row of coaches parked in the middle of the carriage way.

To the north stood several great houses, although these were to change owners and decline in status as their aristocratic original builders moved away from the encroaching streets. Bingley House, facing Cavendish Square, was described by Ralph's *Critical Review* as 'rather a convent than the residence of a man of quality', from its eccentric plan. Also fronting Cavendish Square was the uncompleted mansion of the Duke of Chandos, of which the side-wings only were erected before his death in 1744. Both can be seen in this detail.

This section of Oxford Street has been transformed by Nash's creation of Oxford Circus and Portland Place; Balsover Street disappeared and Portland Place now runs up Ogle Street to the pivot of All Souls Church, opened in 1824, and across the Marylebone Basin. The Portland estate was one of the first to build deliberately not only elegant terraces for the prosperous, but also subsidiary alleys and a market for tradespeople; Oxford market functioned from 1731 to 1876.

Place names on the maps emphasise the significance of the horse as the basic force in all passenger and goods traffic; mews and stable yards were a necessary evil in every part of the metropolis, however fashionable. The modern map shows today's equivalent, a car park, within a few yards of Stable Yard and Blenheim Mews, opposite Market Street.

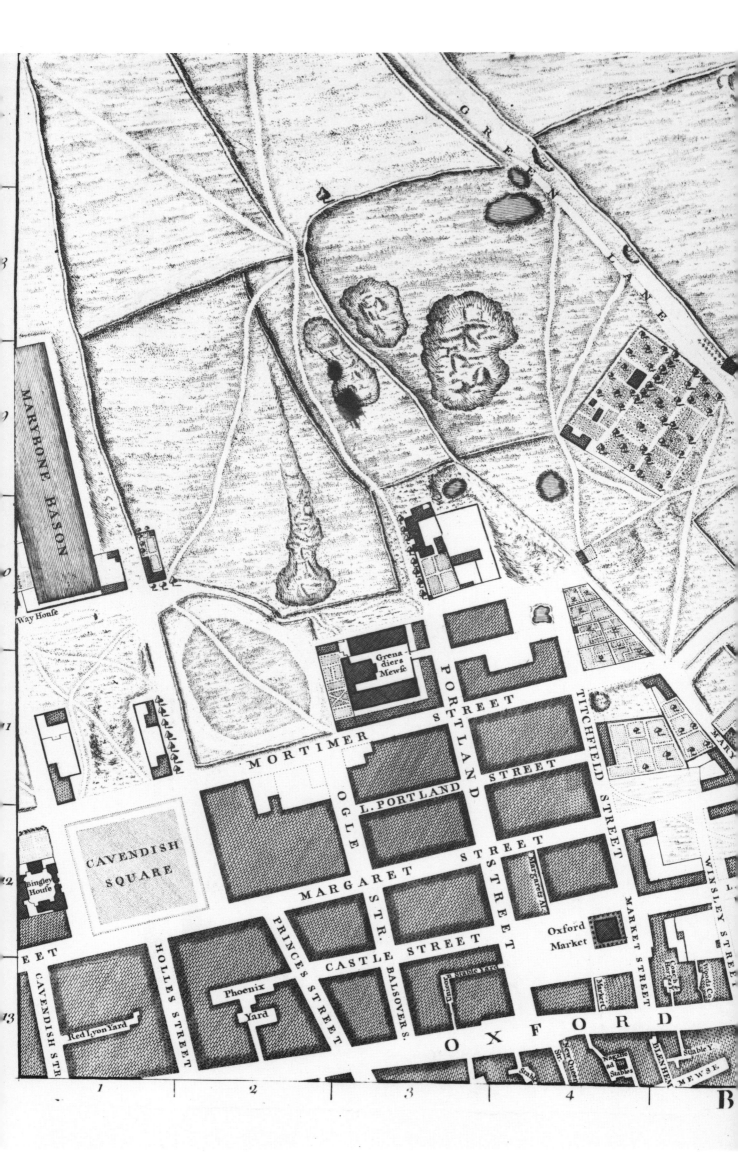

GREEN LANE

MARYBONE BASON

Way House

Grena-
diers Mewse

PORTLAND STREET

TITCHFIELD STREET

MARY

MORTIMER

L. PORTLAND STREET

OGLE STR.

Margarets Alley

WINSLEY STREET

CAVENDISH
SQUARE

MARGARET STREET

STREET

Bingley
House

Oxford
Market

MARKET STREET

CASTLE STREET

PRINCES STREET

BALSOVERS.

Stable Yard

Broad

St.

Pophams Ct.

EET

HOLLES STREET

Phoenix
Yard

O X F O R D

CAVENDISH STR.

Red Lyon Yard

New Queen
Str.

Stable

Nag's Head
ad
Stables

BLENHEIM

Stable Y.

MEWSE

1   2   3   4   B

PLATE 27

Park Lane from a *Plan of the Cities of London & Westminster etc.*

by John Rocque, 1746

Howgego and Darlington, no. 96

Rocque's large-scale map of London in the mid-18th century is justly famous, both as the first since the post-Fire years and as an expression of the Georgian expansion of London.

The great land-owners to the west of London were quick to appreciate the new demand for elegant town houses, and Mayfair was created in the first half of the century; Hyde Park, though open to the fashionable world for promenades, blocked the building frontier to the west, and the land to the north of Oxford Street was to be developed in the following half-century.

Grosvenor Square, largely created by 1725, had from the first an aristocratic reputation. Its connection with the United States began in 1785, when the first American minister to Great Britain, John Adams, moved into number 9. In spite of its noble inhabitants, however, the area retained the public gallows at Tyburn, to which vast crowds streamed out of London when a popular or notorious criminal was to be executed. The lack of civilian police and the danger of urban riot required that troops should be permanently stationed around London's outskirts, and the barracks at Knightsbridge, together with those at Horse Guards, were occupied at all times. The extensive stabling required had to be spread among the surrounding streets for ease of access; three stables can be seen off Tyburn Lane.

A point of interest in the map is Rocque's indication of the impact of London's new buildings; within the wall of Hyde Park are diggings, either for road-mending material or for brick-earth to supply the brick kilns south of Knightsbridge. Within the avenue of ornamental trees lies a reservoir supplying water to the inhabitants of the west end. Rocque himself may have taken his water from the Chelsea Company's Reservoir; his shop stood next to the Duke of Grafton's Head, at the Hyde Park end of Piccadilly.

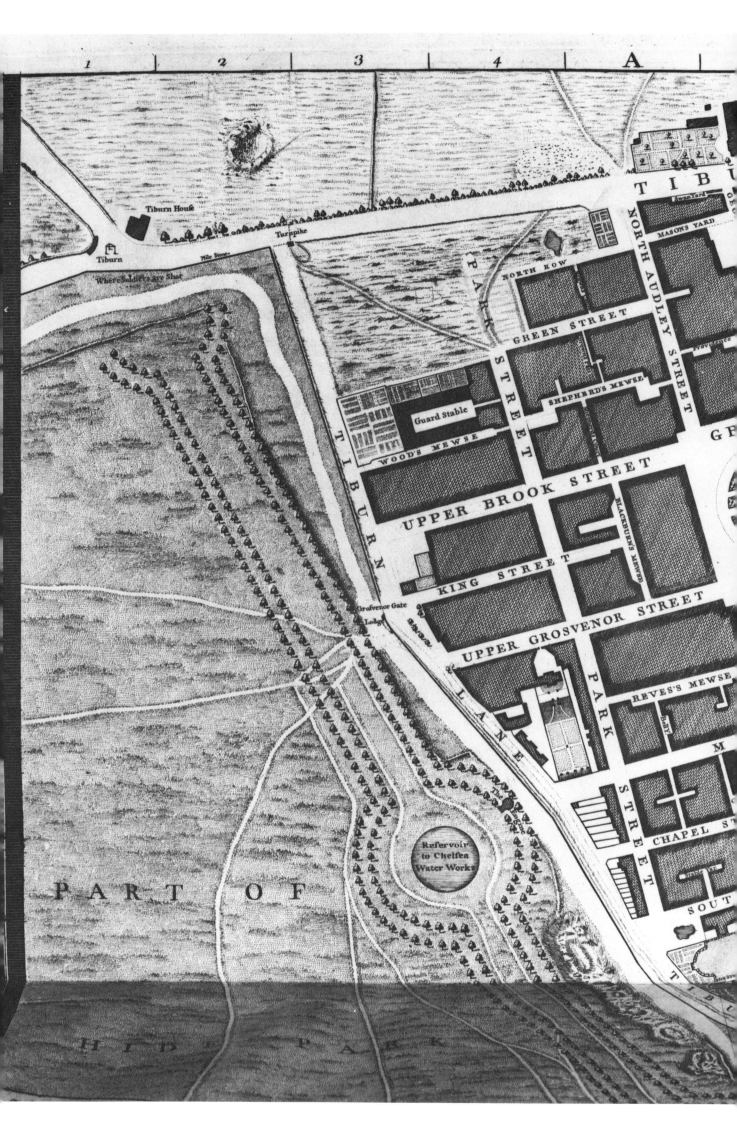

Tiburn House

Tiburn

Where Soldiers are Shot

Turnpike

Mile Stone

TIB

TIBURN

MASONS YARD

NORTH ROW

PARK

GREEN STREET

NORTH AUDLEY STREET

Providence

G

GR

SHEPHERD'S MEWSE

Guard Stable

WOOD'S MEWSE

TIBURN

UPPER BROOK STREET

BLACKBURN'S MEWSE

KING STREET

UPPER GROSVENOR STREET

LANE

Grosvenor Gate

Lodge

PARK

REVES'S MEWSE

M

STREET

CHAPEL ST

Reservoir to Chelsea Water Works

PART OF

SOUT

TIB

HIDE PARK

PLATE 28

Greenwich from *An Exact Survey of the City's of London, Westminster . . . and the Country near Ten Miles Round*

by John Rocque, 1746

Howgego and Darlington, no. 94

This section of Rocque's famous map includes several of the new features he introduced to English cartography. The hilly ground behind the Royal Hospital here shows to dramatic effect in his technique of *hachure*, while most of his land use symbols are included – marsh, market garden, orchard, ploughland, park and common.

Deptford and Greenwich were dominated by the navy and by sailors in retirement. The very place names are redolent of the activities of the naval yards – Archersmiths Alley and Home Pitt Hole, Lime Kiln Lane, Butt Lane, the Stowage. The Kings Yard had been founded by Henry VIII in 1513, and the hospital for distressed sailors by Mary II in 1694 on the site of the Tudor royal palace of Greenwich. Elsewhere industry dictated the character of the district. Mills working corn, leather and armour stood along the river Rother, with others grinding corn on Millwall. The Isle of Dogs, although as yet without permanent inhabitants, was a famous grazing ground, described by Strype as 'a fine rich level for fattening of cattle', and the horse-ferry to Greenwich was one of the busier cross-river links in the 18th century. The flats were to disappear in the next hundred years, partially excavated for docks and partially covered by new houses – many built by the ubiquitous Thomas Cubitt.

Many of the houses marked by Rocque still stand, notably along Crooms Hill, and the flavour of the winding streets of a small nautical community can still be felt in Greenwich.

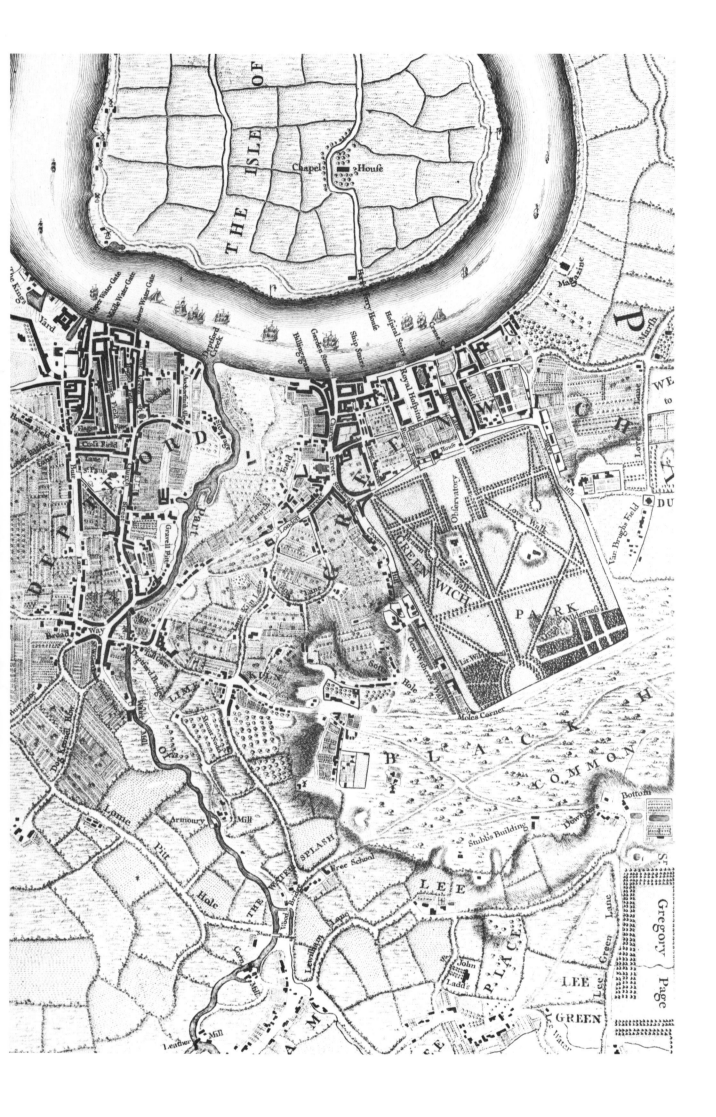

PLATE 29

South London

c 1740–50

British Museum, Map Room K 27.48.2

This manuscript plan of roads in Lambeth and Southwark, drawn and coloured on parchment, is from the royal topographical collections now in the British Museum Map Room. The precise purpose for which it was prepared is not indicated, but it differentiates between the new and old roads in the area and shows Lambeth Marsh and St. George's Fields before the modern road system was created, long before Dance erected his obelisk at St. George's Circus.

Because of the elaborate system of turnpikes on the few roads crossing the marsh between Westminster and Southwark, goods waggons found it expedient in the mid-18th century to take short-cuts across the marsh and so avoid the weigh-houses at the turnpikes, several of which are marked.

St. George's Fields were regarded as open to Londoners for enjoyment and for assemblies when public opinion was disturbed. Lord George Gordon's 'Good Protestants' paraded there in their thousands in June 1780. The earliest balloon ascents took place there. The Dog and Duck, so called from the shape of two ponds nearby, provided tea and ale, but was closed down in 1799 as the area lost its rural character. All common rights still existing in St. George's Fields were extinguished in 1810, and the builders moved in.

The mill, merrily turning upside-down in St. George's Fields, was a well-known south London landmark, and may have been the very one referred to by Justice Shallow when reminiscing with Falstaff. William Gardiner, the probable model for Shallow, was an Elizabethan justice of the peace of unpleasant character who acquired substantial properties in this area by various devices of dubious legality.

R I V

THE

LAMBETH

K. Arms

Pine Street

Orange

Falcon

The Banks Side

LONDON BRIDGE

WESTMINSTER

Lambeth Marsh

Turn-pike

St SAVIOURS

St Margaret

BOROUGH OF SOUTHWARK

St Olives Ch.

St Thomas's

St Tooly's Street

St GEORGES

Alms Houses

Mint Street

St Georges Church

St Johns Church

PALACE

LAMBETH Church.

RIDGE ROAD.

Alms Houses

FIELDS.

Blackman Street

Long Lane.

Free Iron Lane.

Dog and Duck

St Mary Mag

Bermon

Townsend

Fishmongers Alms Houses

Turn Pike.

THE

Kent Street

Three Coney Walk.

Lambeth Butts.

NEWING-

TON.

BRIDGE ROAD.

Lock Hospital

The Grange Ro

Vaux Gardens.

Kennington Lane.

The Turn Pike

Road.

Cock

Bull a

Turn Pike

Vaux Hall Bridge.

Turn Pike.

To Kennington Common.

WALWORTH.

Kent Street

Turn Pike.

To Ward

To SUSSEX.

To Clapham.

To Croydon.

Turn Pike.

Peckham Gap.

THE KEN

Stroms W

PLATE 30 (*opposite*)

Part of Hyde Park from
a *Survey of Kensington and
Hyde Park*

by Joshua Rhodes, engraved
by George Bickham, 1764

This massive picture-map, nine feet long and on a scale of 38 inches to the mile, brings out the essentially rural nature of London's western fringes two centuries ago.

Hyde Park was stocked with deer, and horses and cattle grazed there with them on licence. The two coach roads through the park, indicated by the numbers 95 and 96, were the old and new roads to Kensington Palace; the modern carriage road and Rotten Row continue the line of the latter. The main road at Knightsbridge was uncomfortable for fashionable traffic. It was heavily rutted, and Salway's survey for the turnpike trustees in 1811 shows that there was a considerable problem of surface water, particularly where the West Bourn crossed under the road. It was frequently clogged with traders' carts coming from the market gardens of Brompton and Chelsea with supplies for London; a heavily laden cart is being whipped up almost opposite the site of Harvey Nicholls' store, outside the Swan, 'the last House in Kensington Parish adjoining the City of Westminster'.

Within the Park stood the Ring, the scene of foot and horse races and of a nightly promenade by the coaches of the fashionable, entering by ticket at the gate at Hyde Park Corner. The Park was also the place for military parades and reviews, and a storehouse for gunpowder and ammunition stood in isolation north of the Serpentine. (The present magazine is a later building, erected at the time of the Napoleonic Wars.)

PLATE 31 (*pages 132–133*

East London from
*A Topographical Map of
the County of Middlesex*

by John Rocque, 1754

Gough rated Rocque only fourth among those contemporary map-makers who were publishing county 'surveys on large scales' but without doubt he was the premier in producing maps of the London region, whether specifically of London or, like this one, maps of the home counties which only incidentally included the capital.

Rocque's particular value lies not only in the scale he used but also in his record of land use. The Middlesex map shows quite clearly that the country was still predominantly agricultural, despite the comment by Thomas Coxe in 1724 that 'we may call it almost all London being inhabited chiefly by the citizens . . . that they may breathe a little sweet air, free from the fog and smoke of the City'.

The eastern part of the county was mostly enclosed by this period, apart from the water-meadows along the river Lea, and in the late 18th century turnips grown in Middlesex were feeding London's stall-kept dairy cows.

The parishes of the bills of mortality, enclosed within a dotted line marked by crossed bones, were those whose clerks made weekly returns to the Parish Clerks' Company of all deaths from whatever cause. These crude statistics, first collected by the Crown in the 16th century, have been used as the basis of most later historians' demographic estimates for London. The same area, covering 99 parishes, was later administered by the Metropolitan Board of Works.

The vast extent of, for example, Hackney, Islington and St. Pancras parishes was to be broken up early in the 19th century. The map indicates several developments significant for the future. In St. George's Fields the new roads foreshadow the growth of Lambeth and the first tentative beginnings of a dock system are visible in Limehouse.

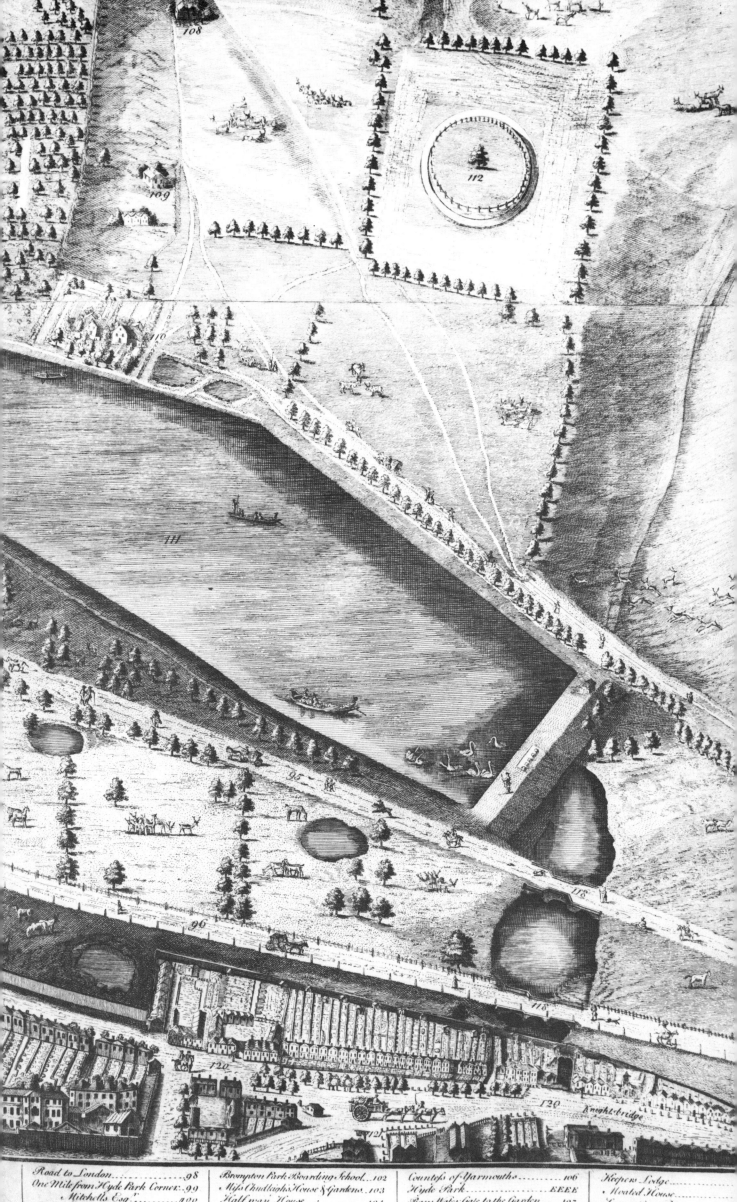

Road to London..................98	Brompton Park Boarding School..102	Countess of Yarmouths..........106	Keepers Lodge
One Mile from Hyde Park Corner..99	Miss Chudleigh's House & Gardens..103	Hyde Park..........EEEE	Moated House
Mitchells Esq.r..........100	Half way House..........104	Bays Water Gate to the Garden..107	Serpentine River
Brompton Park Nursery..........101	His Grace the Duke of Rutlands..105	Powder Magazine..........108	The Ring

Stamford Turnpike

Clay Street

Kemps Mill

Marsh St. eet

Blood House

Morris's Ferry

Marsh

Walthamstow

How hall

WALTHA

Marsh bow

Mead

Walthamstow

in Mead

GTON

Caked Lane

Jeremys Ferry

Lee Bridge

Clapton

Ruckholt hou

klewell and

Marsh Lane

Hackneys

Dalston

Marsh

HACKNEY SHE

Homerton

Wickhouse

Temple

Mills Temple

Nag's head

old Smiths house

BILLS

Bow

Chol

Grove Street

Road

Cambridge Heath

Bow

Ho

Bethnal Green

OLD FORD

Old Ford

Marsh

The George

Madhouse

W

Bear binder La.

Clay-hall

T

Globe Lane

Bencrofts Hospital

Bow

West Ham

MILE END

Whit Chapel St. New Town

Old Town

Halfway house

Bromley Town

B

London Hos

Mapley La.

Bromley Lane

Bromley

Three Mills

Half Way House

Rogues Well

A Mill Street

The River

Abbey

Mar

Shadwell Sta.

N

Salmon Lane

Four Mill

Hanover Sta.

Ratcliff Cro

Globe St.

Lime House

E

Copperas House

Good luck hou

Lime Kiln

P

Orchard House

Lee

9

POPLAR

Poplar Gutt

Blackwall

ITY

Angel Lane

Harrow lane

Cold Harbour

Bow Creek

PU

New Dock

Isle of DOGS

HOUSE

Lane

Wall

PLATE 32

Holborn to Lambeth
from *A New Plan of the
City and Liberty of
Westminster etc.*

by Robert Sayer, Thomas
Jefferys and Carington Bowles,
1766

Howgego and Darlington, no. 122

This, the second edition of Jefferys' map, captures central London just as the impact of two new bridges, Westminster (1750) and Blackfriars (formally opened in 1769), was becoming visible on the south bank.

The contrast between the crowded streets and new squares north of Holborn and the relatively empty lower section of the map was soon to disappear, as new roads were laid out across the marshes in Lambeth. The dotted lines indicate roads crossing St. George's Fields, but they were not all finally carried out as plotted here. The New Road to the Borough is now Westminster Bridge Road, and Lambeth Marsh Road is still so named, with its continuation the Cut to Christ Church, built in 1671 to serve the manor of Paris Garden. St. George's Circus and the Elephant and Castle junction did not yet exist and are not included on the map. (For another version of the proposed layout in Lambeth, see plate 29.)

In the city the new street called Moorgate is marked by a dotted line. The gate itself and the wall on either side had been removed in 1762 and the new street was to run directly from Bethlem Hospital to the Bank.

Jefferys' firm was one of the largest map-publishing houses in London in the second half of the 18th century, with a particular stake in fine maps of colonial America. This map, one of several of London published by him, is a run-of-the-mill simplified street plan, brought up-to-date in respect of the most obvious development such as the new bridge and roads, but ignoring all buildings except for hospitals and prisons, of which there are respectively seven and five in the detail reproduced. The great number of watermen's landing stages, or stairs marked along the river underline the supposition that maps of this general simple type were produced for visitors to London.

THE ARTILLERY GROUND

Tindals Burying Ground

Charter House Square

West Smithfield

HOLBORN

Grays Inn Garden

Lincolns Inn Fields

Portugal Row

Kings Way

Red Lyon Square

Foundling Hospital

Lincolns Inn Fields

FLEET STREET

Ludgate Hill   Ludgate Str.

Kings bench Walk

St. PAULS

CHURCH YARD

THAMES   STREET

BLACK FRYARS BRIDGE

THAMES

THE RIVER

Upper Ground

Willow   Street   Bank

Narrow Wall

Broad Wall

The Green Lane

Gravel Lane

Maid

Eyres Street

Duke Street

Queen   Street

Lowmans Str.

Melancholy Walk

Kings bench Prison

BLACKMAN STREET

WESTMINSTER BRIDGE

Bridge Str.

THE   NEW   ROAD   TO   THE   BOROUGH

Lambeth Marsh

Lambeth Marsh

Kennington

ST. GEORGES

Asylum

FIELDS

Lambeth Palace

Church Street

Lambeth Road

Dog & Duck

Lambeth Common

Fishmongers Alms Houses

Newington Butts

Explanation.
The Limits of the City are Coloured Red.
Intended Streets or New Buildings
not finished . . . . Yellow.
New Roads . . . . Light Brown.
St. Martin's le Grand which is part of
the Liberties of Westminster. . . . Green.

THE   NEW   ROAD   TO   KEN

Parishes in the County of Surry within the BILLS of MORTALITY.
1 St. Mary at Lambeth   3 St. Saviour in Southwark.
2 Christ Church in Surry.   4 St. George in Southwark.

ON BOWLES, at No. 69 in St. Pauls Church Yard.

LONDON, Printed for

Disposition of the Troops and Patroles in and adjoining to London

BOWLES's Reduced NEW POCKET PLAN of the CITIES of LONDON and WESTM

Printed for Carington Bowles, at his

A TABLE of REFERENCES to the CHURCHES and I

CHURCHES			
1 St Alban's, Wood Street	F n	18 St Bennet Fink, Threadneedle Street	G n	36 St James's, Dukes Place	H n	54 St Mary Woolnoth, Sherborn Lane	G o	72 St Ste
2 Allhallow's, Barking Tower Street	G o	19 St Bennet's, Gracechurch Fenchurch Str.	G o	37 St James's, Garlick Hill	F o	55 St Matthew, Friday Street	F n	73 St Sw
3 Allhallow's, Bread Street	F n	20 St Bennet's, Pauls Wharf	F o	38 St Katherine Coleman, Fenchurch Street	G o	56 St Michael Bassishaw, Basinghall Street	F n	74 Tem
4 Allhallow's the Great, Thames Street	F o	21 St Botolph's, Aldersgate	H n	39 St Katherine Cree Church, Leadenhall Str.	H o	57 St Michael's, Cornhill	G n	-5 Trini
5 Allhallow's, Lombard Street	G o	22 St Botolph's, Aldgate	H o	40 St Katherine's, near the Tower	H o	58 St Michael's, Crooked Lane	G o	-6 St Ve
6 Allhallow's, London Wall	G n	23 St Botolph's, Bishopgate	G n	41 St Laurence Jewry, Cateaton Street	F n	59 St Michael's, Queen Hithe	F o	-7 St An
7 Allhallow's Staining, Mark Lane	G o	24 St Brides, Fleet Street	E n	42 St Magnus, London Bridge	G o	60 St Michael's Royal, College Hill	F o	78 St Cl
8 St Alphage, London Wall	F n	25 Christ Church, Newgate Street	F n	43 St Margaret's, Lothbury	G n	61 St Michael's, Wood Street	F n	79 St Ge
9 St Andrew's, Holborn	E n	26 St Christopher's, Threadneedle Street	G n	44 St Margaret Pattens, Little Tower Street	G o	62 St Mildred's, Bread Street	F o	8o St Ge
10 St Andrew's Undershaft, St Mary Axe	G n	27 St Clement's, Eastcheap	G o	45 St Martin's, Ludgate Street	F n	63 St Mildred's, Poultry	G n	81 St Ge
11 St Ann's, Black Friers	F o	28 St Dionis Backchurch, Fenchurch Street	G o	46 St Martin Outwich, Threadneedle Street	G n	64 St Nicholas Cole Abby, Old Fish Street	F o	82 St Ge
12 St Ann's, Aldersgate	F n	29 St Dunstan's in the East, St Dunstan's Hill	G o	47 St Mary Abchurch, Abchurch Lane	G o	65 St Olave's, Hart Street, Crutched Friers	H o	83 St Ja
13 St Antholin's, Budge Row	F n	30 St Dunstan's in the West, Fleet Street	E n	48 St Mary, Aldermanbury	F n	66 St Olave's, Old Jewry	F n	84 St Ja
14 St Austin's, Watling Street	F n	31 St Edmund the King, Lombard Street	G o	49 St Mary, Aldermary, Bow Lane	F n	67 St Peter ad Vincula, in the Tower	H o	85 St Jo
15 St Bartholomew, Royal Exchange	G n	32 St Ethelburga, Bishopsgate Street	G n	50 St Mary, le Bow, Cheapside	F n	68 St Peter's, Cornhill	G n	86 St Jo
16 St Bartholomew, the Great, West Smithf.d	F n	33 St Georges, Botolph Lane	G o	51 St Mary, at Hill, St Mary Hill	G o	69 St Peter le Poor, Broad Street	G n	87 St Jo
17 St Bartholomew the Less, ditto	F n	34 St Giles's, Cripplegate	F n	52 St Mary Magdalen, Old Fish Street	F o	70 St Sepulchres, Snow Hill	F n	88 St Jo
		35 St Helen's, Bishopgate Street	G n	53 St Mary Somerset, Thames Street	F o	71 St Stephen's, Coleman Street	G n	89 St L

The PLAN is divided on the four Sides into Miles and half Miles: And for the easier finding the Buildings referred to in the above Table, every Division or
to look for the Royal Exchange; the Table shews that e in the Plan is the Reference there

━━ a Battali
■ a Statio
● a Post

e late Riots the beginning of June 1780 —

with the BOROUGH of SOUTHWARK, exhibiting the NEW BUILDINGS to the YEAR 1780.

SCALE OF ONE MILE.

9 in St Pauls Church Yard, London. Engraved by J. Ellis, Clerkenwell, London.

BUILDINGS, shewing their Situation in the above PLAN.

G o 90	St Margaret's, near Westminster Abby	C p	H Clifford's Inn. Fleet Street	E n
G n 91	St Martin's, St Martin's Lane	C o	I East India House. Leadenhall Street	G n
E n 92	St Mary, le Strand	D n	J Exchequer. New Palace Yard	C p
H o 93	St Mary, le Savoy	D o	K Excise Office. Broad Street	G n
C n 94	St Mary's, Rotherhith	K p	L Exeter Exchange. Strand	D n
C o 95	St Olave's, Tooley Street	G p	M Fleet Prison Fleet Market	E n
B n 96	St Paul's, Shadwell	K p	N Gatehouse Westminster	C p
B n 97	St Paul's, Covent Garden	D n	O Guild Hall, King Street Cheapside	F n
D m 98	St Saviour's, Southwark	G p	P Herald's Office, Doctors Commons	F o
F m 99	St Thomas's Street	G p	Q Hicks's Hall, St John's Street	E n
	PUBLIC BUILDINGS		R St Luke's Hospital, upper Moorfields	G m
C n A	Admiralty Office, Charing Cross	C o	S Mansion House. Walbrook	F n
B o B	Bank of England, Threadneedle Street	G o	T Marshalsea Prison, Southwark	F p
E m C	St Bartholemew's Hospital, West Smithf^d	F n	U Monument, Fish Street Hill	G o
	D Bernard's Inn, Holborn	E m	V Navy Office, Crutched Friers	H o
I p E	Borough Court, St Margaret's Hill	F p	W New Goal. Southwark	F p
	F Bridewell Hospital & Prison Fleet Ditch	E m	X New Prison. Clerkenwell	E m
F m G	Christ's Hospital Newgate Street	F n	Y Bridewell, Clerkenwell	E m

Z Opera House, Hay Market	C o	a Burlington House. Piccadilly ... B o
a Pay Office, Broad Street	G n	b Carlton House. Pall Mall ... C o
b Physician's College, Warwick Lane	F n	c Devonshire House. Piccadilly ... B o
c Post Office, Lombard Street	G o	d Leicester House. Leicester Square ... C n
d Poultry Compter	G o	e Marlborough House. St James's Park ... B o
e Royal Exchange, Cornhill	G n	f York House, Pall Mall ... C o
f Royal Society House, Crane Co. Fleet Street	E n	g Pantheon Oxford Street ... C n
g Session's House, Old Bailey	F n	
h Sion College, London Wall	F n	
i Skinner's Alms Houses, Mile End	K n	
k Stamp Office, Lincolns Inn	D n	
l Theatre Royal, Drury Lane	D n	
m Theatre Royal, Covent Garden	C o	
n Theatre Hay Market	C o	
n Trinity House, Water La. Tower Street	G o	
o Vintner's Alms Houses, Mile End	K n	
p Westminster Hall, New Palace Yard	C p	
q Wood Street Compter, Cheapside	F n	

Bottom of the PLAN, is markt with a Capital Letter of the Alphabet from A to K: and on the Sides with small Letters from l to q. "Suppose you want
rnhill, and is to be found in the Square formed by the extreme Lines of G and n.

✕ Guards, Piquets or Detachments
—— Horse Patroles
—— Foot Patroles

PLATE 33 (*overleaf*)

The defences of London during the Gordon Riots in 1780

Guildhall Library, Print Room

For a few days in June 1780 London was at the mercy of a riotous, drunken and destructive mob which attacked the Bank of England, burnt down several prisons and damaged over a hundred private houses. The riots started as demonstrations in support of the religious fanatic Lord George Gordon, for whom they are now named, but the blue cockade of his Protestant Association was soon adopted by the restless and dissatisfied proletariat of London, anxious for loot.

The threat posed by angry mobs to a city without a permanent civilian police force was not new, but as Walpole drily commented, 'the justices dare not act'. As an emergency measure, regular troops and militia were moved in from outlying barracks in Chelsea and at Knightsbridge and marched from counties as far distant as Northumberland to protect strategic points within the capital. This map, drawn up after the riots were over, marks in coloured ink on a copy of Bowles' *Reduced New Pocket Plan* the disposition of troops within London, their patrol routes and their encampments. It is supplemented by a manuscript account in the Guildhall library, unsigned but in the same hand, which gives further details of the troops involved.

The compiler of both map and list was obviously well-informed, if not directly concerned in the operation, since he gives the ranks, regiments, stations and duties of all the troops involved. In all some 11,000 rank and file and about 1000 officers were drafted into London during the crisis. The hourly patrols undertaken between 9 p.m. and 3 a.m. by the Third Dragoon Guards on circular routes in the city are reminiscent of a policeman's regular beat and foreshadow the system established when the police forces for the City and Westminster were created half a century later.

Oddly enough, while rioters were burning and looting in the City and Southwark, fashionable life in the west end continued normally. Thus, Walpole wrote, on the night when the Fleet prison was burnt, 'Lady Aylesbury has been at the play in the Haymarket and the Duke of Gloucester and my four nieces at Ranelagh this evening'.

The science of military surveying in England was still in its infancy, although at this date General Roy had started to apply the methods of the later Ordnance Survey in Scotland, and commercially-printed maps were perforce used on occasion for military purposes. In the collected papers of Sir Harry Calvert, Adjutant-General, at Claydon House, is a copy of the 1769 edition of Rocque's map of London's environs which the commander used to draw up the dispositions to be adopted for troops and artillery in case of a Napoleonic invasion. By the date of the threatened invasion, the information given by the map was 40 years or more out-of-date, but no adequate substitute was available which gave a more accurate picture of contour lines, vital information for strategic planning.

PLATE 34 (*opposite*)

The country to the south-west of London from *The Country Twenty-Five Miles Round London*

by William Faden, 1788

Howgego and Darlington, no. 188

Several publishers produced large maps of the country around London in the eighteenth century. Faden's may be compared with Rocque's of a generation earlier (plate 28). The later map has almost the look of an Ordnance Survey sheet, with similar conventions in the symbols and colours used, although the contours were still expressed by *hachure* in the French style introduced by Rocque. Faden specialised in colonial maps, especially those of North America, and at a period when London was becoming the cartographic centre of the world, the quality of his work led to his being appointed briefly official engraver and publisher to the Board of Ordnance, before it set up its own printing establishment in the first decade of the following century.

Faden differentiated between woodland, common and park and identified industrial premises, such as the many mills along the Wandle or 'Vandal' river – copper, snuff, budge [cloth], paper – but this was to remain primarily an area of wealthy private houses and farmland for another half-century or more. In Isleworth and Old Brentford the ducal houses still clustered, although nearer London Chelsea and Kensington were beginning to fill up with squares and terraces; the Brentford Road was built up on one or the other side as far as the eighth milestone from Hyde Park Corner.

The mileages recorded along the main roads are confusing since, although – as Faden claimed in the lower margin of the map – 'The Turnpike Roads are all laid down from an actual measurement with a Perambulator,' no common starting point was used. The important western route through Hounslow was measured from Hyde Park Corner 'on the King's Road', but those routes south of the river from either Westminster Bridge or Cornhill. On the Guildford road Faden, to make it absolutely clear, quoted the mileages as from both starting points.

PLATE 35

Southwark from the
*Plan of the Cities of
London and Westminster
the Borough of Southwark
and Parts adjoining*

by Richard Horwood, 1792–9

Howgego and Darlington, no. 200

In 1550 the City purchased three royal manors at the south end of London Bridge and so, it was hoped, acquired control of the turbulent Borough of Southwark with its liberties and precincts. Traditionally a district of hostelries for travellers and those noisesome industries such as brewing and tanning that were unwelcome within the city, on this late-18th century map it is clear that the atmosphere of the Borough was still rough and smelly.

The famous Quaker-owned brewery of Barclay, Perkins on Park Street, once Deadman's Place, the world's largest in the last century, still exists today, although it was taken over by Courage's in 1955. Only in the last decade or so have the buildings where the hated General Haynau was routed in 1850 been demolished.

The tanyards have also disappeared in the past half-century (their characteristic aroma is vividly recalled in V. S. Pritchett's reminiscences of a south London boyhood). The area was not however considered unsuitable for two large hospitals. The one, Guy's, was founded in 1721 by the bookseller Thomas Guy, as a hospital for incurables. At the time of the map, its buildings had just been extended to include a new four-ward hospital to the south for lunatics. St. Thomas's Hospital, refounded after the Reformation, no longer stands in Southwark – in 1862 the South Eastern Railway required an extension to the new terminus at Charing Cross and purchased the site for a handsome sum, so with its proceeds the hospital was rebuilt on the Albert Embankment, opening in 1871. London Bridge Station now dominates the area by Tooley Street (St. Olave's Street), the lines running almost over Southwark Cathedral.

Horwood's map catches the persistent character of the area before the coming of the railways, with its predominant elements of prisons, hospitals, breweries and squalid back alleys.

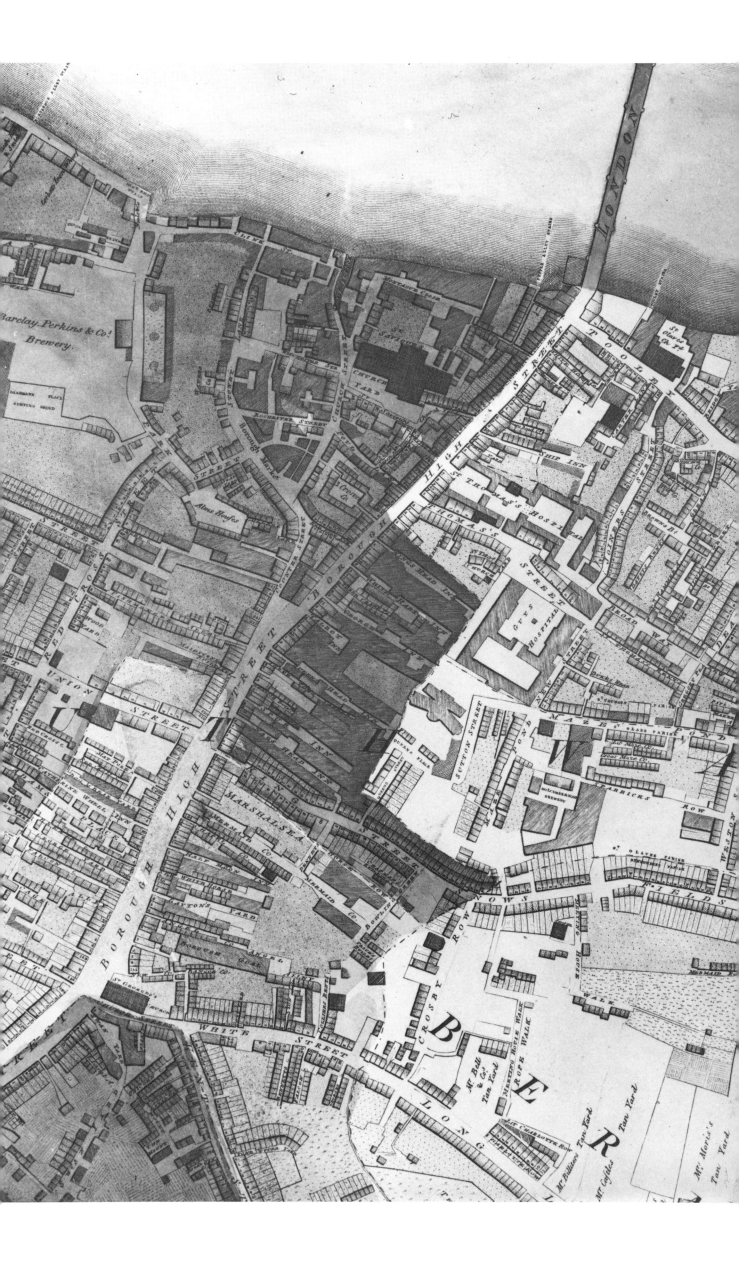

PLATE 36

Finsbury from the *Plan of the Cities of London, and Westminster, the Borough of Southwark and Parts adjoining*

by Richard Horwood, 1792–9

Howgego and Darlington, no. 200

This section of Horwood's map shows a district fast filling up with houses. Its closeness to the city had created in Finsbury an atmosphere of recreation and the green spaces were retained well into the 18th century, partly for military practice and partly for leisure. The Peerless Pool had been described by Stow two centuries before as a popular bathing spot and a fishing pond had been added, but these amenities were soon to disappear under the inexorable pressure from London's population.

The area was socially very mixed, as the varied types of housing indicate. Terraced cottages with small yards or no ground at all stood along Bunhill Row, while larger houses with long gardens elaborately laid out surrounded the recently completed Finsbury Circus. This was a traditional centre of nonconformity in London, home of Quakers and the followers of Wesley and Whitfield. Wesley's chapel still stands on the City Road today, pacifically confronting the Victorian castellated gateway of the Honourable Artillery Company.

The foreign community in the area had been considerable since the Huguenot influx of the late 17th century, and in 1718 the French Hospital had been opened for 'distressed French Protestants'. The London Hospital, founded in the healthy fields of Finsbury in the 1740's, was by the time of this map becoming surrounded by houses.

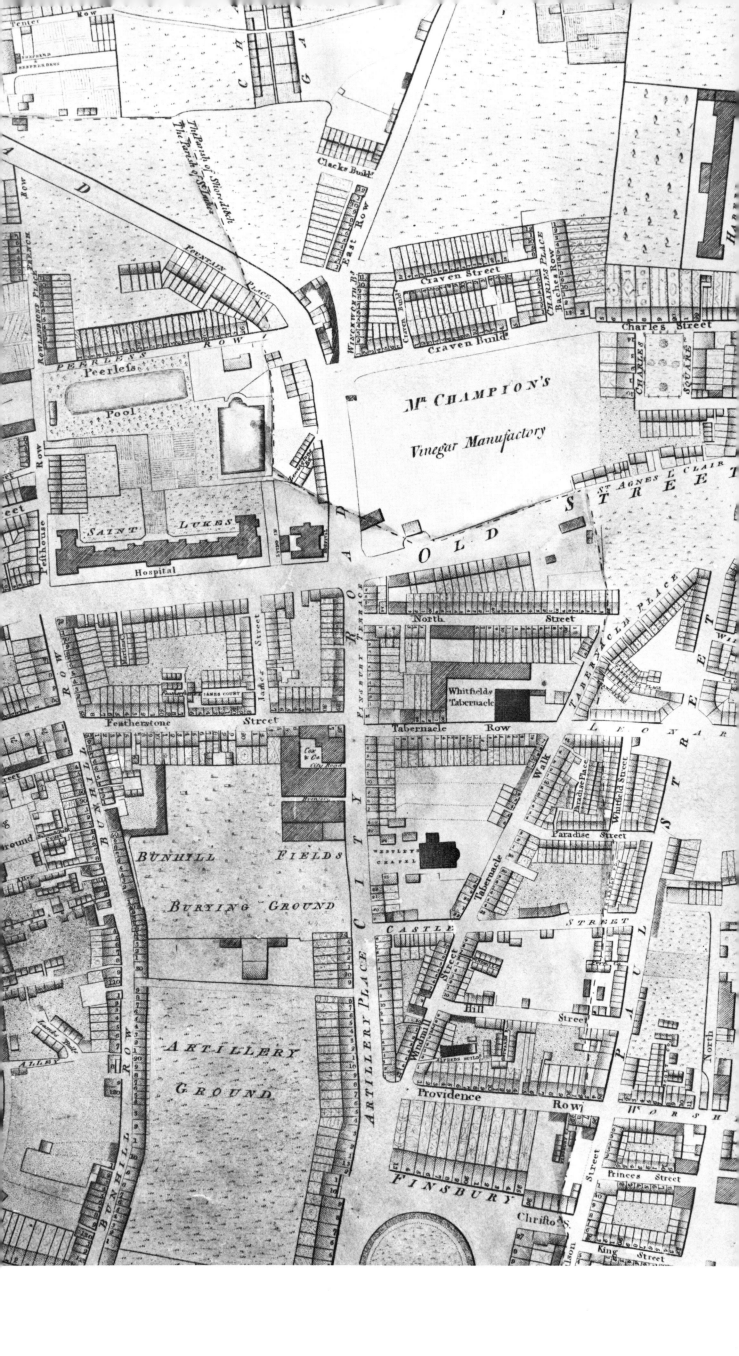

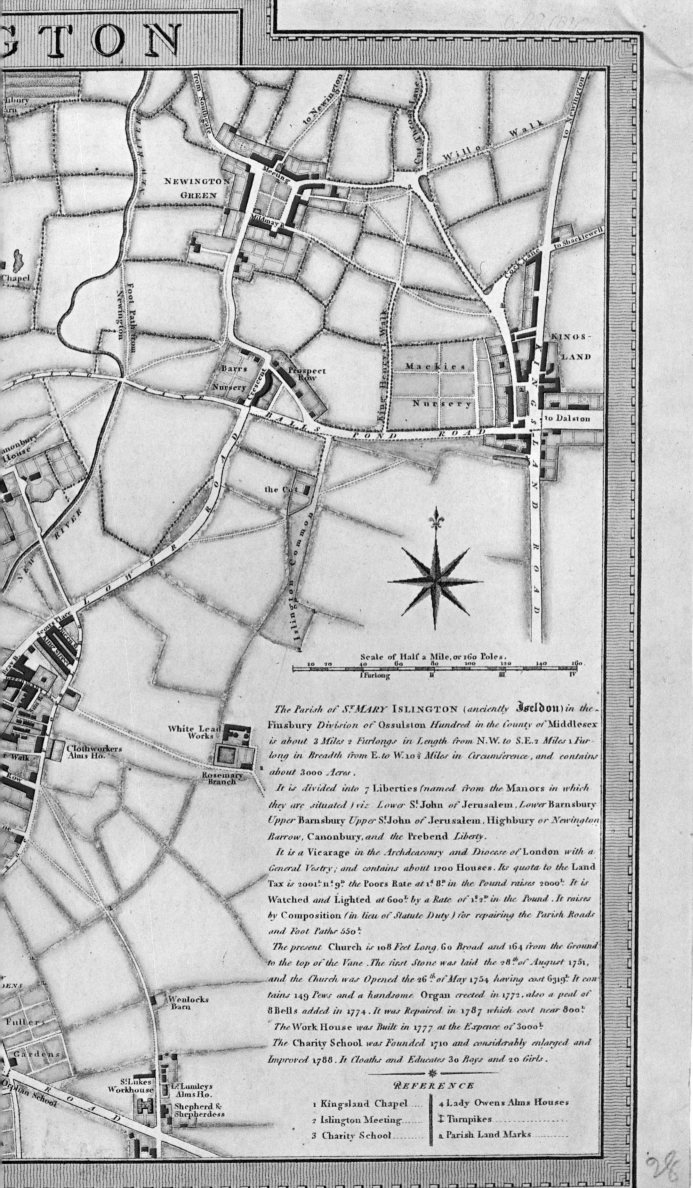

TON

NEWINGTON
GREEN

Meeting

Mildmay R.

to Newington

Willow Walk

to Shacklewell

KINGS-
LAND

Barrs
Nursery

Prospect
Row

Mackies

Nursery

to Dalston

BALLS POND ROAD

Foot Path from Newington

Chapel

NEW RIVER LOWER ROAD

anonbury
House

Islington Common

the Cot

Scale of Half a Mile, or 160 Poles.

10   70   40   60   80   100   120   140   160
I Furlong   II   III   IV

White Lead
Works

Clothworkers
Alms Ho.

Walk

Rosemary
Branch

Scotts Place

The Parish of St MARY ISLINGTON (anciently Iseldon) in the
Finsbury Division of Ossulston Hundred in the County of Middlesex
is about 3 Miles 2 Furlongs in Length from N.W. to S.E. 2 Miles 1 Furlong in Breadth from E. to W. 10½ Miles in Circumference, and contains
about 3000 Acres.

It is divided into 7 Liberties (named from the Manors in which
they are situated) viz. Lower St. John of Jerusalem, Lower Barnsbury
Upper Barnsbury Upper St. John of Jerusalem, Highbury or Newington
Barrow, Canonbury, and the Prebend Liberty.

It is a Vicarage in the Archdeaconry and Diocese of London with a
General Vestry; and contains about 1200 Houses. Its quota to the Land
Tax is 2001ᴸ. 11ˢ. 9ᴰ. the Poors Rate at 1ˢ. 8ᴰ. in the Pound raises 2000ᴸ. It is
Watched and Lighted at 600ᴸ. by a Rate of 1ˢ. 2ᴰ. in the Pound. It raises
by Composition (in lieu of Statute Duty) for repairing the Parish Roads
and Foot Paths 550ᴸ.

The present Church is 108 Feet Long, 60 Broad and 164 from the Ground
to the top of the Vane. The first Stone was laid the 28ᵗʰ of August 1751,
and the Church was Opened the 26ᵗʰ of May 1754 having cost 6319ᴸ. It contains 149 Pews and a handsome Organ erected in 1772, also a peal of
8 Bells added in 1774. It was Repaired in 1787 which cost near 800ᴸ.

The Work House was Built in 1777 at the Expence of 3000ᴸ.

The Charity School was Founded 1710 and considerably enlarged and
Improved 1788. It Cloaths and Educates 30 Boys and 20 Girls.

Wenlocks
Barn

Fullers

Gardens

DENS

Orphan School

ROAD

St Lukes
Workhouse

Lumleys
Alms Ho.

Shepherd &
Shepherdess

REFERENCE

1 Kingsland Chapel ....   4 Lady Owens Alms Houses
2 Islington Meeting ....   ‡ Turnpikes ....
3 Charity School ....   ⌐ Parish Land Marks ....

B. Baker sculp.

PLATE 37 (*overleaf*)

Islington

by E. and B. Baker, 1793

The movement of London's wealthier inhabitants into the outlying villages of Middlesex, first noted by John Norden in the 16th century, was particularly rapid in the late Georgian period, before cheap transport brought a flood of mass-development in these areas. These genteel inhabitants were ready purchasers of maps and histories of their home parishes, and four maps of Islington were published between 1793 and 1820, of which this is the earliest.

The ancient parish of Islington stretched from Battle Bridge (which acquired its more familiar name of King's Cross from a statue of George IV placed there in 1836) to Highgate and Kingsland, its area indicated on the map by small boundary stones in the fields. At this date it was still rural and the dairy farm to London; in 1803 nearly 3000 acres in Islington were given over to meadow and grazing land. Part was used by cattle in transit to Smithfield Market to put on flesh, after their journey on foot from the farms of northern and eastern England. In 1855 Copenhagen Fields, Islington, was to become the live cattle market for London, when Smithfield had become an intolerable nuisance.

Islington's reputation for health had led to its being chosen by builders of almshouses; six private institutions, as well as the school and workhouse maintained by the parish, are marked on the map.

A rash of terrace housing was to spread throughout Islington in the first half of the 19th century, but its impact had hardly been felt at the date of this map. The village remained one of large houses standing in substantial grounds – of which the tower of Canonbury House is the sole survivor today – of market gardens, and of cottages lining the roads. Middleton's New River bisects the map, and several famous 'spas' and 'wells' indicate its favoured position on the line of springs, which drew Londoners to the parish. (For the picture of the parish given to travellers out of London, see plate 40.)

PLATE 38 (*opposite*)

East London from the manuscript drawings for the first Ordnance Survey of Essex

1799

R. A. Skelton 'The Ordnance Survey 1791–1825' *British Museum Quarterly*, vol. 21, 1958

In its early years the Ordnance Survey, true to its initial military purpose, concentrated its work on the coastal counties, potentially threatened by Napoleon's armies of invasion, and for this reason London was not at first surveyed specifically. Parts of it were included in the surveys of Essex, Kent and Middlesex; sheet 7, covering London as a whole, was published in 1822. This drawing shows the boundary of Middlesex and Essex along the river Lea.

Just at this date the first docks were being constructed in the Isle of Dogs. Authorised in the year of this drawing, they were opened for traffic in 1805. The wide flood plain of the Lea dominates the area, which was still predominantly rural, the corn mills at Stratford-le-Bow supplying flour for London's bake-ovens as they had since the middle ages. Limehouse Cut, the canal linking Bromley by Bow with the Thames, had been opened in 1770, to speed up the movement of bulky water-carried goods from Essex and Hertfordshire into London. On Ratcliffe Highway and in Stepney are two rope walks, reminders of the ship-building industry which flourished on the Middlesex bank between the 16th and 19th centuries.

The Ordnance Survey drawings, deposited in the Map room of the British Museum in 1955 by the Director General of the Survey, bear the signatures of the officers concerned (in this case Lt. Col. W. Twiss) and their date of completion, together with triangulation points, which for the London area were high-standing buildings such as the British Museum and the roofs of St. Clement Danes, St. Giles-in-the-Fields and St. Paul's Cathedral.

The published sheets of the first Ordnance Survey are to the familiar one-inch scale, but in the field the surveyors drew to larger scales – two, three or even six inches to the miles; Essex, a county considered to be at risk from invasion, merited the three-inch scale. The fair copies, revised from the field drawings, were complete in May 1799, but the four sheets covering Essex were not published until 1805, when the field boundaries and ridge and furrow recorded in the surveyors' initial drawings were omitted from the reduced printed maps. General Roy himself had directed that 'in the enclosed parts of the County all the Hedges and other Boundaries of Fields are to be carefully laid down'.

London Printed for & Published by Thomas Milne N.º 7 New-street Knightsbridge, as the Act directs; 11.ᵗʰ March 1800.

PLATE 39 (*overleaf*)

Land use in the London region from the *Plan of the Cities of London and Westminster*

by Thomas Milne, 1800

Howgego and Darlington, no. 221

G. B. G. Bull: 'Thomas Milne's Land Utilization Map,' *Geographical Journal*, 122, 1966

Milne's map is an attempt unique in its period to express a complex range of land uses, anticipating a method of cartography not fully developed until the present century. Only one copy is known, now in the British Museum Map room, with contemporary hand-applied tints supplementing the elaborate system of lettered references used in the map to distinguish 17 varieties of land usage. Two years before, John Middleton in his *View of the Agriculture of Middlesex* had included a map on which he used only three colours to differentiate arable, pasture and nursery land.

Thomas Milne trained as an estate surveyor, but had also the considerable advantage of working with William Faden on the first county map of the Ordnance Survey, that of Kent, published in 1801; Milne had tried unsuccessfully to join the Board of Ordnance in 1791, and continued to keep abreast of the Board's techniques. He certainly used for this map General Roy's primary and secondary triangulations radiating from Hounslow Heath, and given in the margins numerous trigonometrical points laid down by the Survey between 1791 and 1799, including Bromley Church, together with the 'Parellel of Gen'l Roy's station on Norwood' and the Greenwich Meridian. (Compare plate 38.)

The as yet undrained state of the river-bank parishes to the west and south of London is apparent on the map. Milne used the letters 'ma' for marsh, and they are sprinkled liberally in Battersea, Fulham, Rotherhithe and Greenwich; part of a possible explanation for their condition is implied in the neighbouring fields marked with the letters 'caf' or 'cmf', arable or meadow land still farmed at least nominally in common. The first General Enclosure Act was passed in the year this map was published, and the commons near London, which in Middlesex had first been attacked in the 16th century, were to disappear finally in the 19th. Market gardens and nurseries, indicated respectively by 'g' and 'n', predominated in the riverside parishes, creating that 'green and open tract which gives a pleasing rural character to the immediate vicinity of the town', but over the entire area of the map, about 240 square miles, half the land was taken by meadow and pasture, and only a fifth by those growing directly for the kitchens of London.

Milne's uncertainty about the layout of the future docks in the East End is clear; he merely marked a broad channel short-circuiting the river bend and left it unnamed and without locks. His definition of land use contained little hint of the rapid growth of industry in and around London which was already taking place.

PLATE 40 (*opposite*)

The roads from London to Hendon and London to Finchley from the *Survey of the High Roads from London*

by John Cary, 1801

In publishing maps of the roads out of London Cary was following a profitable precedent set by the Stuart cartographic publisher John Ogilby. His intention was to convey to the traveller 'that kind of information which will give pleasure to his peregrinations,' and with this in view he identified the gentlemen's residences along the road, 'to which the Travellers' enquiry is naturally directed'. (Compare plate 13.)

Cary took little care to indicate the quality of the road surface, which might reasonably be of interest to the intending traveller, confining his geographical references merely to high ground, heath and rivers, and the symbols he used show no awareness of the Ordnance Survey conventions which were being used at this date by such map-makers as Milne and Faden. The milestones and turnpikes were indicated, the latter 'often complained of from the uncivility as well as imposition of the toll-gatherers', with the object of enabling travellers to achieve the maximum distance for their tickets, once purchased. Turnpike areas overlapped, and the rates for some were more favourable than others, so that Cary's notes on tolls were of considerable practical value.

The techniques used by contemporary map-makers and urban surveyors are rarely explained in detail (although see pages 63–65), but for Cary's methods there is ample evidence in a case brought in 1801 which challenged the originality of his road-books; he employed a French surveyor, Louis Hèbert, who had learnt his trade in France, where road-books were more sophisticated than the English ones. He earned ninepence a mile for measuring with a perambulator: 'the orders he received from the plaintiff were to ascertain the whole of the turnings branchings or runing out of the road . . . and to note the exact distance of one stationary object from the other, wherever it could be in any degree useful; and to inform himself of the name of the resident of the different seats'.

No original survey by Hèbert survives, but it is unlikely that, given his instructions, they approached in quality the superb survey prepared by Joseph Salway in 1811 for the Kensington Turnpike Trustees of their road from Hyde Park Corner to Counter Bridge His drawings, now in the British Museum, combine a flat plan with a vertical section of the road, indicating the quality of the surface and its drainage, both natural and man-made.

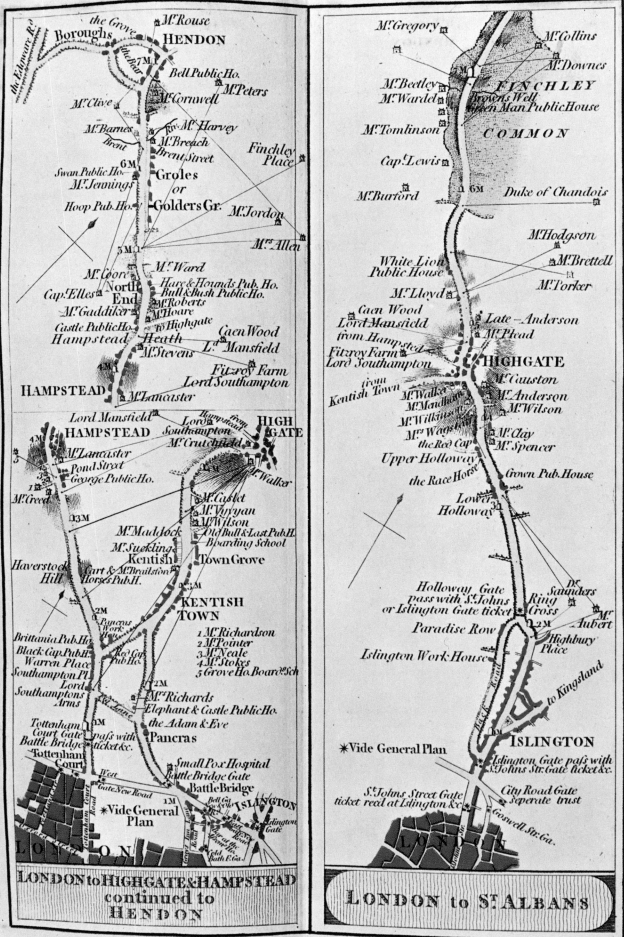

LONDON to HIGHGATE & HAMPSTEAD continued to HENDON

LONDON to St ALBANS

Published by J. Cary, July 1st 1801.

PLATE 41

The Isle of Dogs from *London and Westminster*

by John Fairburn, 1802

Howgego and Darlington, no. 203

This, the sixth or seventh edition of a map first published in 1795, demonstrates the dramatic changes in east London in the intervening period, changes which a map-seller could not afford to ignore. Fairburn's original map stopped short at Limehouse; he added a section in later editions to show the various 'Alterations and Improvements now making or intended to be made'.

The most significant of these for east London was the creation of the East and West India docks in the Isle of Dogs, and the Commercial Road linking them with the city. Some recently-built houses had to be removed for the docks, but behind the countryside lay open to the north, apart from the lines of houses along Poplar High Street, an ancient highway. Before the docks were built, traffic ran along the river and much further north, on the old Roman road to Old Ford. Traffic to Limehouse was further increased when the eastern extension of the Regent's Canal was opened there in 1820. (Compare plate 22.)

This section of Middlesex, between the river Lea and the Tower, was transferred to the County of London in 1889, in recognition of its urban character. The river Lea (or Lee) had come within London's orbit as early as the 16th century, with the need for a navigable waterway up to Ware, to bring corn and other bulky commodities to the markets of the capital. Later it not only powered mills and factories, but also supplied drinking water to thousands in the east end. This function has now been taken over by vast reservoirs, and the Lea may eventually be allowed to revert to a place for fishermen and bird-watchers, as industry moves out of London and the polluted river clears again.

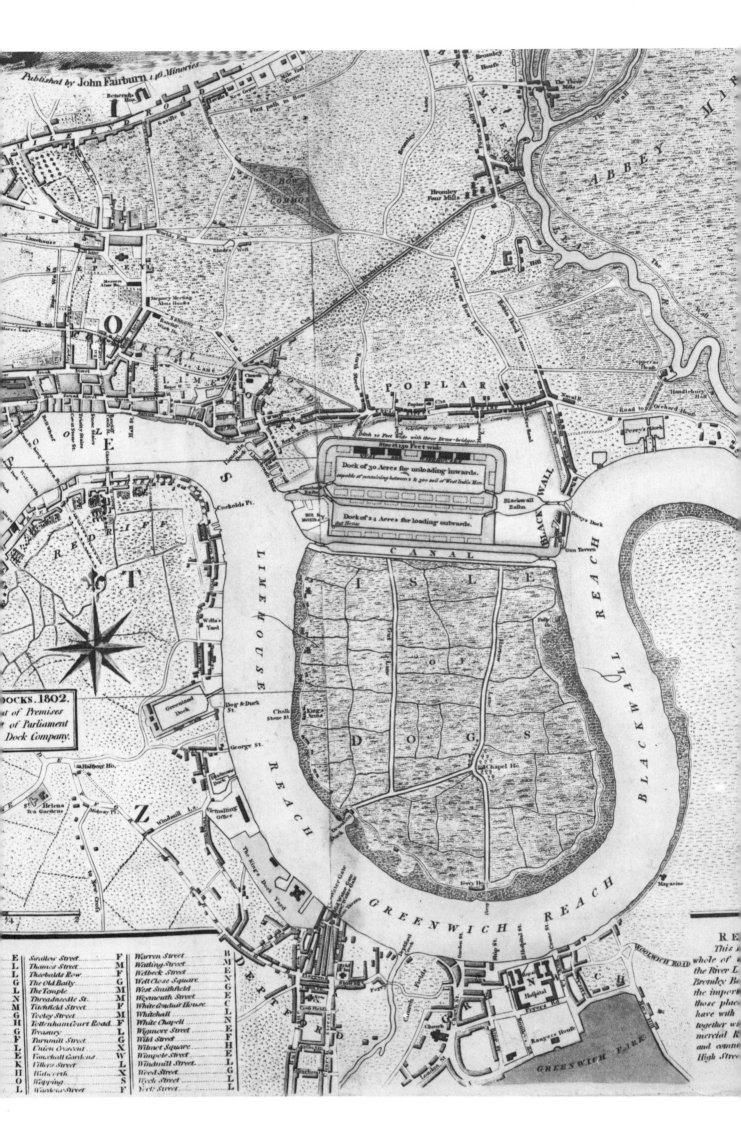

Published by John Fairburn 146 Minories.

MILE END ROAD

STEPNEY

LIMEHOUSE

POPLAR

ABBEY MARSH

Bromley House

The Three Mills

BOW COMMON

Bromley Four Mills

Bromley Hall

Handlebury Hall

Road to Orchard House

Percy's Dock

Ditch 40 Feet wide with three Draw-bridges.
Street 130 Feet wide

Dock of 30 Acres for unloading inwards.
capable of containing between 5 & 300 sail of West India Men.

Dock of 24 Acres for loading outwards.

Blackwall Basin

Blackwall

BLACKWALL REACH

George's Dock

Gun Tavern

CANAL

ISLE OF DOGS

Folly Ho.

King's Arms

Chapel Ho.

LIMEHOUSE REACH

REDRIFF

Cuckolds Pt.

Wells's Yard

Greenland Dock

Dog & Duck St.

Chalk Stone St.

George St.

St. Helena Tea Gardens

Windmill La.

Victualling Office

The King's Dock Yard

GREENWICH REACH

Ferry Ho.

Magazine

WOOLWICH ROAD

Hospital

Fryers

Church

Ranger's House

GREENWICH PARK

DOCKS. 1802.
of Premises
of Parliament
Dock Company.

E	Swallow Street	F	Warren Street	M
L	Thames Street	M	Watling Street	B
L	Theobalds Row	F	Welbeck Street	E
G	The Old Baily	G	Well Close Square	N
L	The Temple	M	West Smithfield	G
N	Threadneedle St.	M	Weymouth Street	C
M	Titchfield Street	M	White Conduit House	L
G	Tooley Street	F	Whitehall	N
H	Tottenham Court Road	F	White Chapel	E
G	Treasury		Wigmore Street	F
F	Turnmill Street	L	Wild Street	H
L	Union Crescent	G	Wilmot Square	E
E	Vauxhall Gardens	X	Wimpole Street	L
K	Villers Street		Windmill Street	G
H	Walworth	L	Wood Street	L
O	Wapping	X	Wych Street	L
L	Wardour Street	F	York Street	F

RE
This
whole of
the River L
Bromley Be
the imper
those place
have with
together wi
mercial R
and comm
High Stree

PLATE 42

Edgware Road to
Chelsea from the
*New Two-Sheet Plan of
the Cities of London &
Westminster*

by Bowles and Carver, 1805

Howgego and Darlington, no. 206

This map, although published in the early years of the 19th century, is in every respect typical of those sold throughout the Georgian period (see plates 32, 33). The symbols, the lettering, the use of stippling and colour, all are characteristic, and show no awareness of the arrival of modern map-making under the influence of the Ordnance Survey. It is interesting both as an example of its genre and as an illustration of the reluctance of contemporary map publishers to engrave fresh plates when an old one could be adapted; copper-engraving represented a substantial element in the cost of map production.

In a wish to demonstrate to potential customers the value and accuracy of their London map the publishers extended into the borders to show sections of Chelsea, Brompton and Paddington newly built since the plates were first cut. To the east, the docks were added on an inset below Greenwich, at a lesser scale. To the north the inoculation hospital at Battle Bridge, Islington, straddled the margin. London refused to be confined. No wonder maps were popularly derided; 'such sorts of things could give no information'.

Chelsea and Pimlico, still as shown here largely outside London, were slow to succumb to the builder; their proximity to the capital was offset by the lack of a direct connecting road and by their low-lying ground. When the West Bourn flooded below Knightsbridge in 1809 all road traffic between Westminster and Chelsea was necessarily brought to a standstill, a hazard not experienced by the traveller to Paddington, Marylebone or other settlements along the gravel ridge to the north. Not only was the marshy nature of the soil a deterrent to drainage and sewage disposal (a problem only resolved half a century later by Joseph Bazalgette, who learnt his trade as an engineer in Chelsea), but it also made the district a valuable growing-ground for market gardeners, so that land values were high. Each of the 200 fertile acres between the riverside and Westminster known as the Neat Houses produced several hundred pounds-worth of produce a year for London's hungry markets, and also acted as a convenient dumping-ground for the potentially fertile dung and nightsoil of London.

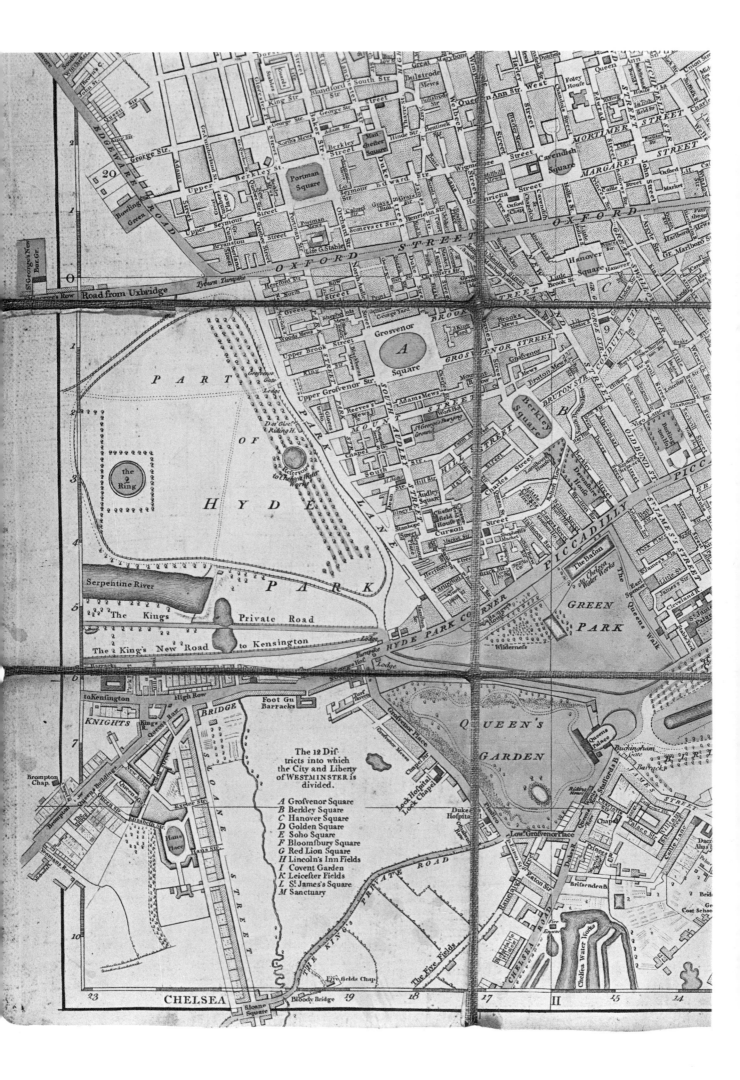

The 12 Districts into which the City and Liberty of WESTMINSTER is divided.

A Grosvenor Square
B Berkley Square
C Hanover Square
D Golden Square
E Soho Square
F Bloomsbury Square
G Red Lion Square
H Lincoln's Inn Fields
I Covent Garden
K Leicester Fields
L St James's Square
M Sanctuary

PLATE 43

Regent's Park to Pimlico
from the *New and
Accurate Plan of London*

by John Cary, 1815

Howgego and Darlington, no. 184

Twenty-five years before, when Cary published the first edition of this map, much of this area was still rough pasture land. Lisson Grove, Paddington, for example, has clearly been added to the plate subsequently, but the plate had not been erased thoroughly and the symbol for grass continued under some of the buildings marked here and in Brompton. The first of Cary's London maps appeared in 1782; they were to continue on the market for many years, since some of his plates were acquired by Cruchley after Cary's retirement from publishing. After 1800 they looked increasingly oldfashioned by comparison with the products of that new school of publishers working under the stimulus of the Ordnance Survey such as Faden, Milne and Bryant (compare plates 39 and 40). The scale of the map, at 6½ inches, is large for its time, almost as large as Greenwood's (plate 47), but the amount of detail shown by Cary is far less and his lettering heavy and clumsy.

The best-known of the Regency improvements to the metropolis, the creation of Regent's Street to link Carlton House with Regent's Park, was intended as a royal carriage route different only in scale from the king's private roads to Kensington, Chelsea and Richmond from St. James's. It became, however, a major north-south artery in central London and set the pattern for further large-scale road works undertaken by the Board of Works later in the century. Royal and private enterprise was far in advance of civic responsibility in such major public expenditure. Incidentally, Cary still referred to as 'new' one major 18th-century road improvement, the coach road linking Paddington and Islington (the Marylebone and Euston roads).

The basic outlines of this area of London have changed in essence very little. Royal parks defined the course of growth in west London from the 16th century. Belgravia and Tyburnia, estates north and south of Hyde Park, were to be created out of farmland in the 19th century; the first signs of the latter are visible along the Edgware Road. The churchyard of St. George's Chapel, marked on Bayswater Road, having been for many years disused and a popular place for games of tennis, has now, a century and a half later, fallen to building speculators and has become a site for blocks of flats.

PLATE 44

Holborn and the Strand from the *Plan of the Cities of London and Westminster*

by William Faden, 1819

Howgego and Darlington, no. 200

Faden's map, the fourth edition of Horwood's of 25 years before, demonstrates the pace of change in central London in the intervening years, which was to intensify later in the century and transform this area by the outbreak of the First World War. (Compare plates 10, 52.)

Waterloo Bridge was completed, with Wellington Street, in 1817. From 1828 King's College was to occupy the space to the east of Somerset House, which the engraver has used for the titles of the departments using it, and congestion in the Strand was to be considerably eased a year later by the removal of the Exeter Exchange, at the foot of Burleigh Street, which had been opened in 1679 to supply the fashionable Westminster customer with fancy goods.

Somerset House had been designed by Sir William Chambers in 1780 as a home for government departments, the Royal Academy and the Society of Antiquaries, all long since moved elsewhere, apart from the remnants of the Inland Revenue. Its superb position overlooking the river has not been exploited recently, but there is now some hope that it may again become a place of public resort.

In Covent Garden the market stalls were still free-standing but in 1831 they were to disappear inside Fowler's splendid market house. The communications between the market and its rural suppliers remain congested and inadequate, but access was even more difficult before the widening of the Strand and the building of Aldwych and Kingsway early this century.

The overcrowding and the unsavoury reputation of the inhabitants in this area led eventually to considerable public pressure for improvements merely as a justification for rehousing; in clearing the five-and-a-half-acre site now occupied by the Law Courts from 1866, 4000 residents were shifted, who had lived in a rat run of 33 separate alleys and courts.

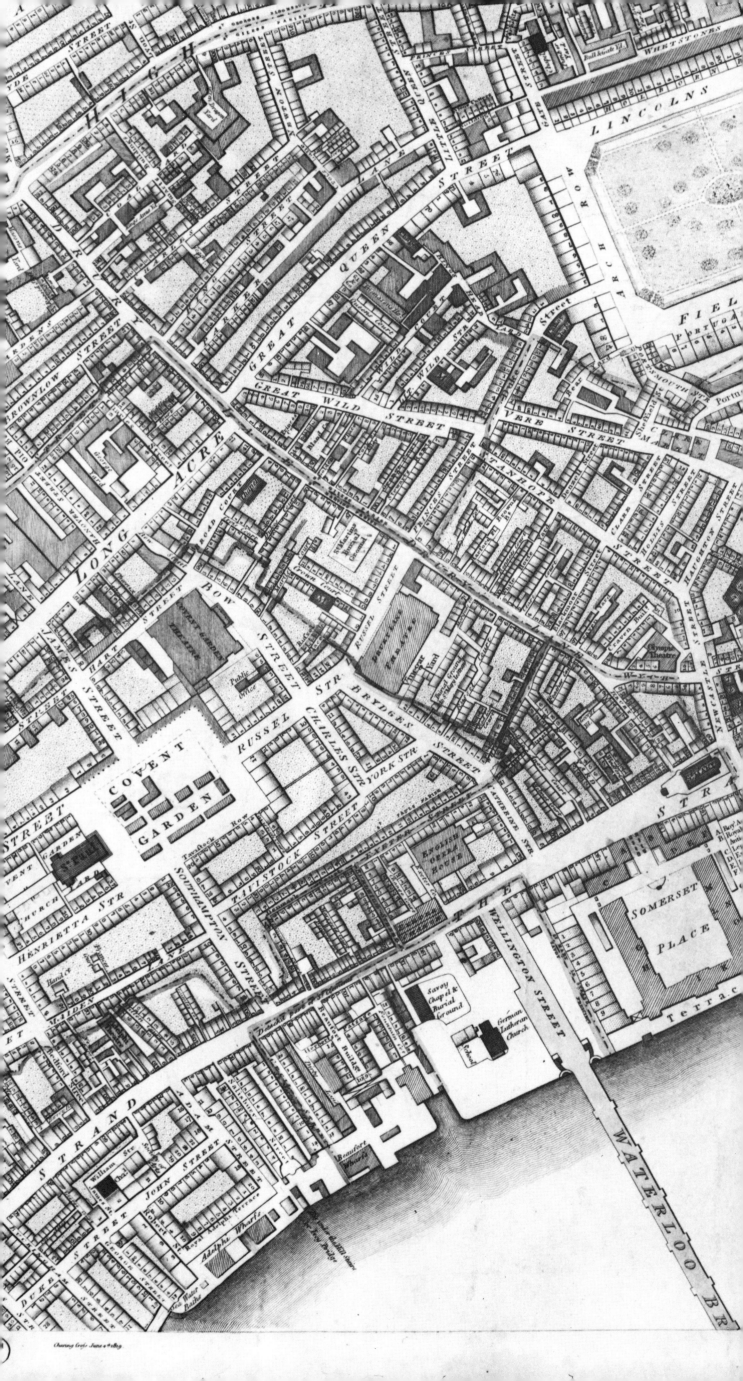

PLATE 45

Central Kensington
from the *Plan of the
Parish of St. Mary
Kensington Reduced from
Actual Survey*

by T. Starling, 1822

The old parish of Kensington stretched from Ladbroke to the river; it acquired its present status as a royal borough early in this century, when Edward VII granted the title in memory of his mother's long association with the area. A few years earlier the boundary between the parishes of St. Margaret's, Westminster and St. Mary Abbots, Kensington had been moved to the Broad Walk to bring Kensington Palace and part of the Gardens into the parish, and at the same time the detached portion on the riverside on which the Royal Hospital stood was passed to Chelsea.

Thomas Starling, who engraved this map, specialised in publishing parish surveys. He published a map of his home parish of Islington in the same year, with a comparable emphasis on field acreages, although by that date Islington was beginning to fill up with terraces – Trafalgar, Aboukir, Copenhagen – patriotically named after Nelson's heroic victories. Kensington had not yet been penetrated by the developer, although Earl's Terrace and Phillimore Place were indications of the invasion to follow. So little was there of interest to the potential purchaser in the northern section of the parish, beyond Notting Hill or 'Kensington Gravel Pits', that the engraver included the area at a reduced scale. These open fields were to be the site for estates planned and built wholesale in the 1840's and 1850's, but at this date the total population of the parish did not exceed 4000, most of whom were market gardeners and nurserymen, occupations traditional to Kensington since the late middle ages. In 1635 an aldermanic report to the City commented that the inhabitants 'be husbandmen by profession . . . they sow for parsnips, turnips and carrotts and the like in their commonfields'; the common fields had vanished by the 19th century and the nurserymen had turned their attention to more glamorous seeds and cut flowers. The 'King's Forcing Ground' in Church Street, attached to Kensington Palace, was until very recently used as a barracks, and is now a car park.

PLATE 46

North-east Surrey from the county map

by Andrew Bryant, 1823

Bryant was one of a new generation of surveyors and map-makers which emerged in the first 30 years of the 19th century, heavily influenced by and drawing on the techniques and conventions of the Ordnance Survey. He and the Greenwood brothers (compare plate 47) were contemporaries and rivals in the production of large-scale county maps, and on many occasions their respective surveyors must have been treading on one another's heels, so close were their publication dates. This map of Surrey was published by Bryant 1 June 1823, and Greenwood's of the same county exactly three months later.

Publishers of county maps in the Regency were supplying a considerable need; as Greenwood commented in 1823, looking back at the beginning of the century, 'few maps of any of the Counties of England and Wales could be found to be depended upon'. This was due partly to improvements in techniques, but also to the immense changes in the face of England, with the coming of canals and the machine age 'from the Great Increase of Population and the consequent additional number of Villages, Hamlets, Gentlemen's seats, Manufactories and Mills'.

In Surrey these changes were less dramatic than in the Midlands, but this corner of the country was bisected by the Surrey Iron Railway from Croydon to the Thames at Wandsworth, and the Croydon canal to the Grand Surrey Docks at Rotherhithe, opened in 1803 and 1809. The railway, so-called, was more accurately an iron tram road carrying heavy commodities to and from the river, and was superseded in the 1830's by a true railway; the canal closed in 1836, when the bed was bought by a railway company as a ready-made track.

Along the Surrey bank at Battersea a line of factories and mills indicates the increasing industrialisation of the environs of south London, and the black scatter of houses in Southwark and Lambeth demonstrates the density of population within walking distance of the city. Beyond the limit of the paved streets, where the protected monopoly of the hackney coaches ended, local public transport was limited to slow, lumbering coaches, continually stopping, like a Green Line bus, to drop and pick up passengers. A French traveller, L. Simond, took two hours to cover the distance from Richmond to Hyde Park Corner in 1810 in a public coach, so that working men with neither time nor money to spare had to live within walking distance of their daily work until the coming of the railways, 15 years after this map was published.

Bryant supplied his map with a key of 21 symbols, ranging from castles to bridleways, and gave an additional piece of information, the ecclesiastical divisions of the county, from parishes to deaneries.

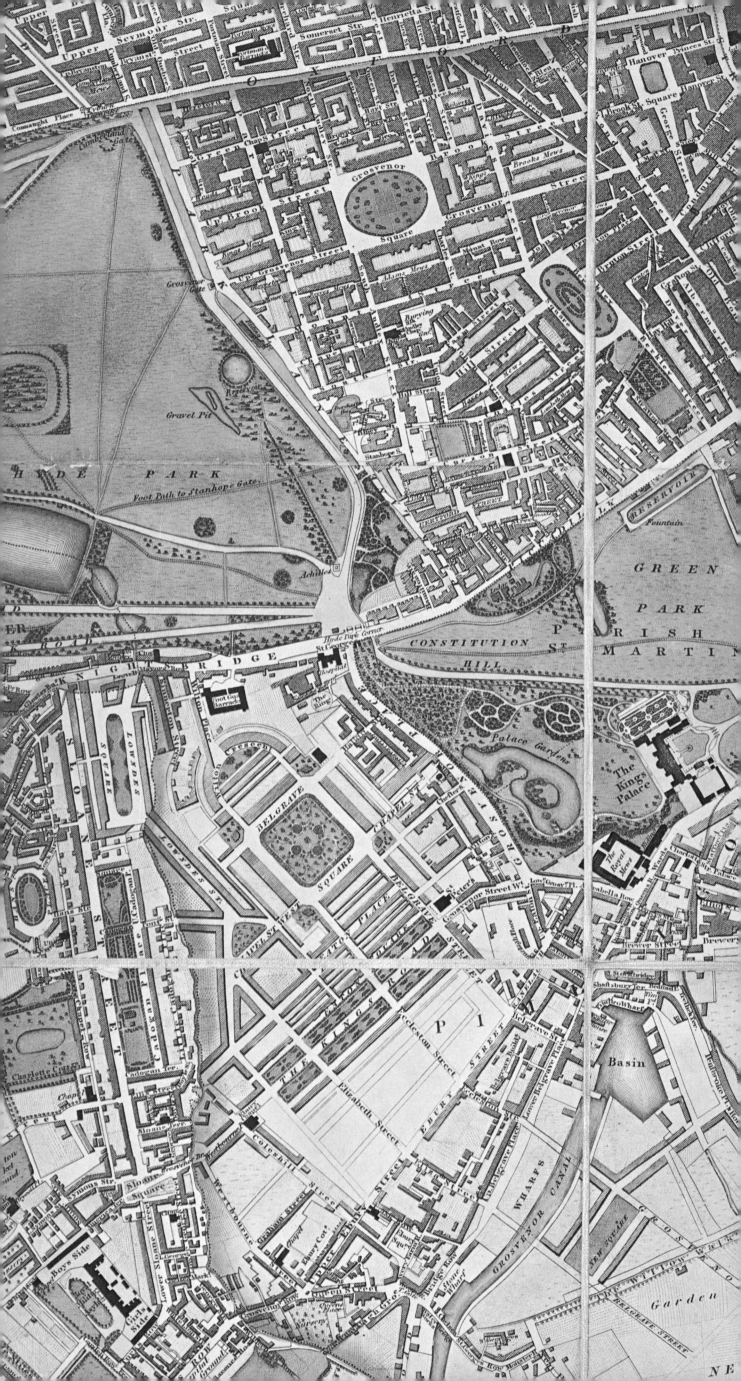

PLATE 47 (*overleaf*)

Westminster from the *Map of London from an Actual Survey*

by C. and J. Greenwood, 1827

Howgego and Darlington, no. 309
J. B. Harley, *Christopher Greenwood, County Map-Maker*, 1962

Greenwood's magnificent 6-sheet map of London, superbly engraved by Josiah and James Neele, was the first to be published on a large scale (7 inches to the mile) for many years, and the first to a standard of accuracy comparable with modern large-scale maps of the capital. The colour was still a wash applied by hand and was used to emphasise the chain lines marking the bounds of parishes and liberties, as well as the boundaries of the city and Westminster. Greenwood abandoned contour lines within the built-up area, so that he marked Primrose Hill, still then in a semi-rural district, but ignored the steep rise from the Fleet valley to St. Paul's.

The presence of monarchy still dominated Westminster; the yellow roads in the parks were private, reserved for those ticket-holders generously permitted entry by the king, so that for the general public a trip from for example Knightsbridge to Charing Cross followed a devious route; the ancient privy garden of Henry VIII's palace still flanked Whitehall. Behind Buckingham Palace Thomas Cubitt's Belgravia, recently laid out for the Duke of Westminster on five fields between Grosvenor Place and Chelsea, was beginning to rise from the ground. Along the Grosvenor Canal, cut in 1824, lay the wharves where stone and brick were unloaded for his elegant terraces. Until 1852 the canal served also as feeder to the reservoir of the Chelsea Water Works.

The maze of streets and squares eastwards from Hyde Park is apparent here, which arose from the many landowners in this area each developing his estate piecemeal; Nash's Regent Street stands out clearly as the innovation it then was, a stroke of planning possible only to a man backed by the financial and legal support of Crown agencies. Later in the century the Board of Works was to create other equally dramatic improvements, slashing through the muddled centre of the capital, and in this century so wholesale has the cutting of new routes become that Nash's loses all impact. At Charing Cross Greenwood illustrates the general uncertainty about the future of that ancient junction; while the royal mews had gone, a plan for what was to be Trafalgar Square had not yet been agreed upon; Somerset House remained the home of the Royal Academy, and Burlington and Northumberland Houses were still in private hands. (Compare plates 51, 52.)

Greenwood's map was superb, but did not make his fortune; about 1835 he was forced to hand over the plates to a rival, E. Ruff, and quit his Regent Street premises. Ruff republished the map, with minor changes, for another 20 years, by which date its quality had been surpassed and new methods of printing and machine colouring introduced.

PLATE 48 (*overleaf*)

Marylebone from the
*Topographical Survey of
the Borough of
St. Marylebone*

by B. R. Davies, 1834

The streets east of Edgware Road shown on this map had been largely created out of dairy farmland in the previous 30 years, as London spread out to the New Road (the present Marylebone and Euston roads). Indeed the creation of Regent's Park was welcomed by Leigh Hunt for this very reason, 'it has checked in that quarter at least the monstrous brick cancer that was extending its arms in every direction and has prevented Harley and Wimpole Streets from going further (north)'

Further northward building was effectively blocked by the park, and Portland Place remained a relatively isolated backwater for the next half-century. West of the park the Eyre estate in St. John's Wood had a character very different from the streets and squares nearer Hyde Park; the large detached villas, each in its own substantial garden, had a truly suburban air and contrasted markedly with the formal town terraces around Baker Street and those which were to fill Tyburnia later in the century. Most of these villas have disappeared today, swallowed up in the vast Lisson Green estate.

The tip of the basin of the Grand Junction Canal juts into the map to the left below the Harrow Road; the canal itself loops northwards at this point and reappears beyond Alpha Road. Little Venice has acquired today a certain reputation as being the home of luxurious houseboats, but its very existence was threatened a few years after this map was published; the flat, regular bed of a canal could be cheaply and easily converted to railway track and in 1845 the Regent's Canal narrowly escaped the fate of the Croydon Canal, which had become the site of a south London railway line.

Madame Tussaud's and the Planetarium, the first operating originally in Portman Square and in Marylebone Road only from 1884, had predecessors in the district, the Diorama on Park Square and the Colosseum on Albany Street. The Zoological Gardens in Regent's Park, a further attraction, were opened in 1828.

The ancient parish of St. Mary on the Bourne had been growing rapidly throughout the previous century, when it had acquired two new cemeteries and several chapels of ease. In 1817 the old church was superseded by Hardwick's semi-classical building; both are marked on the map opposite York Gate, with those other necessary adjuncts to urban life, the parish workhouse and a police-office, close at hand.

PLATE 49

Kentish Town and
Regent's Park from the
*New Plan of London and
its Vicinity*

by John Cary, 1836

Howgego and Darlington, no. 279

The crude engraving and colouring of this cheap folding map of London may be compared with the quality of the survey of Marylebone parish published two years before, which includes much of the same area (plate 48).

The first edition of this particular publication, one of literally scores of London maps put out by the Cary brothers and their successors in the Georgian and early Victorian periods, appeared in 1820. It was brought up-to-date by the addition of that new venture, the railway line from Birmingham to Euston Square, which was to be opened in 1837 but is here shown terminating at a depot in Primrose Hill. (Elsewhere on the map is shown the other line already built at this date, that from Greenwich into south London, but merely as a dotted line, with no terminal points, although the station at London Bridge was to be opened in December of this same year, 1836.)

This section of London was slow to fill up with houses because of the block to direct communication created by the Regent's Park and its attendant terraces; building had not yet reached the limit of the twopenny post delivery in the London district, indicated here by a broad red line. This line also served as the outer limit of metropolitan hackney carriages; as Cary warned, 'Hackney Coachmen are allowed by the New Act of Parliament to charge both fares from all places outside the same circle'.

The Bedford estate in Bloomsbury, carefully protected by its owners from railway and industrial invasion, was beginning to acquire its intellectual flavour; Wilkins' classical building, called London University on the map, but now University College on Gower Street, was opened in 1827, and Smirke's new British Museum building four years before.

Outside the built-up area nurseries flanked the main roads, as they did in Fulham and Islington, supplying fresh fruit and vegetables to London's inhabitants. Before the coming of steam, when urban retailers could rely only on the horse and cart for their supply of perishable foodstuffs, the capital was closely ringed with dairy farms, market gardens and nurseries. That marked on the map at the centre of Regent's Park is now the magnificent rose garden called after Queen Mary.

PLATE 50

Proposed changes on
the Chelsea waterfront
from the *First Report of
the Commissioners for
Improving the
Metropolis*

1844

The need for a satisfactory direct link between Chelsea and Westminster, a principal recommendation of the Commissioners' report, to 'conduct to the health and recreation of the public', was recognised by most local landowners, but no-one wanted it across his land.

Objections varied from the bitter complaint of the Governor of Chelsea Hospital, that it would detract from the therapeutic privacy of the hospital grounds, to the white-lead-maker's reaction that it would destroy his vital access to the river bank. Apothecaries objected to the removal of Sir Hans Sloane's physic garden to Kew, on the grounds that it would be inaccessible to the medical students for whom it was intended, and only the developers of building land made no outcry. The advantages to them were obvious; their riverside sites could and did become attractive and expensive once the hazards of flooding and the picturesque but smelly foreshore disappeared with the building of an embankment to take the proposed road.

The embankment was not completed until 1874, by the Board of Works, and was preceded by Chelsea Suspension Bridge in 1858, an additional amenity not contemplated by the Commissioners when this plan was prepared.

Chelsea still retained its historic character as the home of nurserymen, but they were gradually being squeezed out by developers and by factories. The persistent industrial flavour of the riverside between Vauxhall and Chelsea bridge is already clear on this map, although Battersea Power Station now occupies the extensive site of the Southwark water-works. Battersea already possessed several tea-gardens and a shooting ground, soon to be formalised into a public park, but the south bank had still a predominantly rural flavour.

This plan is of interest both as an example of the work of that new class of urban surveyor which was to contribute so much to the practical improvement of Victorian London, and also as an early piece of colour lithography, whose value in such heavily illustrated reports as this one the Government was quick to realise.

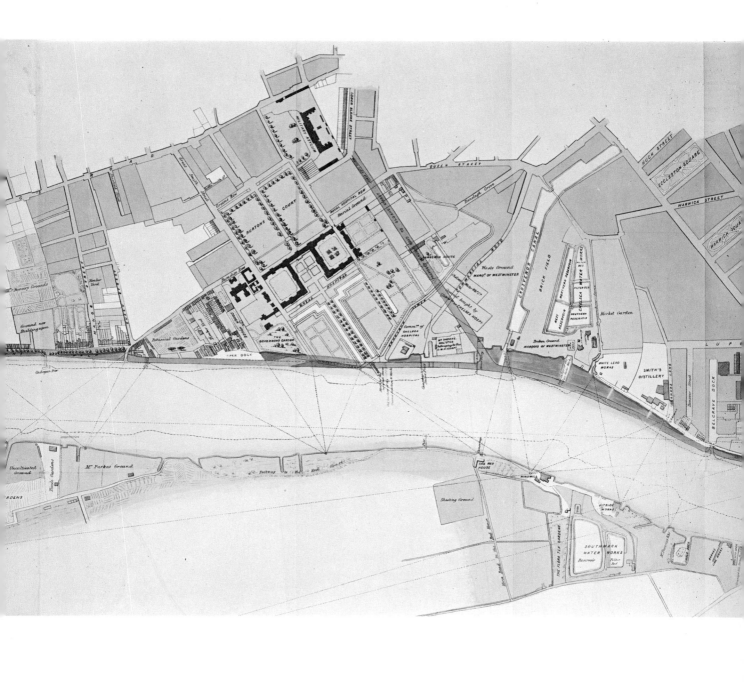

PLATE 51

Central London from a
*Balloon View of London as
seen from Hampstead*

1851

This map of London in the year of the Great Exhibition, taken from an unfamiliar angle, is a novelty inspired by the mid-Victorian passion for ballooning. It recalls the bird's-eye views of the Elizabethans; the technique allows individual buildings to be distinguished, and the relationship between railway viaducts and the houses over which they soared is clearly seen on the South Bank. Central London was not yet recognisable in its modern state. A rural air still pervaded Wandsworth and Camberwell; behind the houses lining the main roads lay open fields, soon to be covered in small terraces.

The shot towers flanking Waterloo Bridge have both disappeared in this century, one in 1937, the other in 1962. Northumberland House still dominated Charing Cross, Wyld's short-lived Great Globe occupied Leicester Square, and no direct route led as yet from Trafalgar Square to Tottenham Court Road. The enclave between Grosvenor Place and Whitehall remained separate and inaccessible, closed off by gates to all but the military and visitors to Buckingham Palace. At Hyde Park Corner Decimus Burton's screen, erected in 1825, faced the Constitution Arch, originally planned as a grand approach to Buckingham Palace but moved as part of the Hyde Park Corner rearrangement in the early 1960's.

Hungerford Suspension Bridge 'only for foot passengers' linked the north and south banks of the river; its piers were used in 1862 for the Charing Cross rail-bridge, built to serve the new north-bank terminus. As the railways moved into central London, so the pressure on river steamer services eased. Several steamers are seen in the balloon view, but the peak of their prosperity had passed in the 1840's.

PLATE 52

Bloomsbury to
Whitehall from *London*

by Edward Weller, 1862

The interest of Weller's map, published in a fruitful period for London cartography, lies in his choice of information to be included. He names insurance offices, banks, clubs, government offices and newspaper offices, and such oddities as the Bath and Washhouse in Endell Street and Aldridge's Horse Repository in St. Martin's Lane.

Oxford Street marked a social as well as a topographical distinction; to the north lay the Bloomsbury estates of the Bedfords, adorned with Smirke's British Museum and elegant squares, closely controlled, with their tenancies restricted to exclude 'any noisy, noisome or offensive trade or business whatsoever'. This determined policy kept the squares of Bloomsbury 'all modern, middle class and devoid of associations to tempt us to linger in them', as Charles Knight commented in 1844.

To the south lay the confused hinterland of St. Martins's, St. Giles's, and St. Paul's, Covent Garden, divided among many landlords and therefore not susceptible to wholesale improvement. It required, according to an agitated *Church Times* reporter in 1864, the attention of 'both the policeman and the philanthropist'. The network of breweries, workhouses, hospitals, dispensaries and board and ragged schools seen on the map between Lincoln's Inn Fields and Wardour Street tells its own story.

PLATE 54

Railway Proposals and Miscellaneous Improvements from the *Library Map of London*

by Edward Stanford, 1862

In the 1860's and 70's Stanford's made a lucrative business from their monopoly of publishing maps to show statutory changes in London and throughout the country. Every year new sets of proposals for railways and roads were laid before Parliament; their complexity can be gauged from the section of central London reproduced, which includes not only sanctioned and proposed railway lines, but also street improvements (shaded), notably the Embankment and a street connecting it with Charing Cross which foreshadows Northumberland Avenue, opened in 1876.

On the Key to this edition of Stanford's map are listed 58 railway lines and 19 miscellaneous alterations in London, some major, such as the Holborn Valley scheme and Cromwell Road, others relatively minor, such as the Royal Arcade proposed to connect Regent Street and New Bond Street. The new railway lines varied in length from a mere mile to 36 miles, an ambitious extension of track planned by the Metropolitan District Company which was currently extending its activities in West London. (Compare plate 59.)

In the same year one company proposed running a line from Paddington to Charing Cross, partly underneath Hyde Park and bisecting Green Park. Fortunately the scheme was resisted, and it is still impossible to take a direct line between the two stations.

ARY MAP OF LONDON AND ITS SUBURBS

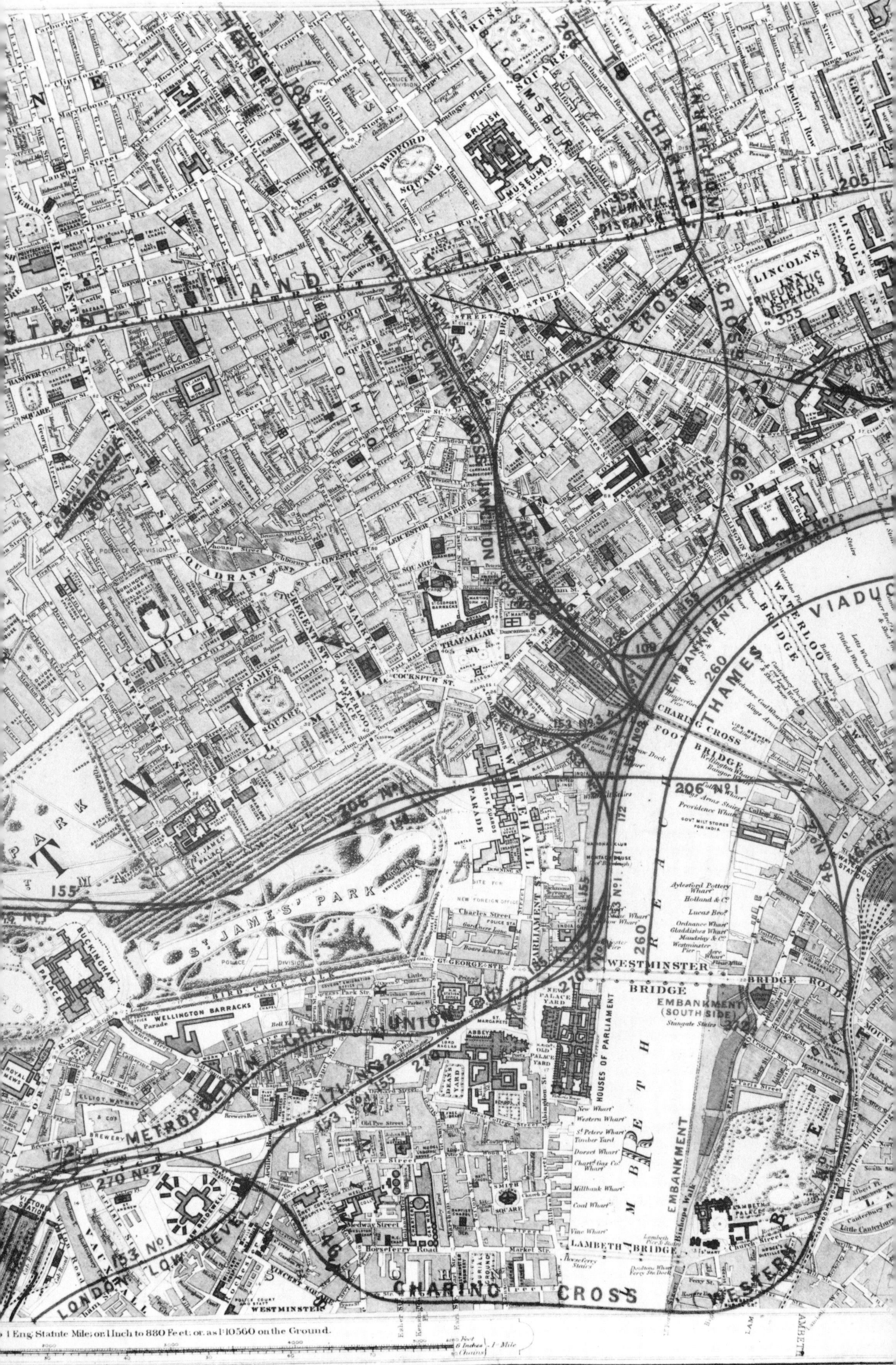

BRITISH MUSEUM

BEDFORD SQUARE

RUSSELL SQUARE

BLOOMSBURY SQUARE

LINCOLN'S INN

LINCOLN'S INN PNEUMATIC DISPATCH 355

CHARING CROSS

QUADRANT

SOHO SQUARE

LEICESTER SQUARE

TRAFALGAR SQ.

COCKSPUR ST.

ST JAMES SQUARE

ST JAMES PALACE

ST JAMES' PARK

THAMES

WATERLOO BRIDGE

THAMES VIADUCT

CHARING CROSS FOOT BRIDGE

EMBANKMENT 260

BUCKINGHAM PALACE

WELLINGTON BARRACKS

WHITEHALL

DOWNING ST

PARLIAMENT

WESTMINSTER

WESTMINSTER BRIDGE

BRIDGE ROAD

HOUSES OF PARLIAMENT

OLD PALACE YARD

ABBEY

GRAND UNION

METROPOLITAN

EMBANKMENT (SOUTH SIDE)
Stangate Stairs

New Wharf
Western Wharf
St Peters Wharf
Timber Yard
Dorset Wharf
Chared Gas Co. Wharf
Millbank Wharf
Coal Wharf
Vine Wharf

SMITH SQUARE

Horseferry Road

LAMBETH BRIDGE

VAUXHALL

LOW LEVEL

VICTORIA STATION

CHARING CROSS

WESTMINSTER

Aylesford Pottery Wharf
Holland & Co.
Lucas Bro.
Ordnance Wharf
Gladdishes Wharf
Maudslay & Co.
Westminster Pier

GOV.T MILT STORES FOR INDIA

LAMBETH

REGENT STREET

WEST

1 Eng: Statute Mile; or 1 Inch to 880 Feet: or, as 1:10560 on the Ground.

hed by Edward Stanford, 6, Charing Cross, Feb.15.th 1862
Additions Dec.r 21.st 1863.

SANCTIONED LINES ———— PROPOSED LI

PLATE 55

St. John's Wood from
Sheet XVI of the first
edition 6 in. Ordnance
Survey of London

1870

The Ordnance Survey was slow to turn its attention to London, partly perhaps because of the vociferous opposition from civilian surveyors and map publishers in the first half of the century, which reached a peak in 1848 at the time of their employment by the Metropolitan Commissioners for Sewers. Not until 1872 was London covered on both the 25-inch and 6-inch scales, a massive undertaking, but one which in the nature of the task required revision almost immediately its results appeared in print. Colonel Pilkington White, writing in 1886 on the progress of the survey, commented wryly:

round about London the survey ... lasted from 1863 to 1873 so that it is now from a dozen to 20 years old – the accessions in the way of buildings north, south, east and west must be something enormous

The second edition was prepared in the 1890's.

The first spurt of building in St. John's Wood had been the development of the Eyre estate, between 1794 and 1830, a rash of semi-detached villas marking the beginnings of middle-class outer suburbia beyond the Marylebone Road. The population grew so fast in this section of St. Marylebone parish that in 1814, after several years of pressure, the vestry founded St. John's Wood Chapel. At the turn of the century the old parish church had been serving a community of almost 70,000 people. (Compare plates 48, 49.)

West of the Edgware Road, here called also Watling Street and Maida Hill, running straight out into Middlesex, lay Paddington and Kilburn, gradually declining socially under the influence of the railway lines cutting the area, but still in parts semi-rural.

PLATE 56

Sydenham from the
Library Map of London

by Edward Stanford, 1877

Stanford's large-scale maps of London, published both as separate sheets and bound into volumes, are an essential source for the historian of late Victorian London. Their careful engraving was equalled by their accuracy, comparable with that of Ordnance Survey publications (compare, for technical similarities, plate 55). Revised editions were issued annually and gave an immediate picture of the developments on London's outskirts as railway companies opened up the home counties.

Although the old village centre is still distinct in the top right-hand corner of this plate, Sydenham was beginning to acquire its present character as an outer London suburb; speculative builders were creating terraces in Penge, Sydenham and Anerley close to the stations, in contrast to the wealthier free-standing houses on Sydenham Hill and northwards to Dulwich. Brickfields and kilns point to the immediate future of the district, but in 1877 it was still a pleasantly rural outing for Londoners, with even a tollgate surviving off Penge Lane. Two million people a year poured out of the two main stations, the High and Low levels, to visit the Crystal Palace, that temple to Victorian leisure crowning Sydenham Hill.

The Crystal Palace had been moved to Sydenham and re-opened as a winter park and amusement centre by Queen Victoria in 1854. Its five storeys towered over a 200-acre park filled with fountains, exotic trees, life-sized prehistoric monsters and casts of classical statues. Within the building were concert halls, exhibition galleries and an aquarium. The Palace survived, although in decline in the 20th century, until a disastrous fire in 1936. One attempt to revive public enthusiasm was the annual Cup Final, held there from 1895, which brought thousands of football supporters to Sydenham. The scale of this map, 6 inches to the mile, permits the elaborate layout of the pleasure park to be seen in its prime.

PLATE 57

Administrative
Boundaries in East
London from the
*Administrative Map of
London and the Suburbs*
by Edward Stanford, 1884

Anomalies in London's government had throughout the 19th century stimulated criticism and suggestions from would-be reformers. The ancient separatism of the City, retained virtually intact, was in some respects alleviated by the continued shift of its residents outwards, so that the administrative problem gradually removed itself, but the chaotic multiplicity of administrative boundaries outside its liberties was not to be resolved until the present century. Stanford's map of borough boundaries was one of a set of several sold together and showing the limits of bodies responsible for London's needs: municipal districts, gas and water companies (eight of each, all supplying different areas), parliamentary boroughs and poor law commissions. The thick red line marks the outer limit of the Metropolitan Board of Works, forerunner to the L.C.C.

Gladstone attempted in the year this map was published to introduce a London Government Bill rationalising some at least of the absurdities, but there was considerable opposition to it. The idea of an elected local authority for London was persistently rejected, and the fear was frequently expressed, before the L.C.C. was created in 1889, that London would become 'a popular and democratic community with enormous powers of taxing the richer classes, a gigantic seat of intense and interested agitation'.

Even after the County of London came into being, anomalies remained. The L.C.C. boundary did not coincide with those of the Metropolitan Police, the school and asylum boards and the Thames Conservancy, and many other distinct districts survived, such as those for inspecting weights and measures, cowhouses and dairies, shop hours and lodging houses. Within the City the tiny ancient parishes still governed themselves, although one, St. Christopher le Stocks, had lost its church in 1781 and was almost entirely covered by the Bank of England. Ely Place, Holborn, retained its medieval seclusion as a private liberty, the inhabitants laying their own paving-stones and refusing entry to policemen.

The largest parish in the county of London was Islington, with more than 300,000 inhabitants, the smallest Staple Inn, with only ten. Such dramatic variation in scale was unusual, but in east London the relative areas of the ecclesiastical parishes of Ratcliff, for example, and Poplar, reflect their respective histories; the Isle of Dogs was slow to fill up with houses and had only a chapel in the marsh until its early 19th-century expansion, whereas Ratcliff had been already a thriving and crowded ship-building community in the 16th century.

PLATE 58 *(overleaf)*

Routes in Central London from the *District Railway Map*

c 1886

The rapid growth in inner London railways during the last quarter of the century demanded annual editions of the popular Victorian route map illustrated here. In this year the proprietor proudly advertised in the margins of the street that the District routes 'to Windsor via Ealing' and to Hounslow and Osterley were now open. By this date the impact of the transport revolution was draining residents from the old inner London; as the chairman of the London Tramways Company claimed in 1884, 'We have relieved London of an immense number of poor people by carrying them out to the suburbs'.

At this time underground trains were still hauled by steam locomotives; the first schemes for electrification were in the air, but the earliest true electric underground railway did not come into operation until December 1890. It ran for almost two miles between King William Street in the City and the Elephant and Castle. The later lines, such as the Central and Piccadilly, were able to run almost entirely underground, and both their stations and their tracks were far more deeply buried below London than their mid-Victorian predecessors. Today the interchanges between the District, the Circle and the Central at, for example, Notting Hill Gate or Bank, emphasise this essential difference in their respective origins. Few of the old Inner Circle stations are more than a short flight of steps below pavement level, and their platforms are often open to the sky, although pressure on central London is increasingly closing them in.

The overprinted colours on the map distinguish between inner and outer London railways and their linking omnibus routes. These by no means give a true picture of the public transport system operating in central London at this date, since the extensive network of independent omnibus and tram routes is omitted. The railway directors were anxious primarily to link termini that were otherwise only circuitously connected by the Underground, such as Baker Street with Victoria and Charing Cross, and to provide spurs to the fashionable shopping districts of Bond Street and Knightsbridge. Even today it is impossible to travel directly between all of the mainline stations, although the Victoria Line has made the journey from King's Cross to Victoria far more convenient.

PLATE 59 *(opposite)*

Public Houses in Central London, from *The Modern Plague of London*

published by the National Temperance League, *c* 1885

This map, on which licensed premises are indicated by red circles, is an illustration of those twin Victorian passions, for social reform and for classification. Welfare workers were convinced and unanimous in their condemnation of the demon drink; in the last year of the century a Westminster district visitor, with more practical experience than most reformers of the problems it enhanced, listed alcohol as the prime cause of poverty in London. 'Drink is the chief evil to be combated'; pawnshop and public house, he noted, were conveniently close to one another, even next door, and the women, among whom public drinking was on the increase, in central London at least, went directly from one into the other.

The distribution of public houses in central London was by no means even. This was due in part to the deliberate policy of exclusion followed by certain great landowners; the steward of the Bedford estates in Bloomsbury had always been careful in his choice of tenants, and public houses were and to some extent still are virtually prohibited. Their property between New Oxford Street and the Strand was run on different lines. Not only the porters of Covent Garden, but also the pleasure-seekers visiting brothels, theatres and restaurants along St. Martin's Lane required refreshment. Soho, divided among many landlords and traditionally a home of entertainment, had the highest density of public houses in central London, out of all proportion to its resident population, and as a Victorian observer commented, 'many are noticeable for their elaborate and beautiful exteriors'.

Further west the Duke of Westminster, in a successful attempt to enhance the value of his Mayfair estates, where leases were falling in and rebuilding going on, had been actively abolishing the numerous public houses around Shepherd Market, leaving only a few open for the thirsty building workers swarming in the area.

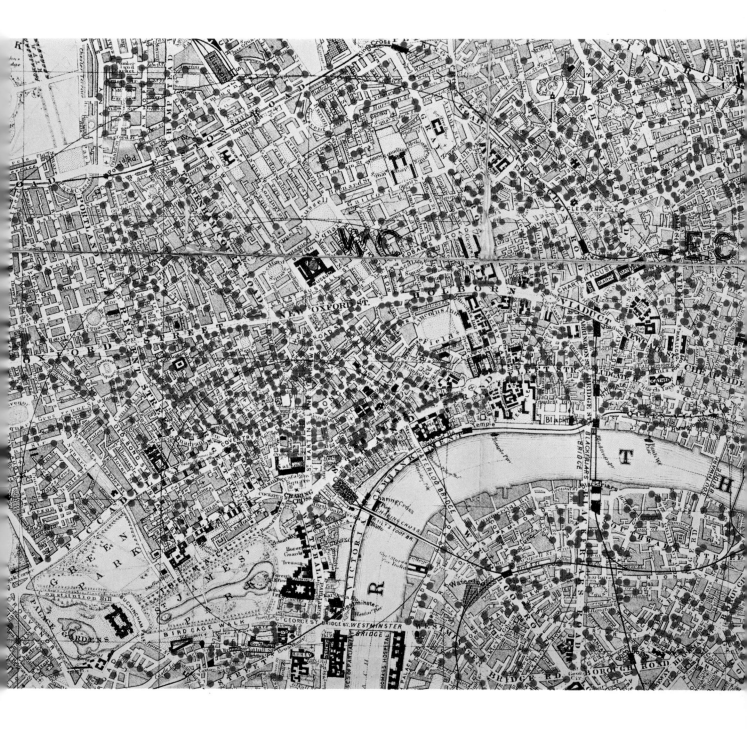

PLATE 60

Diphtheria cases in East
London from *A Map of
London Shewing the
Several Sanitary Districts*

1891

The improvements in public health characteristic of the late Victorian period provoked a mass of statistical material on infectious diseases. The Metropolitan Board of Health published annually a series of maps marking cases of scarlet fever and other diseases such as diphtheria in its district. Diphtheria had first been defined and separated from other throat diseases such as scarlatina in the late 1850's, when a ferocious epidemic hit London. It recurred with great severity in the early 1890's, with particular virulence in east London and West Ham, which lay outside the Metropolitan district. Here the death-rate was the highest in England – 340 per million in 1891 (compared with 173 for the rest of the country) rising to a peak of 740 in 1893. Contemporary medical opinion was divided on the causes of this concentration in east London, attributing it partly to changes in the water table, which increased humidity in low-lying areas, and partly to contamination in cow's milk; certainly the incidence of cases in the map suggests a link with the docks and the Thames. The spots cluster around London Dock and in Cubitt Town on the Isle of Dogs, a notoriously ill-drained development, while there are relatively few in north Stepney, where a line of springs flanks the Mile End Road.

These maps were among the large class of administrative and local government maps prepared and published by the firm of Edward Stanford at Charing Cross and later in Long Acre. The firm is still agent for the Ordnance Survey.

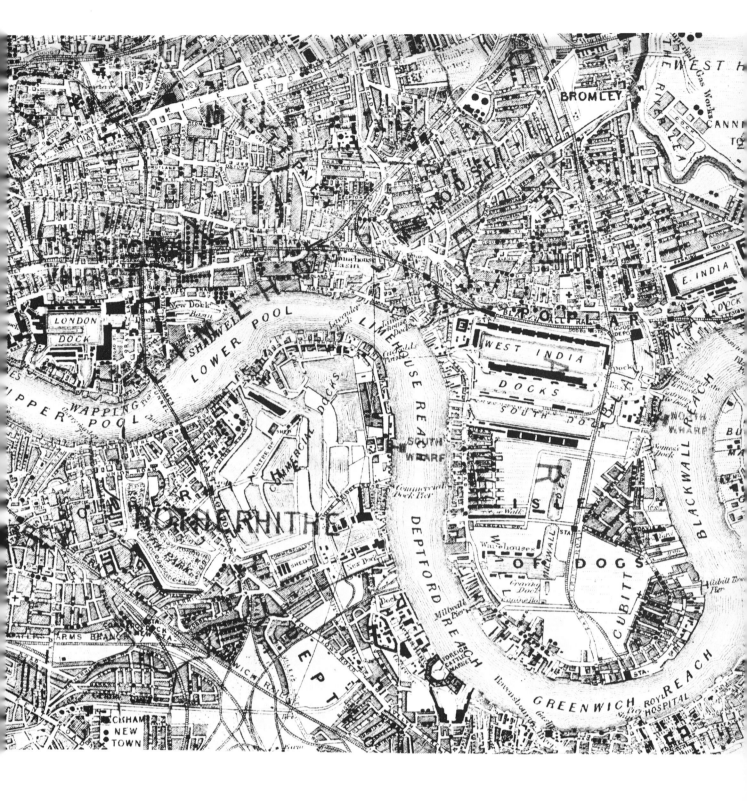

PLATE 61

*Proposed New Road from
Charing Cross to the Mall*

1896

L.C.C., *History of London Street Improvements
1855–1897*, 1898

The L.C.C. was as anxious as the Office of Works to ensure that the proposed new carriage road linking Charing Cross (Trafalgar Square) and the Mall should be sanctioned, since the Council had expanded far beyond the capacity of its original building in Spring Gardens Passage, built for the Metropolitan Board of Works in 1861, and hoped, in the carve-up of Spring Gardens, to expand its offices over the entire area between the Trafalgar Square street frontage and Carlton House Terrace, as indicated on this plan. Its anxiety is understandable; between its formation in 1889 and 1896 its office staff had more than doubled, from 160 odd to 370, not to speak of messengers and temporary staff, and these were scattered in outlying premises up to half a mile away. 'The strain upon the officers . . . can hardly fail to be most prejudicial'.

Although the new road was finally opened just in time for the 1911 Coronation, the L.C.C. failed to establish itself permanently at Charing Cross. Given its growth during this century, the site would never have been adequate for long, and in 1922 the Council moved to the massive building by Sir Ralph Knott on the South Bank.

Admiralty Arch, planned as a national memorial to Queen Victoria, was completed in 1910.

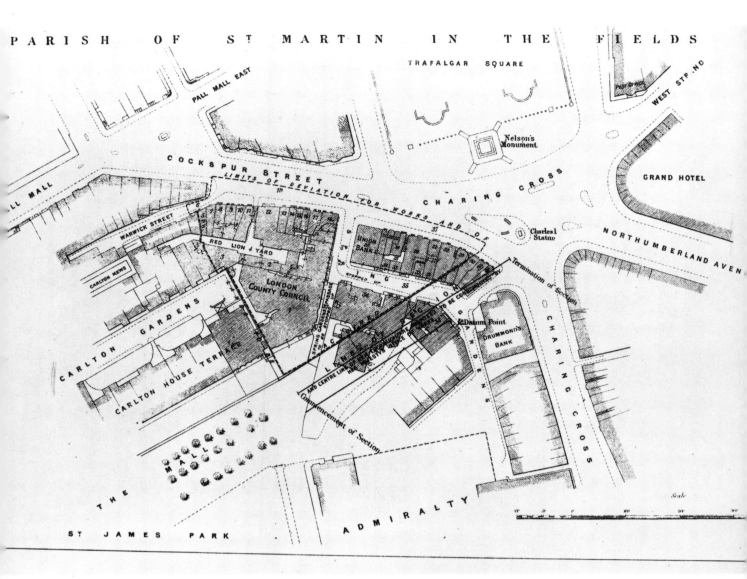

PLATE 62

Old Westminster from the social survey map of London

by Charles Booth, 1899

In his massive series of house-by-house enquiries into the economic life of Victorian London, Booth distinguished seven main classes, from wealthy through degrees of comfort and poverty to the lowest class. In central London and especially in Westminster the social mixture was dramatic; the black areas on the map inhabited by the poor and semi-criminal class, and the dark blue occupied by those only one degree above them, rub shoulders with the red of the well-to-do and even the gold identifying London's wealthiest residents. 'The disreputable classes are still very much in evidence in Westminster', despite the presence of a royal palace, government offices, the Houses of Parliament and Westminster Abbey.

This mixture was partly due to the piecemeal but continuous redevelopment of property in central London. Mansion flats for the middle classes were erected on the site of former slums, and stood side-by-side with poor tenements awaiting their turn for demolition. This is brought out in the contrasting rents paid; Booth noted that the annual rent of flats in Victoria Street was from £300 upwards at this date, whereas off Great Peter Street a three- or four-roomed working-class tenement cost between six and ten shillings a week.

Persistent attempts were made by individual landlords to raise the low character of the back streets, although this inevitably could only be achieved by driving from their homes the very poorest inhabitants, and the population of Westminster was steadily decreasing at this period. The clergy of St. Margaret's Westminster, for example, had about the time of Booth's enquiry bought leases of 17 houses in Lewisham Street 'a rather black spot', and hoped 'by combining the power of ownership with the exercise of other influence', to change its character. Missionary efforts had already succeeded in improving the tone of Great Peter Street, although cases of daylight robbery still occurred; 'lady cyclists now pass through', a thing they had not ventured to do a few years before. The removal of the penitentiary from Millbank in 1890 had contributed, in that the colony of ex-convicts and ticket-of-leave men which clustered about the prison gates had disappeared.

PLATE 63

Canonbury from the
social survey map of
London

by Charles Booth, 1899

Canonbury, like Westminster (see preceding plate) had at this date a considerable social mixture, although the trend there was in the opposite direction, down in the economic scale. Its nearness to central London made it a residential area for working men pushed out of the desperately crowded or rebuilt streets of St. Giles and Holborn; as they moved in and large family houses were divided into flats or let as lodgings, so the former residents moved out to the north. In living memory this district has seen both a decline and, since the Second World War, a partial and patchy rise in social status. A modern Booth might find in the 1970's· economic contrasts almost as stark between the people of one street and the next, although the Victorian investigator's definition of the poverty line, as 'an income of 21/– a week for a moderate family', would have to be multiplied 15 or 20 times today.

Around Canonbury Square stood large, quiet houses, many detached and all with gardens, coloured red to indicate the relative prosperity of their occupiers, although according to Booth, few kept their own carriages, an observation underlined by the presence of a cab stand in Canonbury Place.

Further south, in contrast, and especially east of the Essex Road, lay a patch of poverty-stricken black and blue, where missionaries, district visitors and the police concentrated their attentions. The buildings along Popham Street in particular were noted for the 'moral subnormality' of their inhabitants. This was not due, as so often elsewhere in London, to their being old and tumbledown; the estate had been built only 15 years before, but was administered by an investment company with little interest except in the income. At the time of Booth's first visit a considerable experiment in social welfare was in progress here, employing 20 voluntary workers in a library, women's club and boys' brigade, and on his return in 1899 he noted 'a considerable improvement in the tone' of the inhabitants. Many had no doubt moved on. The population here was continually shifting. (Compare plate 37.)

PLATE 64

Central London from the *Monumental Map of London (Industrial & Commercial)*

by G. W. Bacon, *c* 1900–1905

In this map one aspect of London, its commercial and industrial significance, is stressed, with a resulting sacrifice of all but the most basic topography. A grossly simplified street plan was used as background to a series of vignettes of over a hundred buildings, important not merely for the visual contribution they made to the London street scene but also for the activities they contained. The selection was wide, both in the area included and in the institutions considered suitable for inclusion. Ranging from the marble-tiled premises of Mr Sainsbury at Lewisham, 'Provision Merchant Poulterer and Game Dealer' to the massive Kilburn Brewery on the Edgware Road, they included such non-commercial buildings as the Imperial Institute, Spurgeon's Tabernacle and Newington Public Library.

The perspective views of buildings have a nostalgic charm, since even in the relatively short period of 70 years since the map was first produced, almost all have either disappeared or been altered considerably. Exceptions to this are St James's Palace, Nelson's Column (strictly speaking not a building) and the Charing Cross Hotel, but even the latter has in the intervening years lost the railings protecting its forecourt. A comparison of an earlier series of views of London buildings, John Tallis's *London Street Views*, published in weekly parts between 1838 and 1840, with the street façades of present-day London, shows that rebuilding in central London is no new phenomenon. Only a tiny proportion of the commercial premises identifiable on Tallis's views survives unaltered.

The map was prepared for distribution in France, 'Printed in Paris by Du Frénoy' and 'Engraved by H. Rollet' and is apparently an example of Edwardian advertising techniques.

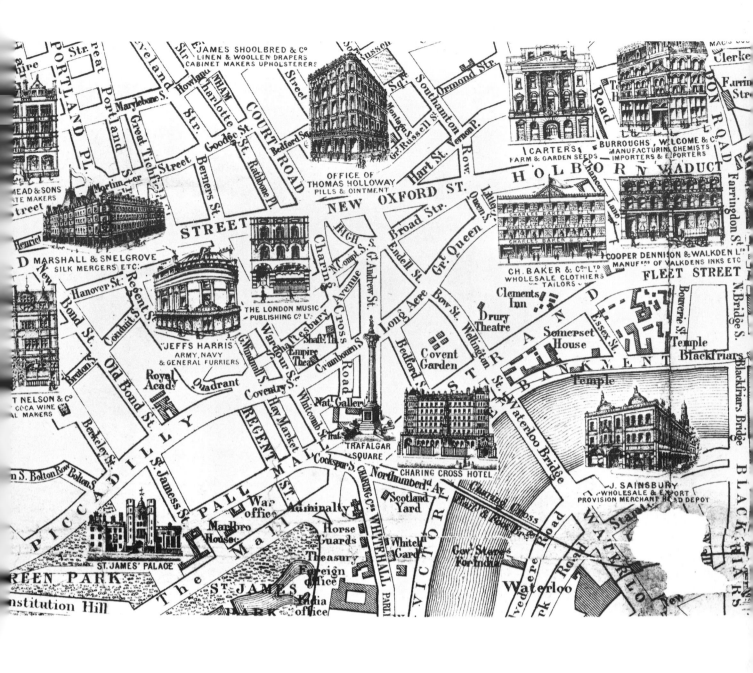

PLATE 65

Section from a *Map of a German night aeroplane raid 31 October 1917*

The First World War saw the emergence as an accepted element in modern mass warfare of the principle of indiscriminate hostility against civilians. In the early stages of the war Zeppelins dropped bombs over English towns, reaching London in April 1915, but from 1915 onwards they were replaced by flights of aeroplanes, often making several forays in one night.

Although by comparison with the following war the effects were slight, in England 1000 civilians and nearly 300 combatants died as a result of German aerial bombardment; features such as lighting restrictions were then enforced at night, forerunners of the later stringent blackout precautions.

The map illustrates the two routes taken by raiders attacking London, across Essex up the Crouch valley, or over Thanet and Sheppey. The dots represent bombs dropped; they cluster in the dock area around Greenwich – perhaps the high land of Blackheath drew the airmens' eye – and surprisingly in residential districts such as Wimbledon and Tooting, whose bombing would noticeably damage neither morale nor vital industries.

In this particular raid some 24 machines took part, dropping 278 bombs, but the damage was slight. Ten people were killed and 22 injured.

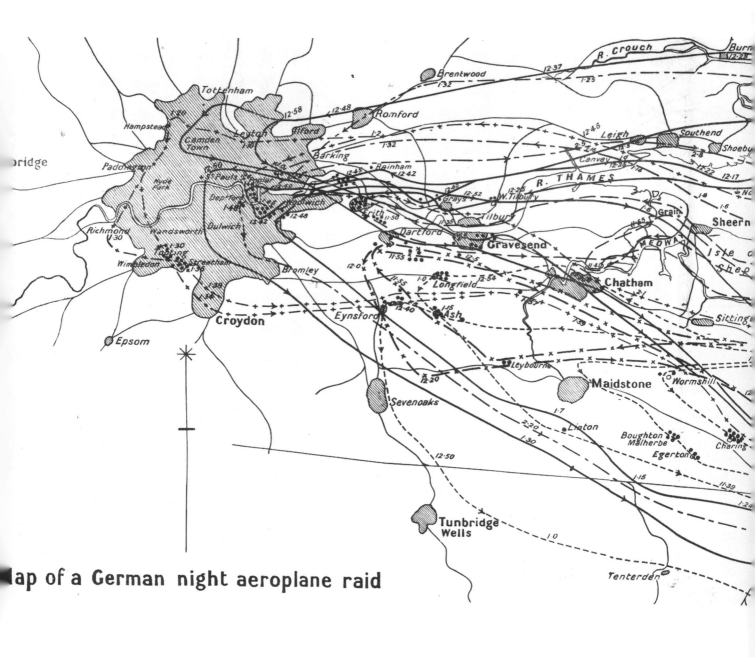

Map of a German night aeroplane raid

PLATE 66

Targets in East London
from the *Stadtplan von
London mit
militärgeographischen
Objekteintragungen*

1941

Between the two world wars bombing of civilian targets became an accepted part of international warfare both for its presumed effect on civilian morale and for the subsequent undermining of the economy in general and the 'war effort' in particular. German preparations were thorough and their information as to potential targets, at least in London, astonishingly accurate. Luftwaffe pilots were issued with lithographed copies on four sheets of the 1933 Ordnance Survey sheets (on the scale 1:20,000), overprinted in colour with symbols representing strategic points.

That these maps were valuable to the bombers, at least in the daylight raids of early September 1940, was obvious in the devastation they achieved. The first full attack on London, in which a flight of 300 bombers concentrated on the docks, Woolwich Arsenal and the oil installations downstream, conformed entirely to the principle of striking at and disabling London's port, although the effects were less drastic than expected. The docks were barely damaged, although thousands of small terraced houses in east London were destroyed and warehouses burned. A week later came the deliberate daylight attack on Buckingham Palace, a target of no economic significance, but one whose destruction was planned as a blow to British morale; the attack, however, had the opposite effect of strengthening public support for the war.

The map of which part of one sheet is illustrated here was prepared for later bombing raids on London; it was corrected to the end of November 1941. The range of potential targets, each outlined in red and with its distinguishing symbol and reference number, was extremely wide. The Tower, a 'Kulturdenkmal' of no economic importance, is flanked by the Mint and Fenchurch Street station. All bridges and tunnels, whether rail or road, were identified by double black lines as prime targets. Even the Albert Memorial, as a historic monument, rated a red star; 40 symbols were used in all, ranging from a posthorn for Post Offices to a miniature house for educational premises.

PLATE 67

Post-war reconstruction
in the City from *A
Report on Improvements
Prepared by the Town
Planning Committee*

1944

In the Blitz some of the oldest and most congested parts of the City were destroyed, especially around St. Paul's, in the raids of December 1940. The opportunity offered for planned rebuilding was rapidly recognised by the city authorities, who in 1941 prepared draft rebuilding proposals, using plans based on town-planning surveys of the 1930's.

These plans bring out the increased pressure on all aspects of urban life in the 20th century: on land values, on transport facilities and on the need for redevelopment, if the upward spiral of prosperity was to be maintained. One map showed the flow of pedestrians along the City's narrow streets; the density on London Bridge and along Old Broad Street from Liverpool Street was over 90 for every 100 feet of pavement, a cold statistical expression of a horrifying congestion experienced daily by thousands of city workers.

The surveys demonstrating proposals for rebuilding the 225 devastated acres are equally interesting. Zoning proposals have had only limited effect, and the limits on office-heights that were proposed seem unrealistically low in the light of the past quarter-century of building.

The plan reproduced brings out the proposed road improvements, most of which have now come into effect, as for example the clearance at the east end of St. Paul's Cathedral and at Holborn Circus. The solid shaded areas at Queenhythe and the great north cross-route by Smithfield market are more drastic changes which have still to be achieved.

PLATE 68

Age/sex structure of the
London boroughs from
The Atlas of London

1969

The *Atlas* comprises a series of maps which combine statistical information drawn from the
1961 census, with a vast range of other data supplied by the Centre for Urban Studies, to
build up a complete picture of the economic, social and physiological structure of the
London region, the first time such a massive compilation has been attempted. For the first
time a determined attack has overcome that fragmentation of information between separate
authorities inevitable in London, where so few responsibilities have boundaries that coincide
exactly or conveniently.

The map reproduced expresses the size of age-groups, male to the left and female to the
right, by five-year bars, in each of the boroughs of inner and outer London. Kensington,
for example, has a significant bulge of 20-30-year olds, living presumably in flats and
peripatetic, whereas Wandsworth and Fulham are rather more top-heavy, with many more
permanently-settled inhabitants of all ages. The birth rate, or rather the size of the children's
age group, is considerably greater in Islington than in Chelsea, an obvious deduction from
the social distinction between the two areas, but one here clearly demonstrated by the
statisticians.

The range of information which the maps as a whole provide is fascinating. Topics
familiar to sociologists, but not normally discussed in terms accessible to the general public,
are here illustrated; one map covers, for instance, the incidence of working wives through
the London boroughs, another the spheres of influence of the modern suburban shopping
centres, such as Croydon, another those areas with families possessing more than one motorcar, with all that implies about prosperity, pressure on roads and parking problems.

PLATE 69

Central London from
the *Greater London* one-
sheet map published by
the Ordnance Survey,
1971

This single-sheet map covers the entire area of Greater London and much of the Home Counties at the one-inch scale, stretching from Tilbury in the east to Egham in the west, and from Caterham to St. Albans, which is shown straddling the northern margin. It is identical in area with four standard Ordnance Survey sheets (160, 161, 170 and 171) and includes parts of five counties around London, together with the whole of Middlesex. So far has London spread since the earliest maps: in the 16th century its entire area could be shown on a double page at a far larger scale (compare plate 3, at 6½ inches to the mile).

The most elaborate development of the use of symbols in modern cartography is evident in the key printed on this sheet, which gives almost a hundred signs in all, differentiated both by form and by colour. The normal range of boundaries, from the civil parish upwards, is extended to six by the inclusion of a broad yellow line to mark the extent of Greater London. Although in the preparation of any map there is inevitably a time lag between the gathering of information and the printing of the map, details of the roads were revised in 1969/70 and the most recent addition to the road system in Central London, the roof-level motorway called Westway, is shown crossing Paddington to connect with the A1 in St John's Wood. The map is not strictly true to scale, so that roads appear to cover more of Central London than is in fact the case.

In the heavily urbanised area reproduced, the full range of physical features distinguished by the Survey, from mudbanks to bridlepaths, is not included, but even in the congested heart of London glasshouses are marked in two places, Hyde Park and Battersea Pleasure Gardens, and that sign familiar to travellers in rural England, NT for National Trust properties, also occurs twice, once in Arundel Street off the Strand, marking the so-called Roman bath (more probably a souvenir of a Stuart nobleman's visit to Italy), and the Blue-Coat School in Westminster, not far from Buckingham Palace.

Acknowledgements

I am extremely grateful to the following institutions for permission to reproduce maps in their collections:

Trustees of the British Museum: Plates 1, 5 (Manuscript Room), 7, 9, 11, 13–15, 19, 21, 25, 29, 30, 32, 34, 38, 39, 41, 46, 55 (Map Room) and 10 (Print Room)

Worshipful Company of Goldsmiths: Plate 20

Greater London Council Map Room: Plates 37, 43, 44, 53, 54, 66

Guildhall Library: Plates 6, 8, 12, 16, 33, 47, 57, 67

Kensington and Chelsea Public Libraries: Plates 42, 45, 49, 56

Trustees of the London Museum: Plates 2–4, 17, 18, 22–24, 26–28, 31, 35, 36, 40, 48, 50–52, 58–65, 68; Endpapers

Ordnance Survey: Plate 69 (Crown Copyright reserved)

ILLUSTRATIONS: My thanks are due to the following for permission to reproduce map details, drawings, etc.:

Trustees of the British Museum: illustrations on pages 24, 31, 32

Trustees of the London Museum: illustrations on pages 11, 16, 18, 29, 34, 37, 40, 42, 56, 60

Guildhall Library: illustrations on pages 22, 49, 65 (cartouche from Bowles' *One-Sheet Plan of the Cities of London and Westminster*)

London Transport: map on page 54

Science Museum: illustration on page 63 (Thomas Tuttell's Advertisement; Science Museum photograph)

Whipple Science Museum, Cambridge: illustrations on title page (from *The Surveyor*, by A. Rathborne, London 1616; and on page 64 (from *The Practical Surveyor*, 2nd Edition, by Samuel Wyld, London, and *Plates to the Geometrical and Graphical Essays by the late George Adams*, 3rd Edition, London 1803)

The Prospect of London

Part of the County of London Midlesex.

Part of the County of Surrey

Greenwich